A PICTORIAL GUIDE
TO THE
LAKELAND FELLS
SECOND EDITION

REVISED BY CHRIS JESTY

being an illustrated account
of a study and exploration
of the mountains in the
English Lake District
by

AWainwright

BOOK SIX
THE NORTH WESTERN FELLS

Frances Lincoln Limited
4 Torriano Mews
Torriano Avenue
London NW5 2RZ
www.franceslincoln.com

First edition published by Westmorland Gazette, Kendal, 1964
First published by Frances Lincoln 2003
Second (revised) edition published by Frances Lincoln 2008

©The Estate of A. Wainwright 1964, 2008
Revisions and additional material ©Chris Jesty 2008
Foreword ©Betty Wainwright 2005

Printed and bound in Singapore

A CIP catalogue record is available for this book
from the British Library.

ISBN 978 0 7112 2712 5

THE
NORTH WESTERN
FELLS

REVISED EDITIONS

THIS REVISED AND UPDATED EDITION PUBLISHED BY
FRANCES LINCOLN, LONDON

the Pictorial Guides, I am delighted that, due to Chris's commitment, the guides are being revised and I give them my blessing. It is with pleasure that I picture Chris re-walking and checking and, where necessary, correcting every route, every ascent and every path. Although most of the individual corrections are minor, the overall impact is huge, and I feel proud and confident — as I am sure AW would be too — that the revised guides will satisfy the needs of the 21st-century walker.

Betty Wainwright
Kendal, January 2005

FOREWORD

The Pictorial Guides have never before been revised,
for the reasons given by AW in his concluding remarks
to the third volume, *The Central Fells*, where he wrote
that by the time he had finished Book Seven, age
would prevent him undertaking the 'joyful task' of
revising the series himself. He went on to write:

> ... Substantially, of course, the books will be useful
> for many years to come, especially in the detail and
> description of the fell tops, while the views will remain
> unaltered for ever, assuming that falling satellites and
> other fancy gadgets of man's invention don't blow
> God's far worthier creations to bits. But, this dire
> possibility apart, the books must inevitably show
> more and more inaccuracies as the years go by.
> Therefore, because it is unlikely that there will ever
> be revised editions, and because I should just hate to
> see my name on anything that could not be relied
> on, the probability is that the books will progressively
> be withdrawn from publication after a currency of a
> few years.

This was written in 1958, when the oldest volume was
only three years old and by the time he had completed
Book Seven in 1965 he was even more conscious of the
little things that had gone out of date in the previous
volumes — cairns demolished or built, screes eroded,
woods felled or grown up, new paths made. As the
years passed and it became apparent that the books
were still in demand, despite these inaccuracies, he
was occasionally approached by people asking for
revised editions. But the core of the problem was that,
as old age approached, he knew he could not
undertake the changes himself, nor did he trust
anyone to do the work as he would have wished.
   When, in 1980, Chris Jesty broached the idea to him,
he was told 'after my lifetime'. This was half the
battle won — AW knew Chris's work well, and did trust
him. Now, given the continuing popularity and use of

FOREWORD
BY BETTY WAINWRIGHT

INTRODUCTION
TO THE
SECOND EDITION
BY CHRIS JESTY

INTRODUCTION TO THE SECOND EDITION

In 1959 I went on an Outward Bound course at Eskdale Green, which involved a lot of walking in the mountains. I found that the depiction of paths on Ordnance Survey maps left definite room for improvement, and I had the idea of producing a guide book that would make it easier for people to find their way around. But in 1961 I was given one of Wainwright's Pictorial Guides to the Lakeland Fells and discovered that he had beaten me to it.

It occurred to me that one day the books would become out of date, and that, as I was presumably much younger than the author, the time might arrive when I would be allowed to revise them. It has taken more than forty years for that dream to turn into a reality.

In the meantime I had made the acquaintance of the author. I collaborated with him on *A Guide to the View from Scafell Pike*, and later on, when his eyesight was failing, I drew the maps for two of his other books (*Wainwright in the Limestone Dales* and *Wainwright's Favourite Lakeland Mountains*). Shortly before he died he requested that if ever the Lakeland Guides were to be revised I should be offered the job.

When, in 2003, following a change of publisher, the proposal was revived, I threw myself into the job with enthusiasm. I had a number of advantages over the author. I had a car, I had satellite navigation equipment, I was able to work on enlargements of the pages, and as I didn't have a job I was able to devote all my time and all my energy to this vast project.

Every feature on the maps and ascent diagrams and every word of text have been checked, but I have not checked every recommended route without a path. Descriptions of natural features and views are virtually unaltered, but the number of changes

INTRODUCTION TO THE SECOND EDITION

that have been made to maps and ascent diagrams is enormous. The decision was taken to print the paths in a second colour so that they stand out from other details, and also so that readers can tell at a glance that it is the revised edition they are using.

Summit altitudes have been corrected where they differ by five feet or more from the latest Ordnance Survey figures. Parking information has been added where appropriate. I have also taken the liberty of adding other information that seems to me to be of interest. No changes have been made to drawings of landscapes, natural features or buildings, or, of course, to Wainwright's 'Personal Notes in Conclusion'.

Occasional references will be found in the books to Bartholomew's maps. These are still available, but they are now published by Collins.

In order to keep the books as accurate as possible and in anticipation of future revised editions, readers are invited to write to me (c/o the publishers) about any errors they find in the revised Pictorial Guides. Emails to chrisj@frances-lincoln.com and letters sent to me c/o Frances Lincoln, 4 Torriano Mews, Torriano Avenue, London NW5 2RZ, will be passed on regularly. Amendments and information about changes that have taken place since publication are available on the Frances Lincoln website (www.franceslincoln.com)

Chris Jesty
Kendal, July 2008

BOOK SIX

is dedicated to
those unlovely twins

MY RIGHT LEG and MY LEFT LEG

staunch supporters
that have carried me about
for over half a century,
endured much without complaint
and never once let me down

Nevertheless, they are unsuitable subjects for illustration

INTRODUCTION

Classification and Definition

Any division of the Lakeland fells into geographical districts must necessarily be arbitrary, just as the location of the outer boundaries of Lakeland must always be a matter of opinion. Any attempt to define internal or external boundaries is certain to invite criticism, and he who takes it upon himself to say where Lakeland starts and finishes, or, for example, where the Central Fells merge into the Southern Fells and *which* fells *are* the Central Fells and which the Southern and *why* they need be so classified, must not expect his pronouncements to be generally accepted.

Yet for present purposes some plan of classification and definition must be used. County and parochial boundaries are no help, nor is the recently-defined area of the Lakeland National Park, for this book is concerned only with the high ground.

First, the external boundaries. Straight lines linking the extremities of the outlying lakes enclose all the higher fells very conveniently. There are a few fells of lesser height to the north and east, however, that are typically Lakeland in character and cannot properly be omitted: these are brought in, somewhat untidily, by extending the lines in those areas. Thus:

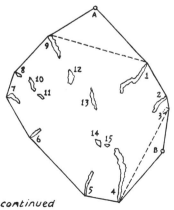

1 : Ullswater
2 : Hawes Water
3 : proposed Swindale Res.
4 : Windermere
5 : Coniston Water
6 : Wast Water
7 : Ennerdale Water
8 : Loweswater
9 : Bassenthwaite Lake
10 : Crummock Water
11 : Buttermere
12 : Derwent Water
13 : Thirlmere
14 : Grasmere
15 : Rydal Water
A : Caldbeck
B : Longsleddale (church)

continued

Classification and Definition

continued

The complete Guide includes all the fells in the area enclosed by the straight lines of the diagram. This is an undertaking quite beyond the compass of a single volume, and it is necessary, therefore, to divide the area into convenient sections, making the fullest use of natural boundaries (lakes, valleys and low passes) so that each district is, as far as possible, self-contained and independent of the rest.

This division gives seven areas, each with a well-defined group of fells, and each area is the subject of a separate volume

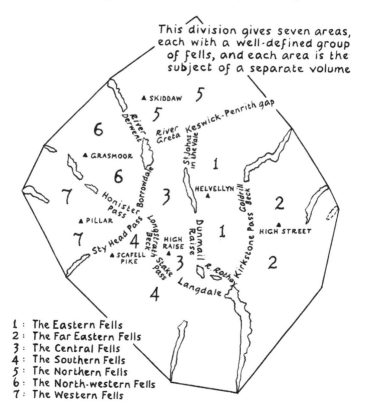

1 : The Eastern Fells
2 : The Far Eastern Fells
3 : The Central Fells
4 : The Southern Fells
5 : The Northern Fells
6 : The North-western Fells
7 : The Western Fells

INTRODUCTION

Notes on the Illustrations

THE MAPS.................. Many excellent books have been written about Lakeland, but the best literature of all for the walker is that published by the Director General of Ordnance Survey, the 1" map for companionship and guidance on expeditions, the 2½" map for exploration both on the fells and by the fireside. These admirable maps are remarkably accurate topographically but there is a crying need for a revision of the paths on the hills: several walkers' tracks that have come into use during the past few decades, some of them now broad highways, are not shown at all; other paths still shown on the maps have fallen into neglect and can no longer be traced on the ground.

The popular Bartholomew 1" map is a beautiful picture, fit for a frame, but this too is unreliable for paths; indeed here the defect is much more serious, for routes are indicated where no paths ever existed, nor ever could — the cartographer has preferred to take precipices in his stride rather than deflect his graceful curves over easy ground.

Hence the justification for the maps in this book: they have the one merit (of importance to walkers) of being dependable as regards delineation of *paths*. They are intended as supplements to the Ordnance Survey maps, certainly not as substitutes.

THE VIEWS.............. Various devices have been used to illustrate the views from the summits of the fells. The full panorama in the form of an outline drawing is most satisfactory generally, and this method has been adopted for the main viewpoints.

THE DIAGRAMS OF ASCENTS.................. The routes of ascent of the higher fells are depicted by diagrams that do not pretend to strict accuracy: they are neither plans nor elevations; in fact there is deliberate distortion in order to show detail clearly: usually they are represented as viewed from imaginary 'space-stations.' But it is hoped they will be useful and interesting.

THE DRAWINGS....... The drawings at least are honest attempts to reproduce what the eye sees: they illustrate features of interest and also serve the dual purpose of breaking up the text and balancing the layout of the pages, and of filling up awkward blank spaces, like this:

Thirlmere

THE
NORTH WESTERN
FELLS

The North Western Fells occupy a compact area, elliptical in plan, with clearly defined boundaries formed by the Rivers Derwent and Cocker. Only at one point, Honister Pass, is there a link with other high country, but even here, quite obviously, one mountain system ends and another begins. In all other places around the perimeter of the area deep valleys sever the North Western Fells from the neighbouring heights.

The Cocker is a tributary of the Derwent, and it follows, therefore, that the North Western Fells are wholly within the catchment of a single river — which further illustrates the geographical unity and separate identity of the group. Elsewhere, no combination of fells of similar extent is so neatly defined.

In size, the area is not very extensive on the map of Lakeland, but because its slopes rise immediately and steeply from the deep surrounding valleys, nothing is wasted: all is mountain country, first-class fellwalking territory. The hills tend to crowd together in the confined space available, but not in confusion and disarray, for connecting links bridge the tops in a pattern of high crests and scarped aretes that are a joy to explore. Indeed, here is to be found some of the finest ridge-walking in the district, smooth going for the most part, none of it difficult, none of it dangerous with ordinary care, all of it very pleasant and providing views of unsurpassed beauty.

THE
THREE
SECTORS

N

MILES
0
1
2
3

Bassenthwaite Lake

Northern

River Cocker

WHINLATTER PASS

Derwent Water

Central

Crummock Water

NEWLANDS HAUSE

South Eastern

Buttermere

River Derwent

HONISTER
PASS

Two motor roads cross the area, attaining their highest points at Whinlatter Pass and Newlands Hause and conveniently making three sectors.

The northern sector may be classed under the general title of Thornthwaite Forest. Slate is the underlying rock of the low rounded foothills comprising the region, but is not much in evidence, being well covered with vegetation and timber. A large part is occupied by the Forestry Commission, and here are being developed the most extensive plantations in the district. Perhaps because of this activity, the sector is less favoured by walkers than used to be the case, but it still offers many routes of unusual interest and charm.

The central sector contains the highest fells, all of them steep-sided and shapely, making arresting and exciting skylines. These, too, are of slate, and in the vicinity of Grasmoor particularly the steep slopes are excessively eroded and exhibit the most extensive wastes of scree in the district. These stony inclines are rarely climbed, but the summits and ridges above are very much frequented by walkers. The western flanks, rich in flora, are a happy hunting-ground for botanists. This sector is bisected by a foot-pass at Coledale Hause.

The south-eastern sector, too, is a place of fine ridges and shapely summits, and a great favourite of discerning walkers. The slate persists, but towards Borrowdale gives place to coarser, rougher volcanic ash.

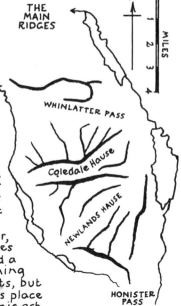

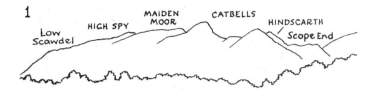

The North Western Fells, as seen from The Heads, Keswick

This geological change is noticeable on the ground and manifests itself in the only tarns amongst the North Western Fells. Rock-climbers appreciate the change and here find their only major interests in the area.

Accommodation is available at several places around the perimeter, being in plentiful supply in Borrowdale, where it is a local industry, but less easy to find at Buttermere and Lorton in summer. Braithwaite is a good jumping-off place, but the finest centre for a fellwalking holiday is Newlands, the only populated valley *within* the area. All the fells in this book may, however, be visited, with the help of the local bus services, from Keswick. It is worth noting that the best approaches to the area are from the north-east, the gradients being easier and the ascending ridges longer in this direction.

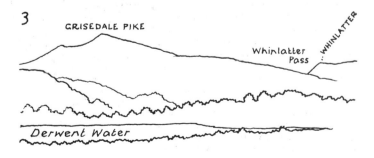

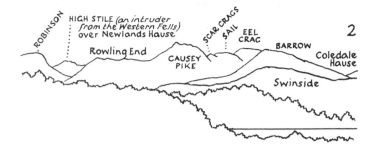

The main watershed lies close above the Cocker, and ascents from the southwest, in consequence, are short, abrupt and steep.

The North Western Fells, with riparian rights in four beautiful lakes, and sharing the proprietorship of the two lovely valleys of Borrowdale and Buttermere, can not be described as characteristic of Lakeland, the underlying slate tending to a smoothness

THE WATERSHED
south of
Whinlatter Pass

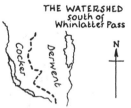

of outline and an absence of tarns, but for walkers who prefer rather easier progression than is to be found amongst the more rugged volcanic fells, even at some sacrifice of romantic scenery, there are none better than these.

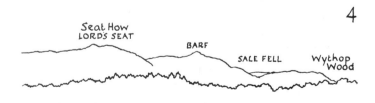

The North Western Fells, as seen from The Heads, Keswick

THE NORTH WESTERN FELLS

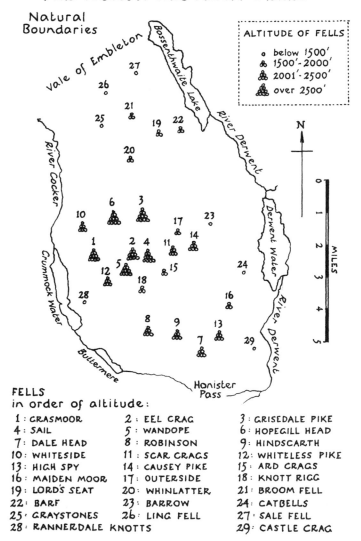

Natural
Boundaries

Vale of Embleton

Bassenthwaite Lake

River Derwent

River Cocker

Crummock Water

Buttermere

Honister Pass

Derwent Water

River Derwent

ALTITUDE OF FELLS

- ○ below 1500'
- ⛰ 1500'-2000'
- ⛰ 2001'-2500'
- ⛰ over 2500'

N

MILES
0
1
2
3
4
5

FELLS
in order of altitude:

1 : CRASMOOR	2 : EEL CRAG	3 : GRISEDALE PIKE
4 : SAIL	5 : WANDOPE	6 : HOPEGILL HEAD
7 : DALE HEAD	8 : ROBINSON	9 : HINDSCARTH
10 : WHITESIDE	11 : SCAR CRAGS	12 : WHITELESS PIKE
13 : HIGH SPY	14 : CAUSEY PIKE	15 : ARD CRAGS
16 : MAIDEN MOOR	17 : OUTERSIDE	18 : KNOTT RIGG
19 : LORD'S SEAT	20 : WHINLATTER	21 : BROOM FELL
22 : BARF	23 : BARROW	24 : CATBELLS
25 : GRAYSTONES	26 : LING FELL	27 : SALE FELL
28 : RANNERDALE KNOTTS		29 : CASTLE CRAG

THE NORTH WESTERN FELLS

in the order of their appearance in this book

Each fell is the subject of a separate chapter

Ard Crags

from Rigg Beck

Rigg Beck

EEL
CRAG ▲   ▲ ARD CRAGS

KNOTT ▲   ● Keskadale
RIGG

⚡ Newlands Hause

● Buttermere

MILES

0   1   2   3

There is one point on the
path alongside Rigg Beck
where the defile ahead is
occupied by the shapely
pyramid of Ard Crags, its
appearance suggesting a
complete isolation from
other fells. At the top of
Rigg Beck, however, a high
pass forms a bridge with
the greater mass of the Eel
Crag range; nevertheless, a
clear identity is maintained
by the ridge of Ard Crags as it
runs southwest over Knott
Rigg to Newlands Hause.
   Both flanks are rough and
exceedingly steep. Erosion
on the south side — facing
Newlands — has been halted
by a plantation to protect
the road and farmstead of
Keskadale at its foot.

MAP

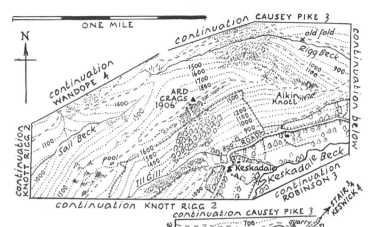

The fell is commonly referred to as Aikin Knott, which is more properly the name of a rocky excrescence on the 1500' contour. This latter name has wrongly appeared as Atkin Knott on some older Ordnance maps.

Rigg Beck

The sharp bend carrying the road over Rigg Beck is *comparatively* new. Formerly the road crossed at a ford lower down (still to be seen). Nearby, but now vanished, was a place of call, the Mill Dam Inn. Rest and refreshment for travellers are now to be found at Birkrigg, Gillbrow and Keskadale.

Higher up the road than the Rigg Beck crossing, at a wooded bend west of Gillbrow, is Bawd Hall, which was for many years in ruins, and Aikin, which was formerly a barn. Both are now occupied dwellings.

ASCENT FROM RIGG BECK
1350 feet of ascent : 1½ miles

Interest in the climb quickens at the foot of Aikin Knott. Bracken is succeeded by heather, through which a neat and charming track winds up the narrow ridge to the east top.

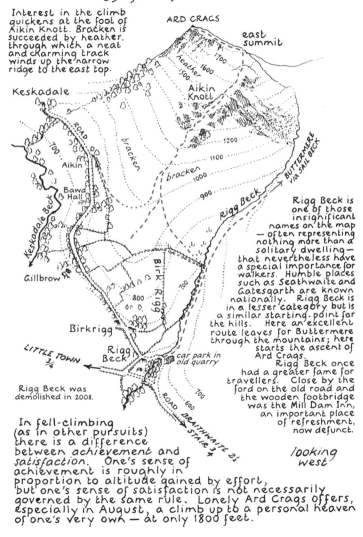

ARD CRAGS

east summit

heather

1700

1600

1500

Aikin Knott

Keskadale

ROAD

700

Aikin

Bawd Hall

Keskadale Beck

bracken

1200

1100

BUTTERMERE VIA SAIL BECK

1000

900

Rigg Beck

Gillbrow

800 or so

Birk Rigg

700

Birkrigg

Rigg Beck

LITTLE TOWN ¾

Rigg Beck was demolished in 2008.

car park in old quarry

700

ROAD

600

BRAITHWAITE STALE 3 2½

Rigg Beck is one of those insignificant names on the map — often representing nothing more than a solitary dwelling — that nevertheless have a special importance for walkers. Humble places such as Seathwaite and Gatesgarth are known nationally. Rigg Beck is in a lesser category but is a similar starting-point for the hills. Here an excellent route leaves for Buttermere through the mountains; here starts the ascent of Ard Crags.

Rigg Beck once had a greater fame for travellers. Close by the ford on the old road and the wooden footbridge was the Mill Dam Inn, an important place of refreshment, now defunct.

looking west

In fell-climbing (as in other pursuits) there is a difference between *achievement* and *satisfaction*. One's sense of achievement is roughly in proportion to altitude gained by effort, but one's sense of satisfaction is not necessarily governed by the same rule. Lonely Ard Crags offers, especially in August, a climb up to a personal heaven of one's very own — at only 1800 feet.

THE SUMMIT

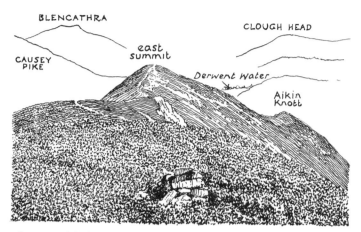

Save a visit here for a warm still day in August, and envy not the crowds heading for Great Gable. This is easier, more rewarding, and *solitary*. The narrow crest is a dense carpet of short springy heather, delightful to walk upon and even better as a couch for rest and meditation. But slumber is a hazard, for crags fall away sharply below one's boots to Keskadale. The highest point is marked by a pile of stones.

DESCENTS : *For Newlands,* follow the ridge over the east summit and Aikin Knott. *For Buttermere,* traverse Knott Rigg and aim for Newlands Hause. The flanks of the fell are too rough for descent.

The summit crags

looking down to Keskadale from the summit

THE VIEW

The highlight of the view is the beautiful detail of Newlands, a picture of bright pastures intermingled with heathery ridges, backed by the Helvellyn range, which is seen end to end in the distance. In other directions, nearby higher fells seriously curtail the view, and this is especially so between west and north, where the massive wall of the Eel Crag range towers above, impressively close. Eel Crag itself impends on the scene overpoweringly. Also of interest is the regular pattern of aretes descending from the long summit of Scar Crags just across the deep valley of Rigg Beck.

Principal Fells

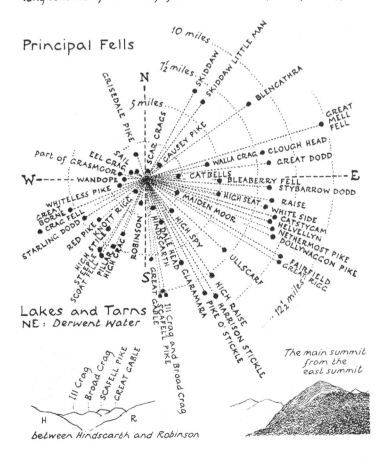

Lakes and Tarns
NE : Derwent Water

between Hindscarth and Robinson

The main summit
from the
east summit

RIDGE ROUTE

To KNOTT RIGG, 1824': 1 mile : SW
Depression at 1660'
130 feet of ascent

This is the natural continuation of the line of ascent over Aikin Knott.

From the cairn a thin track in heather skirts the rim of a gully with a view downwards to Keskadale, and goes on to a depression. The heather is here left behind and a short climb up the facing grass slope leads to a definite ridge with Knott Rigg's cairn at the end of it.

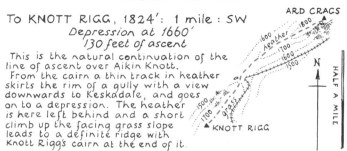

looking southwest along the ridge to Knott Rigg

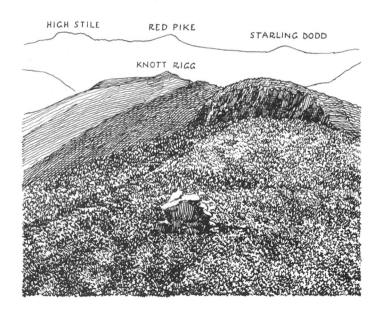

HIGH STILE   RED PIKE   STARLING DODD

KNOTT RIGG

Barf

1536'

from the main road near Beckstones

NATURAL FEATURES

Insignificant in height and of no greater extent than half a mile square, the rugged pyramid of Barf near the head of Bassenthwaite Lake yet contrives to arrest and retain the attention of travellers along the road at its base.   Its outline is striking, its slopes seemingly impossibly steep; the direct ascent from its foot appears to be barred by an uncompromising cliff. There are few fells, large or small, of such hostile and aggressive character, for unrelenting steepness is allied to unstable runs of scree and outcrops. The rough ground is masked by bracken and heather, both enemies of smooth walking and rhythmical progression....
Passers-by look up at Barf with no thought of climbing it.

Barf is really a shoulder of Lord's Seat, which rises beyond but is unseen from the road.   The neighbouring fells on both sides are densely planted with trees, but not so Barf. Crags and steep slopes do not normally deter the forestry workers but significantly they have not acquired any rights on Barf. This little rogue mountain cannot be tamed.

A unique feature that catches the eye from miles distant is the upstanding pinnacle long known as the Bishop of Barf, a venerable figure whose spotless vestments result from regular applications of whitewash.   This is a task not lightly to be undertaken, for the stiff climb to the Bishop's pulpit up shifting scree is a bad enough scramble without the grave added responsibility of balancing a bucket that must not be spilled.   But the job must be done from time to time.

Until recently the whitewash was applied by volunteers from the little community centred on the Swan Hotel directly below, but now the hotel has been turned into flats and the job has been taken over by the Keswick Mountain Rescue Team.

The hamlet is now named Powter How on Ordnance Survey maps.

The Bishop of Barf

BARF

▲

Powter
● How

▲
LORD'S
SEAT

Thornthwaite
▲

MILES

0   1   2

Barf 3

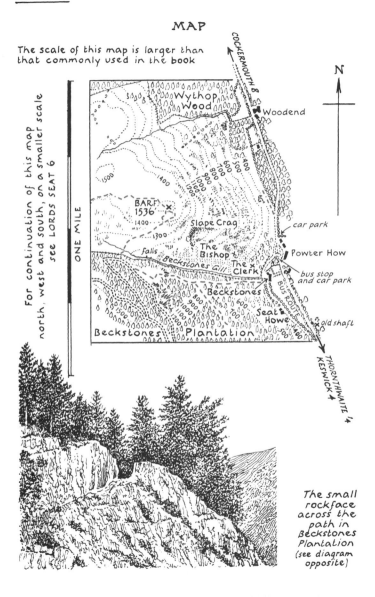

MAP

The scale of this map is larger than that commonly used in the book

COCKERMOUTH 8

N

Wythop Wood

Woodend

For continuation of this map north, west and south, on a smaller scale see LORDS SEAT 6

ONE MILE

BARF 1536 ×

Slope Crag

car park

falls

The Bishop ×

Beckstones Gill

The Clerk ×

Powter How

bus stop and car park

BUS ROUTE

Beckstones

old shaft

Seat Howe

Beckstones Plantation

THORNTHWAITE KESWICK 14

The small rockface across the path in Beckstones Plantation (see diagram opposite)

ASCENT FROM THORNTHWAITE
1220 feet of ascent : 1 mile (from Powter How)

Above the tree-line, easier slopes lead up to Lord's Seat

USUAL ROUTE

The path bifurcates below the top. The highest point is above a white (quartz) rock.

BARF

1400

1300

Blasted out of crags, this road is a considerable engineering achievement

forest road

1200

1100

felled

falls

Fifty yards after joining the forest road take a path on the right leading to a stile (provided with a wooden flap to allow animals through)

Beckstones Plantation

900

800

old forest road

700

600

500

Beckstones Gill

Here scrambling is necessary at a small rockface. A post is provided to show the way, but the route is in no real doubt.

The lower (and younger) plantings are mainly *larch*; higher, *spruce*.

The Bishop

The Bishop is conspicuous from the road, appearing as a detached pinnacle from the vicinity of the bus stop.

Take the path rising through the wood.

400

stile   bracken

Beckstones

looking west

BUS ROUTE

car park

PHEASANT INN 3/4
COCKERMOUTH 8 1/2

Powter How

bus stop and car park

THORNTHWAITE 1/2
KESWICK 4 1/4

Bus route X5 (Keswick – Workington)

This route is much easier to follow and to negotiate than the route described on page 6, and is deservedly more popular.   It is one of the very best of the shorter Lakeland climbs.

The Clerk

In comparison with the commanding figure of the Bishop, the Clerk is a poor drooping individual who attracts little attention to himself. He stands beside the path at the foot of the slope. He too wears white vestments, which are repainted from time to time by the Keswick Mountain Rescue Team.

A visit to the Bishop discloses that, behind the spotless raiment he displays to the road below, his rear quarters are equally brightly annointed. The monolith is not as tall as may be imagined: seven feet on the shortest side. Nevertheless it is to his credit that he has maintained his stately presence, for all around is the debris of shattered and eroded slate; the Bishop is slate, too, although obviously cast in a sterner mould. The time will come, however, when a collapsing pulpit will topple him down the screes.

The Bishop — rear view, looking down to the Swan Hotel

ASCENT FROM THORNTHWAITE
1200 feet of ascent : ¾ mile (from Powter How)

DIRECT ROUTE

BARF

looking west-north-west

Notes arranged from the bottom upwards

1500

grass

second false summit : true summit in view

first false summit : sudden, dramatic view of Bassenthwaite Lake below

heather

1400

Easier slopes now; difficulties over.

sheep track

upper escarpment. Cut up to it from the end of the traverse.

steep heather

Scramble up through the heather, avoiding the gorse.

1200

traverse

The traverse revives lurid memories of Jack's Rake on Pavey Ark, but is short and easy.

Slape Crag

This obstacle can be safely negotiated at one point only. Bear left at its base, across scree, to a rock traverse above an oak and a rowan together.

Oak tree (a surprise!) and a rowan growing together on crags.

steep heather

1000

← At last, a few yards of level walking

Slape Crag is now in view

solitary rowan tree

heather

900

By the time the rowan tree is reached the feeling that one is pioneering a new ascent, treading where no man has trodden before, is very strong, and consequently it is mortifying to find the slender trunk of the tree elaborately carved with the initials of a number of earlier visitors.

Escape left over loose rock to a small arete, then go up an easier heather slope above

800

The scree gully is unpleasant. Its walls of rotten rock cannot be trusted for handholds and fall apart at a touch. The 'tiles' here pull out like drawers.

700

The Bishop

Scramble up to the Bishop and pass behind him to a scree gully beyond

gorse

The Bishop stands on a remarkable pulpit built up of small flat tiles (of slate) lying horizontally.

600

scree

This wide scree slope, although not dangerous, is arduous to ascend, the feet often slipping down two steps for every step up — from which it should not be supposed that better progress will be made by going up backwards. Parsley fern, wood sage and silver birches grow in this area and in June the foxgloves make a colourful display.

Look out for the Clerk, an insignificant figure beside the path, almost hidden amongst trees at the foot of the slope

500

400

The Clerk

kissing gate

BUS ROUTE

→ PHEASANT INN 3¼
COCKERMOUTH 8½

Beckstones

← car park

Bus route X5

← Powter How
bus stop and car park

THORNTHWAITE 2
KESWICK 4¼

Not a walk. A very stiff scramble, suitable only for people overflowing with animal strength and vigour.

THE SUMMIT

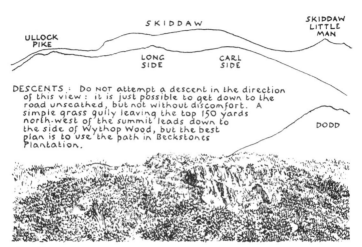

DESCENTS : Do not attempt a descent in the direction of this view : it is just possible to get down to the road unscathed, but not without discomfort. A simple grass gully leaving the top 150 yards north-west of the summit leads down to the side of Wythop Wood, but the best plan is to use the path in Beckstones Plantation.

Heather encroaches almost to the bare top, a small platform with grass growing thinly on underlying rock, which, in places, shows through to form a pavement. There is no cairn, nor facilities for making one. The summit breaks away in an unseen crag on the side facing Skiddaw, a fact to bear well in mind if there are children in the party.

The top of Barf

THE VIEW

The summit of Barf is the one place above all others for appreciating the massive build-up of Skiddaw, here seen, at mid-height, piling up from the shore of Bassenthwaite Lake in three great leaps to the summit 1500 feet above the viewpoint. The lake, too, is exceptionally well displayed directly below — a sensational surprise for those who reach the top from 'behind'. There is a pleasing view of the Vale of Keswick and Derwent Water and an extensive prospect seawards.

Principal Fells

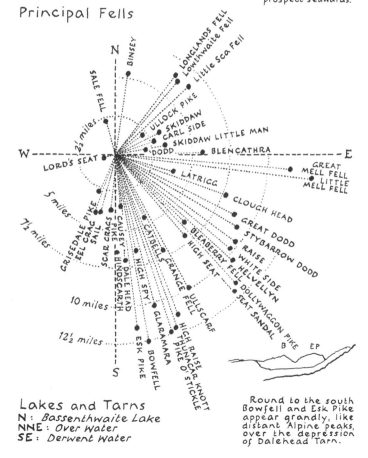

Lakes and Tarns
N : Bassenthwaite Lake
NNE : Over Water
SE : Derwent Water

Round to the south Bowfell and Esk Pike appear grandly, like distant Alpine peaks, over the depression of Dalehead Tarn.

RIDGE ROUTE

To LORD'S SEAT, 1811′ : ¾ mile : W
Depression at 1400′ : 420 feet of ascent

The path starts at the summit, and much of it can be seen winding over an area of grass and heather. There is an indistinct stretch, but it doesn't matter if the path is lost because walking is easy and the heather can be avoided. Even in mist it is not advisable to go down to the fence and follow it up because of thick undergrowth.

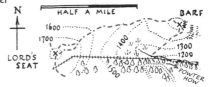

Lord's Seat from Barf

Barf, south side, from a forest road in Beckstones Plantation

Barf, north side, from a dead forest above Wythop Wood

Barrow 1494'

from Outerside
Stile End in the middle
distance; Stonycroft Gill
mine road down on the right

Braithwaite
●
GRISEDALE
▲ PIKE
OUTERSIDE ▲   ▲ BARROW
                ● Stair
   CAUSEY PIKE ▲
            MILES
   0   1   2   3

from
Newlands Beck

NATURAL FEATURES

Barrow occupies an enviable position overlooking a scene as fair as any in the kingdom. In shape a long narrow ridge, rooted in Braithwaite, it rises to present a broad flank to the valley of Newlands before curving west, bounded by Stonycroft Gill, to join the mass of Outerside across the gap of Barrow Door. A great scar on the Newlands face marks the site of the once-famous Barrow Mine; on the opposite flank facing Coledale is another great scar, this one a natural formation, at a point where Barrow Gill, after an uneventful meandering from Barrow Door, is suddenly engulfed in a remarkable ravine, a gorge of amazing proportions for so slender a stream and deeper even than Piers Gill, which continues down, becoming wooded, to the cottages of Braithwaite. Bracken clothes the lower slopes of Barrow, but a dark cap of heather covers the higher reaches.

At Stonycroft Bridge an old water-cut (now dry) can be traced up, first carved in the rock and then following the contour of the fellside, with the gorge steeply below. The old level illustrated, half-hidden by gorse, is alongside the cut in its top part.

This is the setting of the old Stonycroft Mine

Under Stonycroft Bridge. The beck enters the picture from the left. The dry watercut comes down on the right.

Barrow is 'the shivering mountain' of Lakeland. The great fan of spoil from the old mines on the Newlands face sweeps down to the road near Uzzicar and is prevented from burying it in debris only by a retaining parapet with a cleared space behind to accommodate major falls. The spoil is a sandy gravel constantly in slight motion, and the rustle of movement on the slope (no more than a whisper) can be heard on the road below. Note also an air shaft in the small field south of Uzzicar.

Barrow 3

Barrow Gill

looking up the gill to Barrow Door and Causey Pike

looking down the gill to Braithwaite

MAP

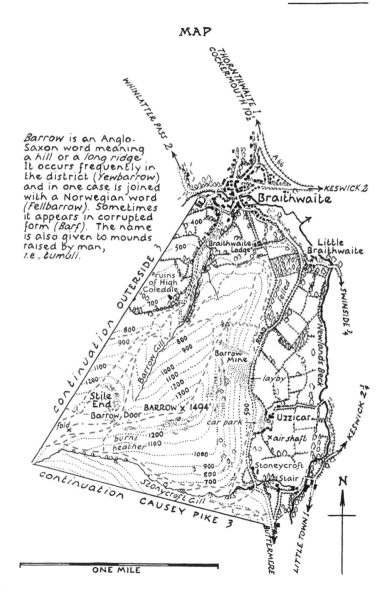

Barrow is an Anglo-Saxon word meaning a *hill* or a *long ridge*. It occurs frequently in the district (*Yewbarrow*) and in one case is joined with a Norwegian word (*Fellbarrow*). Sometimes it appears in corrupted form (*Barf*). The name is also given to mounds raised by man, i.e., *tumuli*.

ONE MILE

ASCENT FROM BRAITHWAITE
1250 feet of ascent : 1½ miles

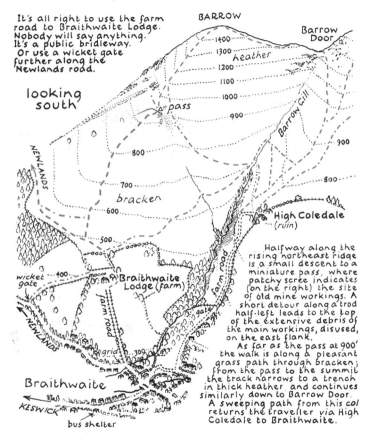

It's all right to use the farm road to Braithwaite Lodge. Nobody will say anything. It's a public bridleway. Or use a wicket gate further along the Newlands road.

looking south

BARROW

Barrow Door

heather

1400
1300
1200
1100
1000
900

Barrow Gill

900

800

NEWLANDS

800

700

800

bracken

600

High Coledale
(ruin)

500

wicket gate

400

Braithwaite Lodge (farm)

farm road

NEWLANDS

gate

grid

300

Braithwaite

KESWICK

bus shelter

Halfway along the rising northeast ridge is a small descent to a miniature pass, where patchy scree indicates (on the right) the site of old mine workings. A short detour along a trod half-left leads to the top of the extensive debris of the main workings, disused, on the east flank.

As far as the pass at 900' the walk is along a pleasant grass path through bracken; from the pass to the summit the track narrows to a trench in thick heather, and continues similarly down to Barrow Door. A sweeping path from this col returns the traveller via High Coledale to Braithwaite.

The ascent of Barrow from Braithwaite by its facing ridge is a favourite Sunday afternoon ramble, in the category of Latrigg and Catbells and Loughrigg Fell, and every step of the way is a joy. The walk can be extended, as indicated, to make a round journey of about two hours.

ASCENT FROM STAIR
1200 feet of ascent : 2¼ miles

looking north·west

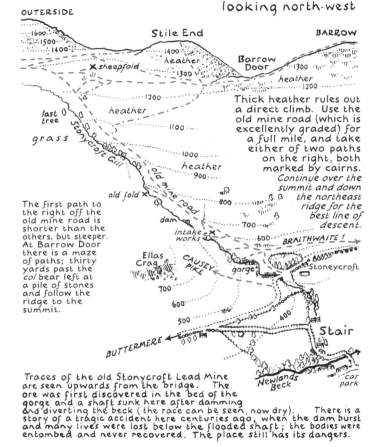

Thick heather rules out a direct climb. Use the old mine road (which is excellently graded) for a full mile, and take either of two paths on the right, both marked by cairns. *Continue over the summit and down the northeast ridge for the best line of descent.*

The first path to the right off the old mine road is shorter than the others, but steeper. At Barrow Door there is a maze of paths; thirty yards past the *col* bear left at a pile of stones and follow the ridge to the summit.

Traces of the old Stonycroft Lead Mine are seen upwards from the bridge. The ore was first discovered in the bed of the gorge and a shaft sunk here after damming and diverting the beck (the race can be seen, now dry). There is a story of a tragic accident here centuries ago, when the dam burst and many lives were lost below the flooded shaft; the bodies were entombed and never recovered. The place still has its dangers.

The old mine road has become a first-class walkers way into the hills, progress being fast and easy, and it lends itself well, coupled with a linking path from Braithwaite, to an ascent of Barrow, while giving an introduction to the quiet upper reaches of Stonycroft Gill. Causey Pike on the left of the valley dominates the walk throughout.

THE SUMMIT

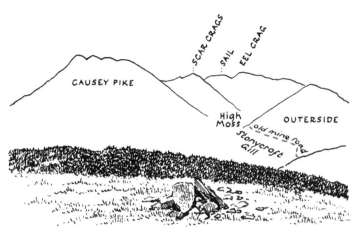

The highest point is situated on a patch of grass with heather all around. There is no cairn. On the right sort of day this is a grand place for settling down and getting the old pipe out for an hour's quiet meditation.

DESCENTS : Use only the track along the ridge, either way. In particular do not attempt a direct route for Newlands.

RIDGE ROUTE

To OUTERSIDE, 1863': 1¼ miles : WSW, then NW and SW

Depressions at 1270' and 1380'
800 feet of ascent
Rough walking in heather

Go down to Barrow Door and up a facing track, which gradually fades away. At the top of Stile End turn left down to Low Moss, across which a charming track mounts through the heather to the top of Outerside.

Not recommended beyond Barrow Door in mist.

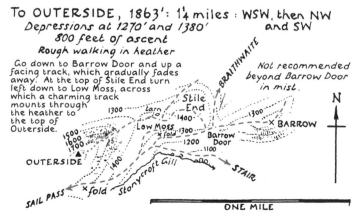

ONE MILE

THE VIEW

This is a splendid panorama, too good really for the small effort involved in earning it.

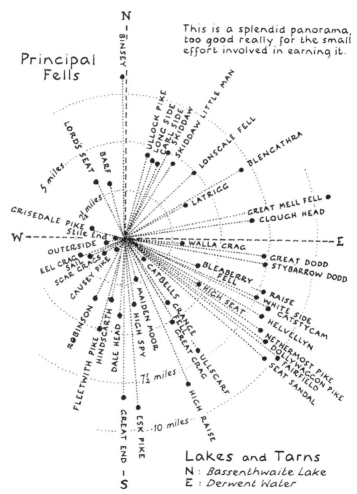

Principal Fells

N

N — BINSEY

ULLOCK PIKE
LONG SIDE
CARL SIDE
SKIDDAW
SKIDDAW LITTLE MAN

LONSCALE FELL

BLENCATHRA

LORDS SEAT

BARF

5 miles

2 miles

LATRIGG

GREAT MELL FELL

CLOUGH HEAD

GRISEDALE PIKE

Stile End

W

E

OUTERSIDE

WALLA CRAG

GREAT DODD
STYBARROW DODD

EEL CRAG
SAIL
SCAR CRAGS

BLEABERRY FELL

CAUSEY PIKE

CATBELLS

HIGH SEAT

RAISE
WHITE SIDE
CATSTYCAM

ROBINSON

MAIDEN MOOR

GRANGE FELL

HELVELLYN

HINDSCARTH

HIGH SPY

GREAT CRAG

NETHERMOST PIKE

DALE HEAD

ULLSCARF

DOLLYWAGGON PIKE
FAIRFIELD
SEAT SANDAL

FLEETWITH PIKE

7½ miles

GREAT END

ESK PIKE

HIGH RAISE

10 miles

S

Lakes and Tarns

N : *Bassenthwaite Lake*
E : *Derwent Water*

There is a remarkable contrast between the smiling Vale of Keswick, where Derwent Water is excellently displayed, and the sombre ring of fells crowded nearby in the west. Away over the head of Newlands is Esk Hause with Esk Pike soaring magnificently to the left of it and looking every inch a mountain

Cockermouth

Wythop
Mill　　　▲ SALE FELL

LING FELL ▲

GRAYSTONES　　▲ BROOM
▲　　　　FELL

Low
Lorton　　● High　　▲ LORD'S
Lorton　　　SEAT

Whinlatter Pass

MILES

0　1　2　3　4

from
Aiken Plantation

NATURAL FEATURES

Broom Fell is the geographical centre of the upland mass rising between Bassenthwaite Lake in the north and Whinlatter Pass in the south, but acknowledges the superiority of a near and higher neighbour, Lord's Seat, to which it is connected by a high ridge. There is little of interest on this rounded grassy hill, and nothing to justify a special visit to the summit; its flanking valleys, however, are sharply contrasted, each having distinguishing features worthy of note. North is the open valley of Wythop, a place of farms and green pastures, but before the descending slopes reach cultivable levels they are halted at a morass, the remarkable mile-wide Wythop Moss — a hopeless, lifeless swamp. At one place a causeway of firmer ground has been laid out and ditched to facilitate a crossing, but this is now as marshy as its surroundings. South is the narrow side valley of Aiken Beck, with the rare distinction of being enclosed on all four sides: a hidden valley, uninhabited, and frequented only for purposes of forestry, most of it being under timber.

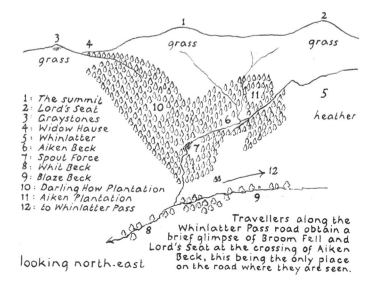

1: The summit
2: Lord's Seat
3: Graystones
4: Widow Hause
5: Whinlatter
6: Aiken Beck
7: Spout Force
8: Whit Beck
9: Blaze Beck
10: Darling How Plantation
11: Aiken Plantation
12: to Whinlatter Pass

grass grass grass heather

Travellers along the Whinlatter Pass road obtain a brief glimpse of Broom Fell and Lord's Seat at the crossing of Aiken Beck, this being the only place on the road where they are seen.

looking north-east

MAP

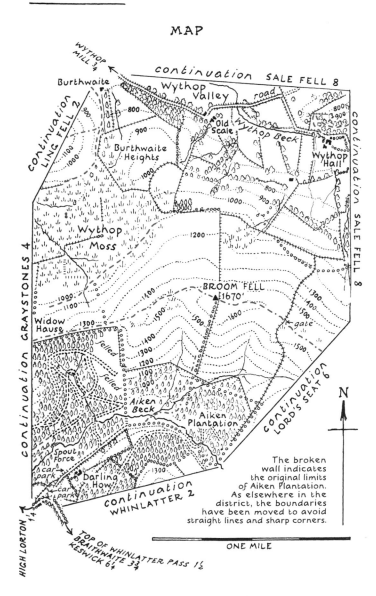

The broken wall indicates the original limits of Aiken Plantation. As elsewhere in the district, the boundaries have been moved to avoid straight lines and sharp corners.

ONE MILE

N

ASCENT FROM WYTHOP MILL
1450 feet of ascent : 4 miles

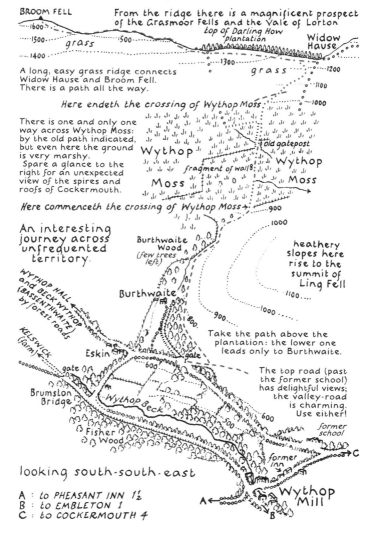

BROOM FELL

....1600....

....1500....   grass   ...500...

....1400....

From the ridge there is a magnificent prospect of the Grasmoor Fells and the Vale of Lorton

top of Darling How plantation

Widow Hause

....1300....   grass 1200

A long, easy grass ridge connects Widow Hause and Broom Fell. There is a path all the way.

....1100

Here endeth the crossing of Wythop Moss 1000

There is one and only one way across Wythop Moss: by the old path indicated, but even here the ground is very marshy.

Spare a glance to the right for an unexpected view of the spires and roofs of Cockermouth.

Wythop

Moss

old gatepost

fragment of wall

Wythop

Moss

Here commenceth the crossing of Wythop Moss → 900

An interesting journey across unfrequented territory.

Burthwaite Wood (few trees left)

....1000

heathery slopes here rise to the summit of Ling Fell

....1100

Burthwaite

WYTHOP HALL and BECK WYTHOP (BASSENTHWAITE) by forest roads

KELSWICK (farm)

Eskin

....800....

....900....

gate

Take the path above the plantation: the lower one leads only to Burthwaite.

....1000

Brumston Bridge

gate

Wythop Beck

....600

The top road (past the former school) has delightful views; the valley-road is charming. Use either!

....600

Fisher Wood

....500

former school

looking south-south-east

former inn

C

former inn

Wythop Mill

A : to PHEASANT INN 1½
B : to EMBLETON 1
C : to COCKERMOUTH 4

A

B

ASCENT FROM HIGH LORTON
1400 feet of ascent : 3 miles

looking east·north·east

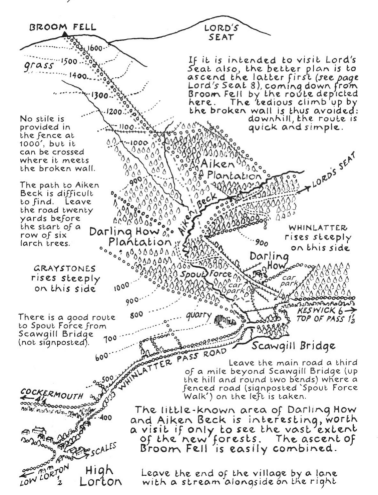

BROOM FELL

LORD'S SEAT

grass

1600
1500
1400
1300
1200
1100
1000
900

If it is intended to visit Lord's Seat also, the better plan is to ascend the latter first (see page Lord's Seat 8), coming down from Broom Fell by the route depicted here. The tedious climb up by the broken wall is thus avoided: downhill, the route is quick and simple.

No stile is provided in the fence at 1000', but it can be crossed where it meets the broken wall.

The path to Aiken Beck is difficult to find. Leave the road twenty yards before the start of a row of six larch trees.

Aiken Plantation

Aiken Beck

LORD'S SEAT

Darling How Plantation

WHINLATTER rises steeply on this side

GRAYSTONES rises steeply on this side

900

Darling How

Spout Force

car park

car park

1000
900
800
700
600

quarry

KESWICK 6 →
TOP OF PASS 1½

There is a good route to Spout Force from Scawgill Bridge (not signposted).

Scawgill Bridge

500

WHINLATTER PASS ROAD

400

COCKERMOUTH 4½

Leave the main road a third of a mile beyond Scawgill Bridge (up the hill and round two bends) where a fenced road (signposted 'Spout Force Walk') on the left is taken.

The little-known area of Darling How and Aiken Beck is interesting, worth a visit if only to see the vast extent of the new forests. The ascent of Broom Fell is easily combined.

SCALES

FROM LOW LORTON ½

High Lorton

Leave the end of the village by a lane with a stream alongside on the right

THE SUMMIT

looking southeast

GREAT DODD

LORD'S SEAT

HELVELLYN

NETHERMOST PIKE

DOLLYWAGGON PIKE

FAIRFIELD

The highest point is marked by a very fine column about seven feet high capped with a quartz stone. Fences stretch both north and south. An old wall comes up the fellside from Aiken Beck to end precisely at the highest point – apparently enclosing nothing, defending nothing, sheltering nothing, marking nothing. It must have some value, however, since now it has fallen into disrepair it has been reinforced by a fence.

DESCENTS : All slopes are easy, the western going down to Wythop Moss, where the old path must be used to cross the morass. *In mist*, let the old wall serve as a guide downhill to Lorton.

GREAT BORNE

GAVEL FELL

BLAKE FELL

BURNBANK FELL

LOW FELL

Darling How Plantation

Vale of Lorton

*looking southwest
to the
Loweswater Fells*

THE VIEW

The gem of the view is the Vale of Lorton backed by the fells around Loweswater — a lovely scene. The Grasmoor group is massed impressively across the gulf of Whinlatter Pass. Beyond Bassenthwaite Lake Skiddaw rises grandly. Northwest is a wide sweep of the Solway Firth and the Scottish hills, with Criffell prominent.

Principal Fells

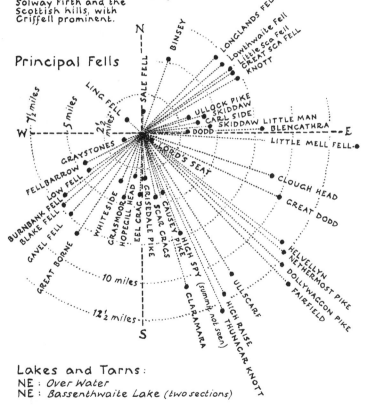

Lakes and Tarns:
NE: *Over Water*
NE: *Bassenthwaite Lake (two sections)*

The skyline to the south

RIDGE ROUTES

To LORD'S SEAT, 1811' : ⅞ mile : SE
Depression at 1586' : 260 feet of ascent
An easy ridge, with nothing of special interest.

The ridge is wide, marshy in places, and carries a path; it has many small undulations, and the actual lowest point, at 1586', just before the ground steepens into the final rise of Lord's Seat, cannot be identified with certainty; not that it matters. This is the slope of Lord's Seat on which the 'seat' is supposed to be found, but its exact location is also in doubt. This doesn't matter either, the author having personally installed himself in every rock-recess hereabouts (anxious as always for the comfort of his readers) and found the process merely painful.

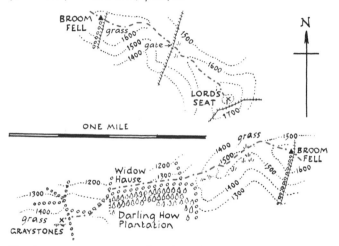

To GRAYSTONES, 1476' : 1¼ miles : WSW
Depression at 1240' (Widow Hause) : 260 feet of ascent
Interest is sustained on this easy walk by the variety of scenery

Starting due west, follow the height of land across a moist depression to firmer ground beyond, which trends south to the corner of Darling How Plantation. Here the crumbling wall that formerly ran solitary along the descending ridge to Widow Hause is now accompanied by a tight forest fence, the plantings here having been carried the full height of the fellside from the valley of Aiken Beck below. The fence continues on to Graystones, and the only place where it can be crossed is at the north-west corner of the plantation, where a short stretch of wooden fence serves as a stile. When the fence finally turns south the summit of Graystones is only two minutes away.

Castle Crag

951'

Grange
●

CASTLE
▲ CRAG

Rosthwaite
●

ONE MILE

from the south

NATURAL FEATURES

Perhaps, to be strictly correct, Castle Crag should be regarded not as a separate fell but as a protuberance on the rough breast of Low Scawdel, occurring almost at the foot of the slope and remote from the ultimate summit of High Spy far above and out of sight. Castle Crag has no major geographical function — it is not a watershed, does not persuade the streams of Scawdel from their predestined purpose of joining the Derwent and interrupts only slightly the natural fall of the fell to Borrowdale: on the general scale of the surrounding heights it is of little significance.

Yet Castle Crag is so magnificently independent, so ruggedly individual, so aggressively unashamed of its lack of inches, that less than justice would be done by relegating it to a paragraph in the High Spy chapter. Its top is below 1000 feet (its 'official' height in 2008 being 951 feet), which makes it the only fell below 1000 feet in this series of books that is awarded the 'full treatment', a distinction well earned.

Castle Crag conforms to no pattern. It is an obstruction in the throat of Borrowdale, confining passage therein to the width of a river and a road, hiding what lies beyond, defying cultivation. Its abrupt pyramid, richly wooded from base almost to summit but bare at the top, is a wild tangle of rough steep ground, a place of crags and scree and tumbled boulders, of quarry holes and spoil dumps, of confusion and disorder. But such is the artistry of nature, such is the mellowing influence of the passing years, that the scars of disarray and decay have been transformed in a romantic harmony, cloaked by a canopy of trees and a carpet of leaves. There are lovely copses of silver birch by the crystal-clear river, magnificent specimens of Scots pine higher up. Naked of trees, Castle Crag would be ugly; with them, it has a sylvan beauty unsurpassed, unique.

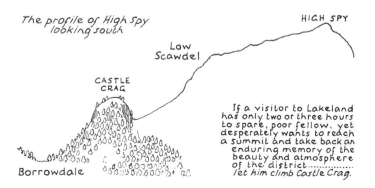

The profile of High Spy looking south

HIGH SPY

Low Scawdel

CASTLE CRAG

Borrowdale

If a visitor to Lakeland has only two or three hours to spare, poor fellow, yet desperately wants to reach a summit and take back an enduring memory of the beauty and atmosphere of the district..............
let him climb Castle Crag.

The summit-quarry

The pedestrian path to the
top goes up the grass
on the right

summit

Quarries and caves of Castle Crag

In addition to the summit-quarry, which is open to the sky
and obvious to all who climb the fell, the steep flank above the
Derwent is pitted with cuttings and caverns and levels, every
hole having its tell-tale spoilheap, but the scars of this former
industrial activity are largely concealed by a screen of trees
and not generally noticed. Much of this flank is precipitous,
the ground everywhere is very rough, and the vertically-hewn
walls of naked stone are dangerous traps for novice explorers.

Of these quarries the best known
is High Hows, the debris of which is
passed on the riverside walk from
Grange to Rosthwaite. A detour up
the quarry road leads to a series of
caverns of special interest because
in one of them Millican Dalton,
a mountaineering adventurer
and a familiar character in the
district between the wars (died
1947, aged 80), furnished a home
for his summer residence, using
an adjacent cave at a higher
level (the 'Attic') as sleeping
quarters. *Note here his lettering
(though now difficult to read) cut
in the rock at the entrance —
'Don't!! Waste words, jump to conclusions'*

The Attic

Millican's Cave

MAP

The thick line forming a square has a special significance. It encloses one mile of country containing no high mountain, no lake, no famous crag, no tarn,

But, in the authors humble submission, it encloses the loveliest square mile in Lakeland — the Jaws of Borrowdale.

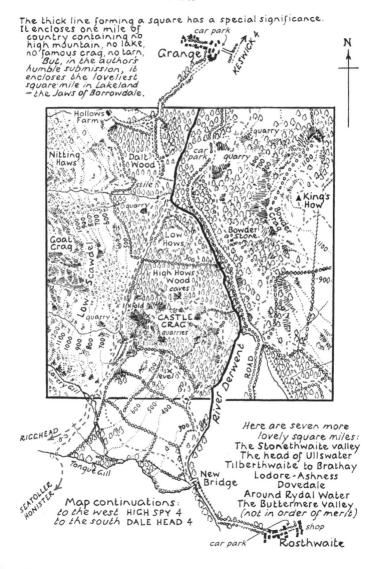

Here are seven more lovely square miles:
The Stonethwaite valley
The head of Ullswater
Tilberthwaite to Brathay
Lodore-Ashness
Dovedale
Around Rydal Water
The Buttermere valley
(not in order of merit)

Map continuations:
to the west HIGH SPY 4
to the south DALE HEAD 4

ASCENT FROM GRANGE

700 feet of ascent
1½ miles

CASTLE CRAG

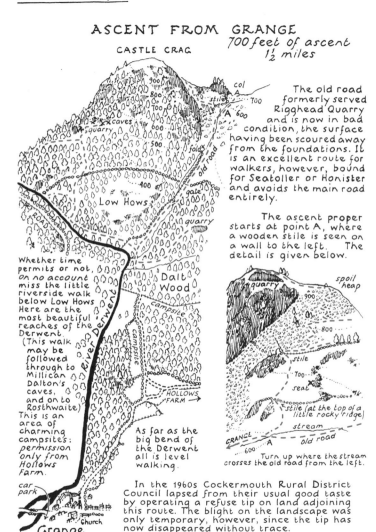

The old road formerly served Rigghead Quarry and is now in bad condition, the surface having been scoured away from the foundations. It is an excellent route for walkers, however, bound for Seatoller or Honister and avoids the main road entirely.

The ascent proper starts at point A, where a wooden stile is seen on a wall to the left. The detail is given below.

Whether time permits or not, on no account miss the little riverside walk below Low Hows. Here are the most beautiful reaches of the Derwent. (This walk may be followed through to Millican Dalton's caves, and on to Rosthwaite). This is an area of charming campsites: permission only from Hollows Farm.

As far as the big bend of the Derwent all is level walking.

Turn up where the stream crosses the old road from the left.

In the 1960s Cockermouth Rural District Council lapsed from their usual good taste by operating a refuse tip on land adjoining this route. The blight on the landscape was only temporary, however, since the tip has now disappeared without trace.

looking south

Leave Grange by a lane (signposted to Hollows Farm) almost opposite the church.

ASCENT FROM ROSTHWAITE

700 feet of ascent
1½ miles

CASTLE CRAG

looking
north-west

From the ridge, the old
Rigghead–Grange 'road'
can be seen ahead and
below in a wild setting.

There are magnificent
Scots pines near the
wall at the top of
the wood.

900

spoil

quarry

B

level
gate

700

level x·x
hut

600

500

400

A

A

300

gate

GRANGE

A quarry path ascends
the big enclosure (A). A
detour of 50 yards to the
old level and stone shelter,
which are typical evidences of
former quarrying operations, is
recommended. Near the top corner
of the enclosure the original path
crossed the wall and proceeded on
the far side to the ridge. This route
is not now used, and it is more
usual to pass through the gate
in the cross-wall to enclosure β
(note another level here in the
corner) and, upon reaching the
ridge, cross the wall to join the
original route: a stile is provided
here. Now the spoil-heap ahead is
climbed by a zig-zag path carved
in the naked stones, after which
the way to the summit is clear.

Stonethwaite
Beck

River Derwent

New
Bridge

ROSTHWAITE ¼
lane

BORROWDALE
Y.H. ½

Leave Rosthwaite by the lane
opposite the village shop, bearing
right at the farm buildings.

An old
level

Old quarry workings, Castle Crag

A typical
stone store
or shelter
hut
(only 3
to 4 feet
high)

THE SUMMIT

The summit is circular in plan, about 60 yards in diameter, and a perfect natural stronghold. Even today, one man in possession, armed with a stick, could prevent its occupation by others whatever their number, there being one strategic point (the place of access to the top) where passage upward is restricted to single-file traffic. Authorities agree that there was once a fort here, probably early British, but it needs a trained eye to trace any earthworks—which, in any case, must have been severely disturbed by an old quarry that has cut a big slice out of the summit and, be it noted, constitutes an unprotected danger. Photographers (who have a habit of taking backward steps when composing their pictures) should take care lest they suddenly vanish.

The highest point is a boss of rock, and this is crowned by a low horseshoe-shaped wall, below which, set in the rock, is a commemorative tablet: a war memorial to the men of Borrowdale, effective and imaginative. Immediately to the west of the summit is a larch tree that blocks out much of High Spy, and other specimens surround the perimeter.

DESCENTS: For the ordinary walker there is only one way on and off, and this is on the south side, by a clump of larch, where a clear track descends between the edge of the quarry (right) and a cutting (left) to the flat top of the spoil-heap, at the end of which a ramp on the right inclines in zigzags to the grass below. Here, if bound for Rosthwaite, cross the wall on the left; for Grange the way continues down, crossing two walls by stiles, to the old Rigghead road.

ENVIRONS OF THE SUMMIT

THE SUMMIT

When this guide was first published, the altitude of the summit (now officially 951 feet) had yet to be determined. It was frequently quoted as 900 feet, but the following reasoning demonstrated that it must actually be in excess of this figure.

From High Doat (927'; 1 mile south) the summit appears to be above the horizontal plane of Latrigg (1203'; 6½ miles), giving a height of not less than 970', and probably 980' or 990'.

Look at High Doat from Castle Crag: it is obviously lower.

THE VIEW

The view is circumscribed but is open to the north, where Derwent Water, backed by Skiddaw, makes a fine scene. The steep fall from the summit on all sides provides an aerial study of the beautiful detail of mid-Borrowdale.

Principal Fells

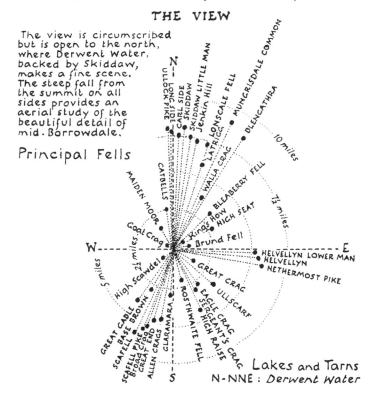

Lakes and Tarns
N-NNE: Derwent Water

Catbells

1481'

Cat Bells
(two words)
on Ordnance maps

from Derwent Water

• Portinscale
   • Keswick

• Stair

▲ CATBELLS
• Little Town
▲ MAIDEN MOOR
  • Grange

MILES

0   1   2   3   4

from the Portinscale path

NATURAL FEATURES

Catbells is one of the great favourites, a family fell where grandmothers and infants can climb the heights together, a place beloved. Its popularity is well deserved: its shapely topknot attracts the eye, offering a steep but obviously simple scramble to the small summit; its slopes are smooth, sunny and sleek; its position overlooking Derwent Water is superb. Moreover, for stronger walkers it is the first step on a glorious ridge that bounds Borrowdale on the west throughout its length with Newlands down on the other side. There is beauty everywhere — and nothing but beauty. Its ascent from Keswick may conveniently, in the holiday season, be coupled with a sail on the lake, making the expedition rewarding out of all proportion to the small effort needed. Even the name has a magic challenge.

Yet this fell is not quite so innocuous as is usually thought, and grandmothers and infants should have a care as they romp around. There are some natural hazards in the form of a line of crags that starts at the summit and slants down to Newlands, and steep outcrops elsewhere. More dangerous are the levels and open shafts that pierce the fell on both flanks: the once-prosperous Yewthwaite Mine despoils a wide area in the combe above Little Town in Newlands, to the east the debris of the ill-starred Brandley Mine is lapped by the water of the lake, and the workings of the Old Brandley Mine, high on the side of the fell at Skelgill Bank, are in view on the ascent of the ridge from the north. A tragic death in one of the open Yewthwaite shafts in 1962 serves as a warning.

Words cannot adequately describe the rare charm of Catbells, nor its ravishing view. But no publicity is necessary: its mere presence in the Derwent Water scene is enough. It has a bold 'come hither' look that compels one's steps, and no suitor ever returns disappointed, but only looking back often. It has only to be seen from Friar's Crag — and a spell is cast. No Keswick holiday is consummated without a visit to Catbells.

from Yewthwaite Comb

Catbells 3

Crags and
Caverns
of Catbells

left: The crags of
Mart Bield,
below the summit
on the Newlands
side of the fell

right: A dangerous hole at
Yewthwaite Mine.
At the end of a rock cutting the
adit suggests a level (horizontal
tunnel) but in fact is the opening
of a vertical shaft.

below: Workings at the
Old Brandley Mine.
A shaft with twin entrances,
overhung by a tree, *left*, and
a nearby level, *right*.

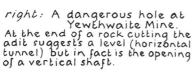

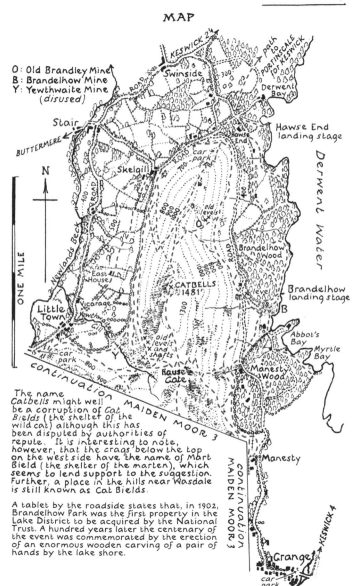

MAP

O: Old Brandley Mine
B: Brandelhow Mine
Y: Yewthwaite Mine
(disused)

The name Catbells might well be a corruption of Cat Bields (the shelter of the wild cat) although this has been disputed by authorities of repute. It is interesting to note, however, that the crags below the top on the west side have the name of Mart Bield (the shelter of the marten), which seems to lend support to the suggestion. Further, a place in the hills near Wasdale is still known as Cat Bields.

A tablet by the roadside states that, in 1902, Brandelhow Park was the first property in the Lake District to be acquired by the National Trust. A hundred years later the centenary of the event was commemorated by the erection of an enormous wooden carving of a pair of hands by the lake shore.

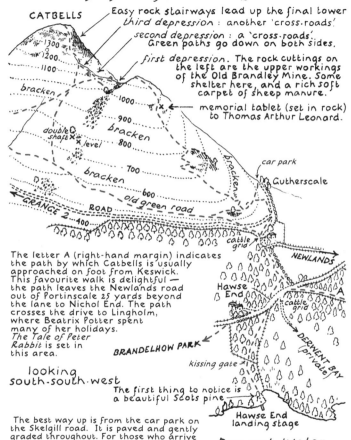

ASCENT FROM HAWSE END
1250 feet of ascent : 1½ miles

CATBELLS

Easy rock stairways lead up the final tower
third depression : another 'cross-roads'

second depression : a 'cross-roads'.
Green paths go down on both sides.

first depression. The rock cuttings on
the left are the upper workings
of the Old Brandley Mine. Some
shelter here, and a rich soft
carpet of sheep manure.

1300
1200
1100

bracken

1000 ─ × ← ─ memorial tablet (set in rock)
to Thomas Arthur Leonard.

900

double
shaft ×   bracken   800
level

700   bracken

car park
Gutherscale

600   old green road

GRANGE 2   ROAD   400

cattle grid

NEWLANDS

Hawse
End

cattle grid

DERWENT BAY (private)

The letter A (right-hand margin) indicates
the path by which Catbells is usually
approached on foot from Keswick.
This favourite walk is delightful —
the path leaves the Newlands road
out of Portinscale 25 yards beyond
the lane to Nichol End. The path
crosses the drive to Lingholm,
where Beatrix Potter spent
many of her holidays.
The Tale of Peter
Rabbit is set in
this area.

BRANDELHOW PARK

kissing gate

looking
south-south-west

The first thing to notice is
a beautiful Scots pine

Hawse End
landing stage

Derwent Water

The best way up is from the car park on
the Skelgill road. It is paved and gently
graded throughout. For those who arrive
by bus or on foot an alternative path
leaves from the road junction and curves
left to join the path from the car park.

Hawse End is served
by motor-launch from
Keswick.

Woodford's Path:
This series of zigzags was engineered
by a Sir John Woodford, who lived near,
and his name deserves to be remembered
by those who use his enchanting stairway.
It starts 80 yards along the old green road.

One of the very best
of the shorter climbs.
A truly lovely walk.

ASCENT FROM GRANGE
1250 feet of ascent : 2 miles

Of course there is no gate at House Gate, just as there is no door at Mickledoor. 'Gate' and 'door' are local geographical terms for a way or opening through the hills or across a ridge. 'Hause' is another good Lakeland name for a pass. 'House Gate' is therefore really a tautological name. 'Hawse End' (with a 'w') is not a mis-spelling, 'hause' being inappropriate to the place.

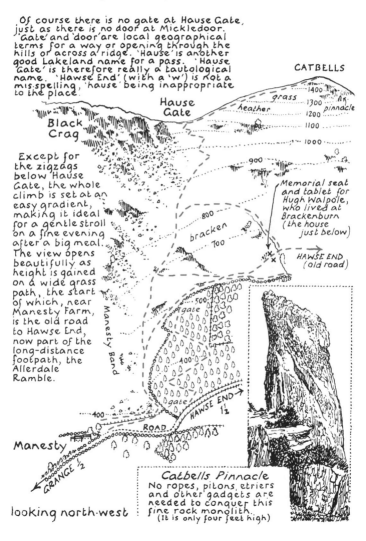

CATBELLS

Hause Gate

Black Crag

grass

heather

pinnacle

1400
1300
1200
1100
1000
900
800
700
500
400

Memorial seat and tablet for Hugh Walpole, who lived at Brackenburn (the house just below)

HAWSE END (old road)

bracken

Except for the zigzags below Hause Gate, the whole climb is set at an easy gradient, making it ideal for a gentle stroll on a fine evening after a big meal. The view opens beautifully as height is gained on a wide grass path, the start of which, near Manesty Farm, is the old road to Hawse End, now part of the long-distance footpath, the Allerdale Ramble.

Manesty Band

gate

gate

HAWSE END 1½

ROAD

Manesty

GRANGE ½

looking north·west

Catbells Pinnacle
No ropes, pitons, etriers and other gadgets are needed to conquer this fine rock monolith.
(It is only four feet high)

ASCENT FROM NEWLANDS

via SKELGILL
1200 feet of ascent : 1½ miles from Stair

via LITTLE TOWN
950 feet of ascent : 1½ miles from Little Town

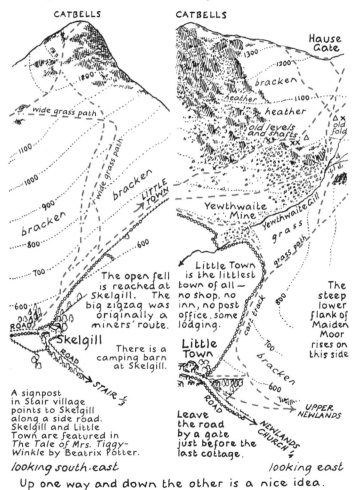

CATBELLS

CATBELLS

Hause Gate

1300

1200

bracken

1100

heather

heather

old levels and shafts

△ x x old fold

wide grass path

1200

1100

1000

wide grass path

900

bracken

800

bracken

LITTLE TOWN

600

700

Yewthwaite Mine

Yewthwaite Gill

grass

grass path

600

600

ROAD

Skelgill

The open fell is reached at Skelgill. The big zigzag was originally a miners' route.

There is a camping barn at Skelgill.

Little Town is the littlest town of all — no shop, no inn, no post office, some lodging.

Little Town

cart track

800

The steep lower flank of Maiden Moor rises on this side

700

bracken

ROAD

STAIR ½

A signpost in Stair village points to Skelgill along a side road. Skelgill and Little Town are featured in The Tale of Mrs. Tiggy-Winkle by Beatrix Potter.

ROAD

Leave the road by a gate just before the last cottage.

NEWLANDS CHURCH ½

600

UPPER NEWLANDS

looking south-east

looking east

Up one way and down the other is a nice idea.

THE SUMMIT

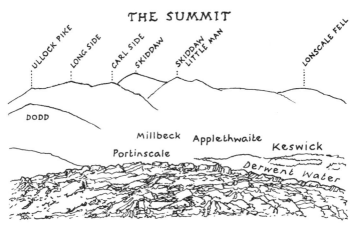

ULLOCK PIKE   LONG SIDE   CARL SIDE   SKIDDAW   SKIDDAW LITTLE MAN   LONSCALE FELL

DODD

Millbeck   Applethwaite   Keswick

Portinscale   Derwent Water

The summit, which has no cairn, is a small platform of naked rock, light brown in colour and seamed and pitted with many tiny hollows and crevices that collect and hold rainwater — so that, long after the skies have cleared, glittering diamonds adorn the crown. Almost all the native vegetation has been scoured away by the varied footgear of countless visitors; so popular is this fine viewpoint that often it is difficult to find a vacant perch. In summer this is not a place to seek quietness. DESCENTS: Leave the top only by the ridge; lower down there is a wealth of choice. Keep clear of the craggy Newlands face.

RIDGE ROUTE

To MAIDEN MOOR, 1887'
1½ miles : S. then SW
Depression (Hause Gate) at 1180'
720 feet of ascent

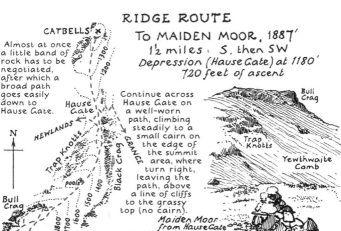

CATBELLS

Almost at once a little band of rock has to be negotiated, after which a broad path goes easily down to Hause Gate.

N

NEWLANDS

Trap Knotts

Hause Gate

GRANGE

Black Crag

pools

Bull Crag

1800 1700 1600 1500 1400

X MAIDEN MOOR

Continue across Hause Gate on a well-worn path, climbing steadily to a small cairn on the edge of the summit area, where turn right, leaving the path, above a line of cliffs to the grassy top (no cairn).

Bull Crag

Trap Knotts

Yewthwaite Comb

Maiden Moor from Hause Gate

HALF A MILE

THE VIEW

Scenes of great beauty unfold on all sides, and they are scenes in depth to a degree not usual, the narrow summit permitting downward views of Borrowdale and Newlands within a few paces. Nearby valley and lake attract the eye more than the distant mountain surround, although Hindscarth and Robinson are particularly prominent at the head of Newlands and Causey Pike towers up almost grotesquely directly opposite. On this side the hamlet of Little Town is well seen down below, a charming picture, but it is to Derwent Water and mid-Borrowdale that the captivated gaze returns again and again.

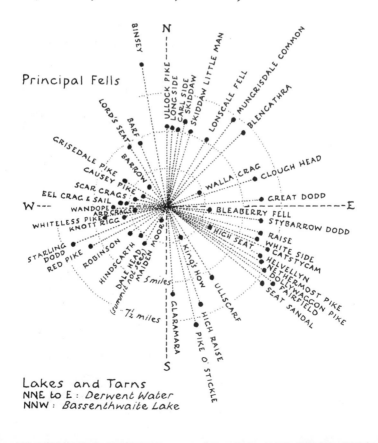

Principal Fells

Lakes and Tarns
NNE to E : Derwent Water
NNW : Bassenthwaite Lake

Hindscarth and Robinson from Catbells

Causey Pike

2090'

Braithwaite

▲ GRISEDALE PIKE

EEL
CRAG ▲

▲ CAUSEY PIKE

● Stair

MILES

0   1   2   3

from Swinside

NATURAL FEATURES

Most fells conform to a general pattern, but some have an unorthodoxy of shape, a peculiarity of outline, that identifies them on sight from wherever they may be seen. These not only help to fix a bearing in moments of doubt but serve also as pointers to neighbouring fells not favoured with distinctive features.

A landmark of this kind is Causey Pike, dominant in the Newlands and Derwent Water scene. The knob of the summit would itself be enough for identification in most views; repeated four times in lesser undulations as it is, like the legendary sea-serpent, the top is quite unmistakable. Even when the lesser ups and downs are concealed from sight, as when the fell is seen end on, the pyramid of the main summit is no less impressive because then it gains in slimness and elegance.

Causey Pike rises very sharply from Newlands but the steepness abates on Rowling End at 1400', whence a half-mile ridge continues easily to Sleet Hause, just below the final tower, where the steepness recurs on a narrowing crest. Rock is in evidence here, and must be handled to attain the summit. Thereafter the top of the fell is a succession of gentle undulations leading on to Scar Crags and the fine ridge that climbs up to Eel Crag and descends beyond to Crummock Water.

Bracken clothes the lower slopes and heather the higher. The confining streams are Stonycroft Beck and Rigg Beck, both feeders of Newlands Beck.

from Whiteless Breast

looking up the valley of
Sail Beck, with Eel Crag
and Sail on the left and
Ard Crags on the right

from Little Town

Causey Pike belongs wholly and exclusively to Newlands but peeps over the watershed of the Cocker, southwest, at several points.

MAP

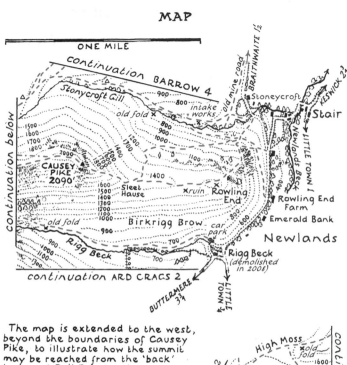

The map is extended to the west, beyond the boundaries of Causey Pike, to illustrate how the summit may be reached from the 'back' by way of Sail Pass (at the same altitude), gaining the pass by using either the Stonycroft mine road or the Rigg Beck path. The Stonycroft route is excellently graded and a very quick way of getting up to 2000' from Newlands; using this route, if Causey Pike is the sole objective, the 'road' can be left on High Moss and a beeline made for the depression between Scar Crags and the Pike. The Rigg Beck route is less satisfactory.

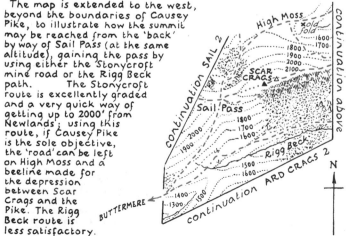

ASCENT FROM STAIR
1750 feet of ascent : 1½ miles

From Sleet Hause to the summit the way lies up the sharp east-south-east ridge: a delightful climb. The final rocktower requires the use of hands: it is easy, but no place for fooling about.

The direct route gains the ridge at Sleet Hause and a splendid view suddenly unfolds to the south.

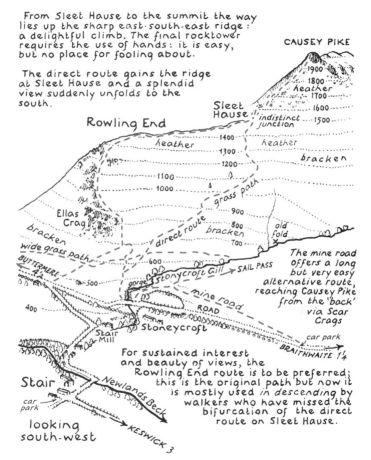

CAUSEY PIKE

1900
1800
heather
1700
1600
1500

Sleet Hause
indistinct junction

Rowling End

heather   1400   heather
1300
bracken
1200
1100
1000

grass path
900

Ellas Crag
800   old
direct route   bracken   fold
700

bracken
wide grass path
600
BUTTERMERE   Stonycroft Gill → SAIL PASS
4½
500   gorge
mine road
400   ROAD

The mine road offers a long but very easy alternative route, reaching Causey Pike from the 'back' via Scar Crags

car park
BRAITHWAITE 1¼

Stair Mill   Stoneycroft

Stair

car park   Newlands Beck

looking south-west   KESWICK 3

For sustained interest and beauty of views, the Rowling End route is to be preferred; this is the original path but now it is mostly used in descending by walkers who have missed the bifurcation of the direct route on Sleet Hause.

Deservedly this is a popular climb, with a heavy summer traffic, the route being quite charming, the views superlative, the finish a bit of real mountaineering, and the summit a place of distinctive character.

ASCENT FROM BRAITHWAITE
2150 feet of ascent : 4½ miles (via Sail Pass)

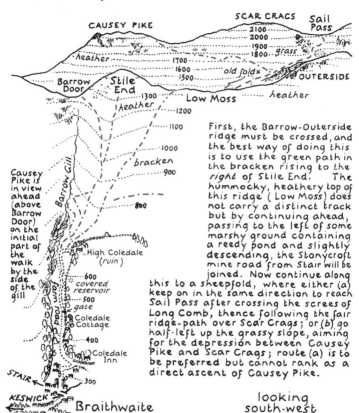

First, the Barrow-Outerside ridge must be crossed, and the best way of doing this is to use the green path in the bracken rising to the *right* of Stile End. The hummocky, heathery top of this ridge (Low Moss) does not carry a distinct track but by continuing ahead, passing to the left of some marshy ground containing a reedy pond and slightly descending, the Stonycroft mine road from Stair will be joined. Now continue along this to a sheepfold, where either (a) keep on in the same direction to reach Sail Pass after crossing the screes of Long Comb, thence following the fair ridge-path over Scar Crags; or (b) go half-left up the grassy slope, aiming for the depression between Causey Pike and Scar Crags; route (a) is to be preferred but cannot rank as a direct ascent of Causey Pike.

*looking
south-west*

Causey Pike is clearly in view from Braithwaite, and its quaint and challenging outline makes it an obvious objective for a day's walk. The route, however, is somewhat 'artificial', as an intervening ridge must first be crossed, and a better plan is to ascend direct from Stair, using the above route for the return journey.

THE SUMMIT

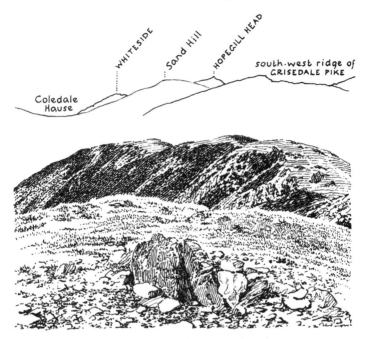

Coledale Hause — WHITESIDE — Sand Hill — HOPEGILL HEAD — south-west ridge of GRISEDALE PIKE

This delightful 'top' is quite unlike any other, its narrow crest undulating over five distinct bumps (meticulous visitors will count seven), the most prominent being the one terminating so abruptly the eastern end of the crest: this is the rocky knob that identifies Causey Pike unmistakably in distant views of the fell. The eastern knob appears to have a slight advantage in altitude, a matter of a few feet or even inches only, over the third bump — the second bump is clearly lower. The third, fourth and fifth bumps have piles of stones on their summits, that on the fourth bump being the largest.

DESCENTS : Leave the top by the path down the east-south-east ridge from the eastern knob; this is rocky at first, needing care in bad conditions, and is not pleasant to descend. At the foot of the steep section, on Sleet Hause, the direct route to Stair goes off to the left at once and the original path over Rowling End continues ahead, the bifurcation at this point being indistinct. It is advisable to use the direct route: the way off Rowling End is on a plain but abominably rough path with no alternative possible.

THE VIEW

In all directions the scenery is of the highest order. Predominantly the view is of mountains, but the severity and starkness of their outlines is softened by the verdant loveliness of the Vales of Keswick and Newlands. Nothing is better than the challenging ridge continuing to Eel Crag. The head of Newlands, displaying the great humps of Dale Head, Hindscarth and Robinson — a magnificent grouping — is exceptionally well seen. The several Pikes of Scafell appear from this viewpoint as separate mountains.

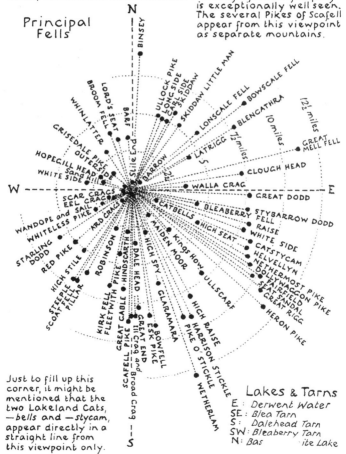

Principal Fells

Just to fill up this corner, it might be mentioned that the two Lakeland Cats, —bells and —stycam, appear directly in a straight line from this viewpoint only.

Lakes & Tarns
E: Derwent Water
SE: Blea Tarn
S: Dalehead Tarn
SW: Bleaberry Tarn
N: Bas....ite Lake

RIDGE ROUTE

To SCAR CRAGS, 2205': ¾ mile: WNW, then W.
Depression at 1915': 320 feet of ascent

Traverse all the bumps and descend a wide stony path to the depression beyond. The ragged edge of Scar Crags now rears imposingly ahead, but the rising track alongside has no difficulties and the flat top is reached after a simple climb, during which striking downward views are available on the left.

HALF A MILE

looking back to Causey Pike from the depression

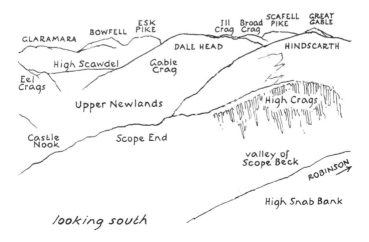

looking south

The valley of Rigg Beck, from Causey Pike

The ridge west from Causey Pike

Key to drawings

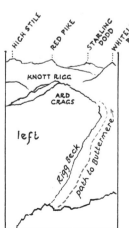

HIGH STILE
RED PIKE
STARLING DODD
WHITELESS PIKE

KNOTT RIGG

ARD CRAGS

left

Rigg Beck

path to Buttermere

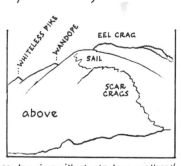

WHITELESS PIKE
WANDOPE
EEL CRAG
SAIL
SCAR CRAGS

above

These drawings illustrate two walkers' ways from Newlands to Buttermere. That *via* Rigg Beck is suitable for a wet day, but the route *par excellence* in clear weather is the ridge from Causey Pike to Whiteless Pike — a magnificent walk.

Dale Head

2473'

Little Town •

HINDSCARTH ▲

DALE HEAD ▲   ▲ HIGH SPY

Gatesgarth •   Rosthwaite •

Honister ≍   Seatoller •
Pass

MILES
0   1   2   3   4

from Castle Nook

NATURAL FEATURES

Dale Head has much in common with Eel Crag in the Grasmoor group. Their summits are focal points of high country, the meeting-place of ascending ridges. Both have craggy northern fronts, darkly shadowed, and easy southern approaches. Both enjoy extensive views of great merit, particularly northwards to Skiddaw. Taking everything into account, these two may be considered the most satisfying summits in the north western area.

Dale Head was named from Newlands, of which valley it commands a remarkable full-length view, and it is in this direction that the best, but not the best-known, items of interest are to be found. There are no walkers' tracks on the rocky northern breast of the fell, but a zigzag path to its copper veins was engineered by miners five or six centuries ago and can still be traced, while recently its steep buttresses have become a climbing-ground. The miners have long since departed from the Yew Crag workings, but on the south side of the pass a beautiful stone is still being won from the Honister Slate Mine.

For the walker, the finest attraction is the north-west ridge leading to Hindscarth, which is excellent. The easy southern slope, rising from the top of Honister Pass, lacks interest. The sharp descent to the east from the summit is soon halted by the extensive plateau of High Scawdel before continuing roughly down to the lovely foothills and woods of Borrowdale.

Dale Head has interest for the geologist, for beneath the carpet of grass there is a fusion of the Skiddaw slates and the volcanic rock of central Lakeland, some evidences of the joint being seen on the actual summit. But perhaps Dale Head's greatest triumph over its north western fellows is that it holds in its lap the only tarns of any size between Bassenthwaite and Honister, a further manifestation of the change in the underlying rock. Streams flow to all directions except west, yet it is in the west their ultimate destiny lies, the fell being wholly within the catchment of the Derwent.

Dalehead Tarn
from
High Scawdel

MAP

Honister Pass is the one (and only) place where the North Western Fells link up with another group (the Western), being otherwise isolated by valleys. Honister Pass is a watershed between the gathering grounds of the Cocker and the Derwent, which form the outer boundary of these fells.

The Honister Slate Mine closed down in 1986 and reopened in 1997. There are frequent guided tours.

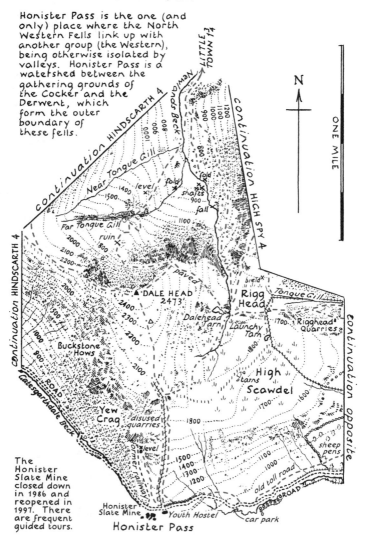

N

ONE MILE

Honister Pass

MAP

Honister Pass can only be reached on foot from Gatesgarthdale by walking along the motor road, but from Seatoller a good alternative is provided by the former toll road, which, being unfit for vehicles, has become a first-class walkers' way, in fact, a pedestrian by-pass. The surface is rough and rutted, but no fellwalker will object to this. It is the smooth hard surfaces of modern roads that tire the legs and feet, the monotony of repeating ad nauseam the same stride exactly. On rough ground no two movements are quite the same.

A good fellwalker never tramps a road that has a bus service.

A level, Righead Quarry

Launchy Tarn

The first big loop of the toll road can be avoided by use of a path in the next field.

Johnny Wood is of particular interest to botanists because of its ferns, mosses and liverworts.

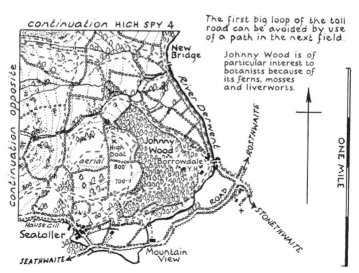

ONE MILE

below: Mine cuttings near the foot of Far Tongue Gill adopted for use with a sheepfold.

Copper Mines and Crags of Dale Head

left: Two mine cuttings near the sheepfold on Newlands Beck at 800'; the upper one is flooded, forming a rocky-sided pool.

below: Dale Head Pillar, Gable Crag, from the ruined mine buildings.

ASCENT FROM LITTLE TOWN

2000 feet of ascent
4 miles via Dalehead Tarn
3½ miles via the copper mine

looking south

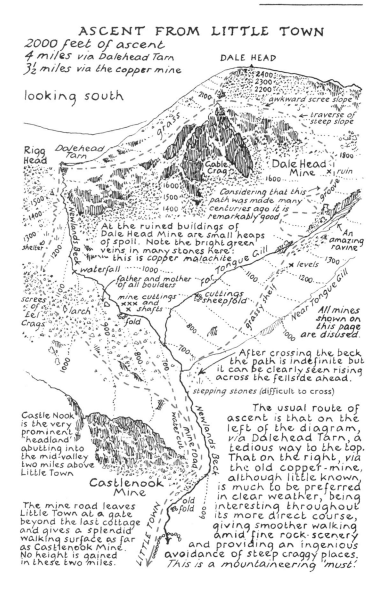

DALE HEAD

2400
2300
2200
2100

awkward scree slope

traverse of
steep slope

Rigg
Head

Dalehead
Tarn

grass

1800

Gable
Crag

Dale Head
Mine × ruin

1600

1600

Considering that this
path was made many
centuries ago it is
remarkably good

groove

1500

1400

An
amazing
ravine

1500

1400

1300

shelter

1200

Newlands Beck

At the ruined buildings of
Dale Head Mine are small heaps
of spoil. Note the bright green
veins in many stones here:
this is copper malachite

Tongue Gill

× levels

1300

1200

waterfall — 1000

father and mother
of all boulders

for

grassy shelf

Near Tongue Gill

1000

scree's
of Eel
Crags

larch

mine cuttings
××× and
× shafts

× cuttings
sheepfold

1100

All mines
shown on
this page
are disused.

fold

900

800

700

After crossing the beck
the path is indefinite but
it can be clearly seen rising
across the fellside ahead

stepping stones (difficult to cross)

Newlands Beck

water cut

mine road

Castle Nook
is the very
prominent
'headland'
abutting into
the mid-valley
two miles above
Little Town

Castlenook
Mine

old
fold

600

LITTLE TOWN

The mine road leaves
Little Town at a gate
beyond the last cottage
and gives a splendid
walking surface as far
as Castlenook Mine.
No height is gained
in these two miles.

The usual route of
ascent is that on the
left of the diagram,
via Dalehead Tarn, a
tedious way to the top.
That on the right, via
the old copper-mine,
although little known,
is much to be preferred
in clear weather, being
interesting throughout
its more direct course,
giving smoother walking
amid fine rock-scenery
and providing an ingenious
avoidance of steep craggy places.
This is a mountaineering 'must!'

ASCENT FROM HONISTER PASS
1300 feet of ascent : 1¼ miles

The first lesson that every fellwalker learns, and learns afresh every time he goes on the hills, is that summits are almost invariably more distant, a good deal higher, and require greater effort, than expected. Fellwalking and wishful thinking have nothing in common.

Here is an exception. This ascent may well be longer than expected, but the climbing is so very simple and the gradients so very easy that the top cairn is reached, unbelievably, before one has started to feel that enough has been done to earn it.

DALE HEAD

2400

2300

cairns

grass

2200

2100

grass

Apparently for no reason at all the fence comes to an end at this point. Of the fence that once led from here to the summit only four posts remain — not enough to justify showing a broken fence.

← This line of fence-posts leads to High Scawdel and Launchy Tarn

looking north-north-east

old level ×

ruins

old quarries

At this point a quarry hole encroaches almost to the fence. Its dangers are obvious when ascending, but could be realised too late in a running descent in mist.

1800

Yew Crag

old quarry

1700

old level

1600

At the summit of Honister Pass is the only working slate mine in England. Altogether there are 11 miles of underground passages.

1500

former railway

quarry road

× sheepfolds

1300

SEATOLLER 1½

1200

1100

1000

BUTTERMERE 4

ROAD

car park

Youth Hostel slate mine

Honister Pass
1190'

No other summit of like altitude is reached so quickly and easily from a motor road. Indeed, if a car be used to the top of the pass, a man of conscience must feel he is cheating the mountain.

Old level where the quarry road meets the former railway.

ASCENT FROM SEATOLLER OR ROSTHWAITE

FROM SEATOLLER:
2150 feet of ascent : 3 - 3½ miles
FROM ROSTHWAITE :
2250 feet : 3½ - 4 miles

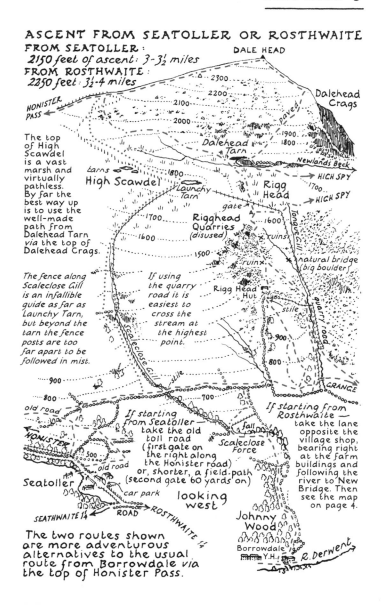

DALE HEAD

△ 2300

2200

2100

2000

1900
1800

Dalehead Tarn

Dalehead Crags

paved

Newlands Beck

HONISTER PASS

The top of High Scawdel is a vast marsh and virtually pathless. By far the best way up is to use the well-made path from Dalehead Tarn via the top of Dalehead Crags.

tarns

High Scawdel

1800

Launchy Tarn

Rigg Head

→ HIGH SPY

1700

→ HIGH SPY

gate

Rigghead Quarries (disused)

1700

1600

1600

1500

ruins

ruins

natural bridge (big boulder)

The fence along Scaleclose Gill is an infallible guide as far as Launchy Tarn, but beyond the tarn the fence posts are too far apart to be followed in mist.

If using the quarry road it is easiest to cross the stream at the highest point.

Rigg Head Hut

stile

900

quarry road

Tongue Gill

900

800

Scaleclose Gill

stile

GRANGE

900

800

700

old road

HONISTER

500

old road

If starting from Seatoller — take the old toll road (first gate on the right along the Honister road) or, shorter, a field-path (second gate 60 yards on)

fall

Scaleclose Force

If starting from Rosthwaite — take the lane opposite the village shop, bearing right at the farm buildings and following the river to New Bridge. Then see the map on page 4.

Seatoller

car park

ROAD ROSTHWAITE 1½

SEATHWAITE 1¼

looking west

Johnny Wood

Borrowdale
Y.H.   R. Derwent

The two routes shown are more adventurous alternatives to the usual route from Borrowdale via the top of Honister Pass.

THE SUMMIT

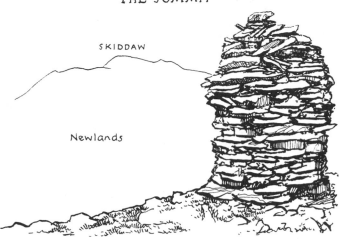

SKIDDAW

Newlands

There are hundreds of unnecessary cairns on the fells and no great loss would be suffered if they were scattered, but those on the summits of the mountains have a special significance: they are old friends and should be left inviolate in their lonely stations to greet their visitors. This was how it used to be, and they were treated with respect. Fellwalkers knew them well.

But not now. Lunatics are loose on the hills; not many, just a few idiots whose limit of bravery is to destroy what others have created. The fine columns on Pike o' Blisco and Lingmell have both been wrecked over the years (and rebuilt by walkers who felt bereaved by their absence, and to whom thanks are due). Dale Head's original cairn fell to the destroyers, too; but in its place arose an even nobler edifice, illustrated here. An expert working party was on the job and the stones appeared to have come from Yew Crag quarry. This cairn was unusual in shape, being wider at mid-height than at the base. It was subsequently rebuilt again, and is now, if anything, even better. Long may it reign over Dale Head.

Its situation is dramatic, immediately on the brink of the great northern downfall, but there is an easy parade on both sides. It is along here that the Skiddaw slates and the Borrowdale volcanic rocks converge, but a knowledge of geology is needed to find evidence of this.

DESCENTS : The way down to Honister Pass, following the cairns and, later, the fence, is fast and foolproof. Do not stray from the fence *in mist* (quarry holes).

For Dalehead Tarn and Borrowdale or Newlands, aim east and find the path that follows the north-east ridge.

For Newlands direct, *via* the copper mine, clear weather is essential unless the way is already known. The place to leave the north-east ridge is marked by a small cairn with steep ground obviously beyond: here turn very sharp left to find a thin track to easy ground.

RIDGE ROUTES

To HINDSCARTH, 2385′: 1¼ miles: WNW, then NNE
Depression at 2156′: 250 feet of ascent
An easy walk, with excellent views.

HINDSCARTH

DALE HEAD

Starting along the top westwards (no path at first), with intermittent fenceposts on the left, a gradual descent soon leads to the finest part of the ridge, which here narrows above a steep gully. A good path now appears and winds round a rocky rise; Buttermere is now in view. Beyond, a big cairn is reached on an outcrop (bit rough) and then the way is clear across a depression to the ridge ahead, where a right-angled turn, leaving the fence, leads easily over the gravelly top of Hindscarth for half a mile to the summit.

The path to the SSW from Hindscarth to the main ridge is going out of use, and nowadays it is more usual to take a short cut that avoids the sharp bend on the old route.

The first rocky rise on the Hindscarth ridge, looking west

N

ONE MILE

NEWLANDS

Eel Crags

HIGH SPY

To HIGH SPY, 2143′: 1½ miles: ESE, NNE
Depression at 1600′: 550 feet of ascent
An interesting journey from one ridge to another

Starting eastwards, a path is soon found following the north-east ridge. After the path bends right it becomes beautifully made, with twists and turns too small to show on the map. Opposite Dalehead Tarn, after passing an old sheepfold, turn left. Across the beck a sketchy path climbs the long slope of High Spy with thrilling views down the crags on the left.

DALE HEAD

Dalehead Tarn

Rigg Head

BORROWDALE

THE VIEW

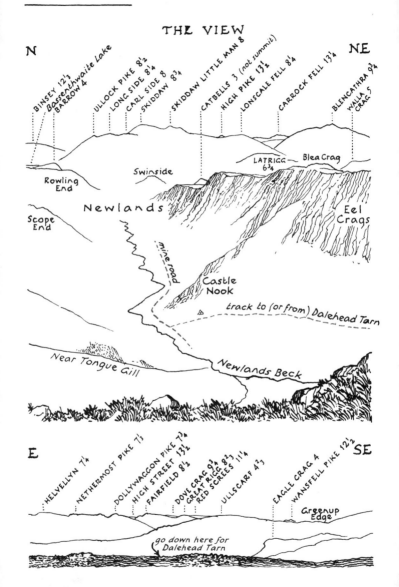

N

BINSEY 12½
Bassenthwaite Lake
BARROW 4
ULLOCK PIKE 8½
LONG SIDE 8¼
CARL SIDE 8
SKIDDAW 8¾
SKIDDAW LITTLE MAN 8
CATBELLS 3 (not summit)
HIGH PIKE 13½
LONSCALE FELL 8¼
CARROCK FELL 13¾
BLENCATHRA 9¾
WALLA CRAG 5

NE

Rowling End

Swinside

LATRIGG 6¾
Blea Crag

Newlands

Eel Crags

Scope End

mine road

Castle Nook

△ track to (or from) Dalehead Tarn

Near Tongue Gill

Newlands Beck

E

HELVELLYN 7¼
NETHERMOST PIKE 7½
DOLLYWAGGON PIKE 7¾
HIGH STREET 13½
FAIRFIELD 8½
DOVE CRAG 9½
GREAT RIGG 8½
RED SCREES 11¼
ULLSCARF 4¾
EAGLE CRAG 4
WANSFELL PIKE 12½

SE

Greenup Edge

go down here for Dalehead Tarn

THE VIEW

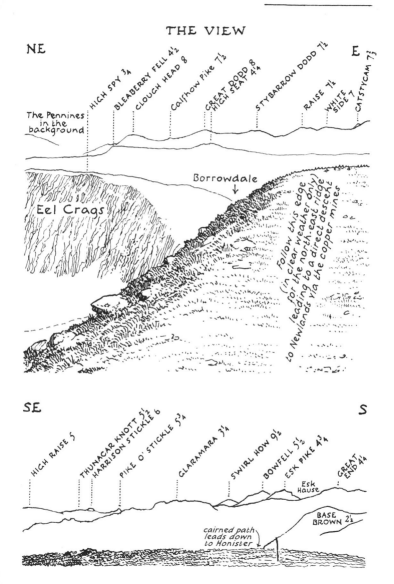

NE

The Pennines in the background

HIGH SPY 3¾
BLEABERRY FELL 4½
CLOUGH HEAD 8
CALFHOW PIKE 7½
GREAT DODD 8
HIGH SEAT 4¼
STYBARROW DODD 7½
RAISE 7½
WHITE SIDE 7
CATSTYCAM 7⅓

E

Eel Crags

Borrowdale

Follow this edge (in clear weather only) for the north-east ridge leading to a direct descent to Newlands via the copper mines

SE

HIGH RAISE 5
THUNACAR KNOTT 5½
HARRISON STICKLE 6
PIKE O' STICKLE 5¾
GLARAMARA 3¾
SWIRL HOW 9½
BOWFELL 5½
Esk Hause
ESK PIKE 4¾
GREAT END 4¼

BASE BROWN 2½

S

cairned path leads down to Honister

THE VIEW

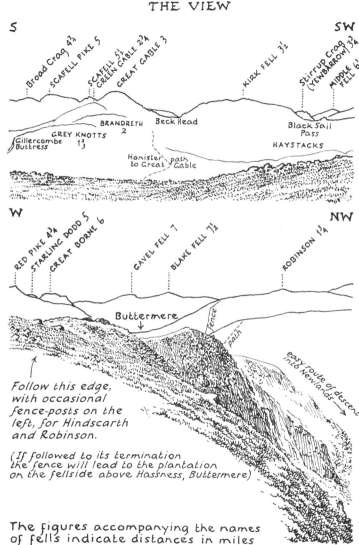

S   SW

Broad Crag 4½
SCAFELL PIKE 5
SCAFELL 5½
GREEN GABLE 2¾
GREAT GABLE 3
KIRK FELL 3½
Stirrup Crag (YEWBARROW) 3¾
MIDDLE FELL 6½

BRANDRETH 2
Beck Head
GREY KNOTTS 1¾
Gillercombe Buttress
Black Sail Pass
HAYSTACKS

Honister path to Great Gable

W   NW

RED PIKE 4¾
STARLING DODD 5
GREAT BORNE 6
GAVEL FELL 7
BLAKE FELL 7½
ROBINSON 1¾

Buttermere

fence

path

easy route of descent into Newlands

Follow this edge,
with occasional
fence-posts on the
left, for Hindscarth
and Robinson.

(If followed to its termination
the fence will lead to the plantation
on the fellside above Hassness, Buttermere)

The figures accompanying the names
of fells indicate distances in miles

THE VIEW

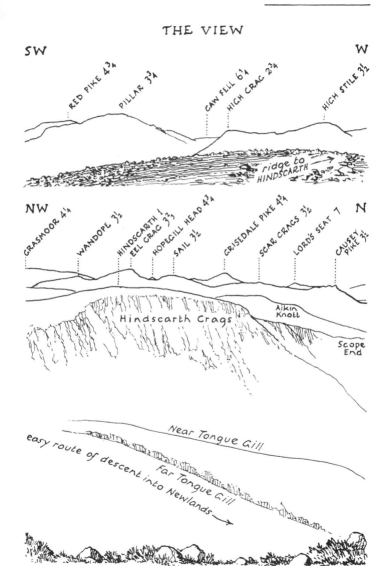

SW

RED PIKE 4¾
PILLAR 3¾
CAW FELL 6¼
HIGH CRAG 2¾
HIGH STILE 3½

W

ridge to HINDSCARTH →

NW

GRASMOOR 4¼
WANDOPE 3½
HINDSCARTH 1
EEL CRAG 3¾
HOPEGILL HEAD 4¾
SAIL 3½
GRISEDALE PIKE 4¾
SCAR CRAGS 3½
LORD'S SEAT 7
CAUSEY PIKE 3½

N

Hindscarth Crags

Aikin Knott

Scope End

Near Tongue Gill

Far Tongue Gill

easy route of descent into Newlands →

Eel Crag

2749'

Crag Hill
on Ordnance
Survey maps

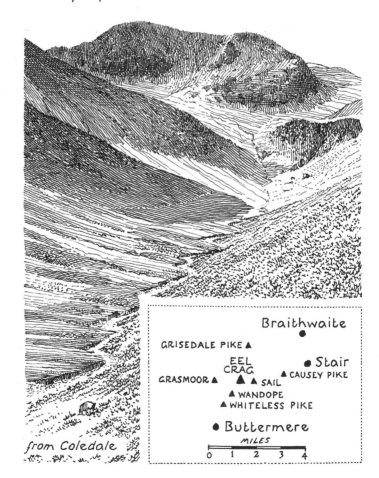

GRISEDALE PIKE ▲

Braithwaite ●

● Stair

EEL
CRAG

GRASMOOR ▲   ▲   ▲ SAIL   ▲ CAUSEY PIKE

▲ WANDOPE

▲ WHITELESS PIKE

● Buttermere

MILES

0   1   2   3   4

from Coledale

NATURAL FEATURES

Although of rather lower elevation than the neighbouring Grasmoor, Eel Crag is more truly the focal point of the concentration of fells rising between the valleys of Newlands and Lorton.   Unlike Grasmoor, Eel Crag is supported by ridges.   Unlike Grasmoor, it stands in the midst of a group of satellites. Unlike Grasmoor, it commands an excellent all-round view.   It is in the centre of things. It is an obvious objective.   Tracks lead up to its stony top naturally and inevitably. It is a traffic junction, while Grasmoor is a cul-de-sac.

The shadowed north-east face of the fell, towering high above the head of Coledale, is a fine sight.   Even steeper, but less familiar, is the craggy southern slope, seamed with gullies, overlooking Sail Beck: this is a no-man's-land. Walkers prefer the exciting ridges, of which a narrowing crest coming up from the east gives the best approach; another, shorter, traverses the summit from Coledale Hause, and a third curves south-west to a grassy depression from which three spurs lead separately to Wandope, Whiteless Pike and the great bulk of Grasmoor. Streams from the fell flow to two main rivers, from Grasmoor to one, and this is the great test of superiority. Eel Crag is a watershed but Grasmoor is not.

The east ridge

The name of the fell is unfortunate and inaccurate. Eel Crag is properly the rocky buttress above Coledale Hause, but for a century or more the whole fell has been popularly known by this name.   The Ordnance maps, in all series, use Crag Hill, and, if adopted generally, this name would avoid the confusion that has arisen due to the recent development of Eel Crags in nearby Newlands as a climbing ground. But walkers are conservative folk: they do not like change in old favourites, and Eel Crag it will remain.

The north-east face, from the lower slopes of Sand Hill

*The south face,
with Sail beyond,
from Wandope*

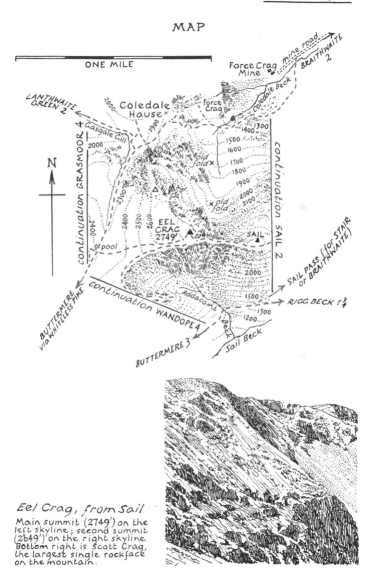

MAP

ONE MILE

Force Crag Mine

mine road

BRAITHWAITE 2

Coledale Beck

LANTHWAITE GREEN 2

Coledale Hause

Gasgale Gill

Force Crag

2000

1900

continuation GRASMOOR 4

N

2000

2000

1300

1400

1500

1600

1700

1800

1900

2000

2100

old fold x

continuation SAIL 2

2300

2400

2500

2600

x *old fold*

2400

EEL CRAG 2749'

pool

SAIL

SAIL PASS (*for STAIR or BRAITHWAITE*)

2000

1500

Addacomb Beck

continuation WANDOPE 4

RIGG BECK 1¾

1300

1200

BUTTERMERE via WHITELESS PIKE

BUTTERMERE 3

Sail Beck

Eel Crag, from Sail

Main summit (2749') on the
left skyline; second summit
(2649') on the right skyline.
Bottom right is Scott Crag,
the largest single rockface
on the mountain.

ASCENT FROM RANNERDALE
2400 feet of ascent : 2½ miles

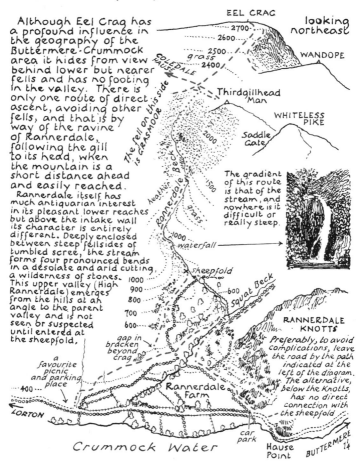

EEL CRAG

looking northeast

2700
2600
COLEDALE HAUSE
grass 2500
2400

WANDOPE

Thirdgillhead Man

WHITELESS PIKE

Saddle Gate

The fell on this side is GRASSMOOR

Heather Beck

Rannerdale Beck

2000

1500

grass

1000

waterfall

sheepfold

1000
900
800
700
600

Squat Beck

600

RANNERDALE KNOTTS

gap in bracken beyond crag

a favourite picnic and parking place

400

LORTON

Rannerdale Farm

car park

Hause Point

BUTTERMERE 14

Crummock Water

Although Eel Crag has a profound influence in the geography of the Buttermere-Crummock area it hides from view behind lower but nearer fells and has no footing in the valley. There is only one route of direct ascent, avoiding other fells, and that is by way of the ravine of Rannerdale, following the gill to its head, when the mountain is a short distance ahead and easily reached.

Rannerdale itself has much antiquarian interest in its pleasant lower reaches but above the intake wall its character is entirely different. Deeply enclosed between steep fellsides of tumbled scree, the stream forms four pronounced bends in a desolate and arid cutting, a wilderness of stones. This upper valley (High Rannerdale) emerges from the hills at an angle to the parent valley and is not seen or suspected until entered at the sheepfold.

The gradient of this route is that of the stream, and nowhere is it difficult or really steep.

Preferably, to avoid complications, leave the road by the path indicated at the left of the diagram. The alternative, below the Knotts, has no direct connection with the sheepfold

Every direct route has something to commend it, if only its directness. Rannerdale additionally is sheltered, has water at hand, and is absolutely unloseable in mist. BUT its charms are few, and, in the upper reaches, the view is limited to the immediate unattractive surroundings.

ASCENT FROM STAIR
2,700 feet of ascent
3½ miles

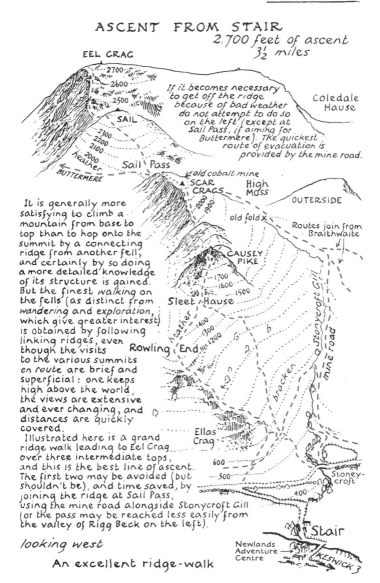

EEL CRAG

2700
2600
2500

SAIL

2300
2100
2000 heather

BUTTERMERE

Sail Pass

Coledale Hause

If it becomes necessary to get off the ridge because of bad weather do not attempt to do so on the left (except at Sail Pass, if aiming for Buttermere). The quickest route of evacuation is provided by the mine road.

old cobalt mine
▲ SCAR CRAGS
2000
1900
High Moss

OUTERSIDE

old fold ✗

Routes join from Braithwaite

CAUSEY PIKE

1700
1600
1500

Sleet Hause

It is generally more satisfying to climb a mountain from base to top than to hop onto the summit by a connecting ridge from another fell, and certainly by so doing a more detailed knowledge of its structure is gained. But the finest *walking* on the fells (as distinct from wandering and exploration, which give greater interest) is obtained by following linking ridges, even though the visits to the various summits en route are brief and superficial: one keeps high above the world, the views are extensive and ever changing, and distances are quickly covered.

Illustrated here is a grand ridge walk leading to Eel Crag over three intermediate tops, and this is the best line of ascent. The first two may be avoided (but shouldn't be), and time saved, by joining the ridge at Sail Pass, using the mine road alongside Stonycroft Gill (or the pass may be reached less easily from the valley of Rigg Beck on the left).

heather
1400
1300
1200

Rowling End

bracken

Stonycroft Gill

mine road

b

Ellas Crag

600
500

Stoney-croft

400

Stair

looking west

An excellent ridge-walk

Newlands Adventure Centre

KESWICK 3

Eel Crag 7

ASCENT FROM BRAITHWAITE
(DIRECT) 2500 feet of ascent
3¾ miles (A); 4 miles (B)

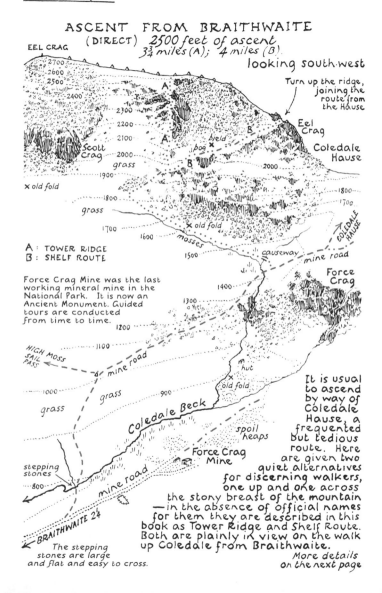

looking south-west

EEL CRAG

2700
2600
2500
2400
2300
2200
2100
2000 grass
1900

Turn up the ridge, joining the route from the Hause

Eel Crag

Coledale Hause

A'
A'
B field
bog ×
B

Scott Crag

× old fold

1800
grass
1700
1600 masses
1500

2000

1800
1700
COLEDALE HAUSE

× old fold

causeway
mine road

Force Crag

A: TOWER RIDGE
B: SHELF ROUTE

Force Crag Mine was the last working mineral mine in the National Park. It is now an Ancient Monument. Guided tours are conducted from time to time.

1400
1300
1200
1100

HIGH MOSS SAIL PASS

mine road

1000
grass
grass
900
m hut
× old fold

Coledale Beck

stepping stones
800

mine road

← BRAITHWAITE 2½

The stepping stones are large and flat and easy to cross.

spoil heaps

Force Crag Mine

It is usual to ascend by way of Coledale Hause, a frequented but tedious route. Here are given two quiet alternatives for discerning walkers, one up and one across the stony breast of the mountain — in the absence of official names for them they are described in this book as Tower Ridge and Shelf Route. Both are plainly in view on the walk up Coledale from Braithwaite.

More details on the next page

The Shelf Route and Tower Ridge

On the ordinary route from Braithwaite, via Coledale Hause, it is usual to tackle the slope of scree 'around the corner' from the Hause (although this can be avoided by continuing forward to the headwaters of Gasgale Gill). This scree is extensive; it is tiresome to ascend and unpleasant to descend.

A way of cutting out this abomination is provided by the Shelf Route, which, rarely used, adds a little thrill of exploration and more interest to the climb. The Shelf, once reached, is obvious ahead: a rising green strip of bilberry and mosses between the broken line of crags facing the head of Coledale. It joins the usual route on the ridge at a point just above the steeper rocks overlooking the Hause. There is hardly any path along the Shelf. Cairns are absent, but a few small ones would be a help in navigation. A guide-cairn never needs to consist of more than two or three stones, placed one on top of another. Siting is more important. From one cairn the next should be visible, preferably on a skyline.

The approach from Braithwaite.

In spring and autumn the Shelf and Tower Ridge are the last two places on the face to be illumined by morning sunlight, the rest then being in dark shadow.

The end of the shelf
Turn up the ridge behind the rocks on the left

Tower Ridge:

Just before reaching the start of the shelf (at a green bog behind a prominent rocky tor) walkers who like a scramble may make their way up the bouldery ridge on the left, which is broad but soon narrows to a well-defined rocky tower, with a secondary buttress alongside on the right. The steeper rises on the ridge can be avoided on the left until the final pyramid of short vertical steps, is reached. A ledge of scree rising 20 yards to the right is now followed and then a grass terrace rising to the left for the same distance, a high stride in a corner here gaining the easy ground at the top of the tower. A simple grassy neck then connects with the summit of the mountain just south of the big cairn on the lower top at 2649'. This variation is direct and cuts out the scree slope altogether. It is necessary in a few places to handle rocks but there is nothing to cause fear or panic, although ladies in ankle-length skirts may find odd places a little troublesome.

Tower Ridge from the end of the shelf

ASCENT FROM COLEDALE HAUSE
850 feet of ascent : 1 mile

looking south-east

EEL CRAG

2700

Prominent path

WANDOPE

2649'

cairns

2600

grass

2500

2400

grass

BUTTERMERE via WHITELESS PIKE

pool

2300

Eel Crag

Shelf Route joins here at a grass platform

2100

old water cut (now dry)

The water cut was made originally to augment supplies to Force Crag Mine

Coledale Hause

2000

Gasgale Gill

BRAITHWAITE

1900

1900

LANTHWAITE GREEN

It is usual to tackle the scree slopes to the lower summit as soon as the upper valley of Gasgale Gill is reached, and to go straight up it — an unpleasant proceeding on steep loose stones. A strip of grass on the right gives better foothold, and then a detour to the left to a gully is to be preferred.
Much easier progress is made by following the good path up the valley, turning left on grass at the head of it.

THE SUMMIT

The top is flat and stony, being littered with slate fragments easy to walk upon so that no clear paths have formed in the vicinity of the survey column marking the highest point (5.5993)

DESCENTS:
All routes of ascent may be reversed, but the bad scree above Coledale Hause ought to be avoided in favour of a direct descent on grass, west, to the headwaters of Gasgale Gill. This is the best line off the top in mist for Braithwaite (path right), Buttermere (path left) or Lanthwaite Green (follow stream).

The route to Stair over Causey Pike (or turning off left at Sail Pass) is picked up at the corner of the summit formed by the north-east and south slopes of the fell, 100 yards south-east of the column; in mist it is quite safe, but under snow or ice care is needed on the rocksteps.

RIDGE ROUTES

To SAIL, 2536': ⅗ mile : E
Depression at 2430'
100 feet of ascent
The best way off Eel Crag

From the survey column head south-east, passing to the right of the big cairn, to the corner of the summit. Thereafter the path is clear, there being no possibility of going astray on the narrow falling ridge. Timid walkers will be aware of their disability at two places where rock must be descended, but may safely venture. Across the depression (not to be mistaken for Sail Pass) a good path climbs up to Sail summit, the small cairn here being half-hidden by vegetation some 25 yards to the left of the path and often passed unnoticed.

looking to Sail from the top of the east ridge.

EEL CRAG   SAIL

N

HALF A MILE

To GRASMOOR, 2791': 1¼ miles : generally W.
Depression at 2350' : 450 feet of ascent
A long moorland tramp, not recommended in mist

Go down the easy slope west to cross the Coledale Hause—Whiteless Pike path near a small pool. Beyond, follow a rising path up the grassy breast to the vast, gently rising top of Grasmoor, the main cairn of which is still a further half-mile distant.

N   GRASMOOR ▲   2700   2600 2500 2400   EEL CRAG ▲
grass   grass   2500
O pool
2400   Addacomb Hole
HALF A MILE

To WANDOPE, 2533': ¾ mile : SW, then S ▲ WANDOPE
Depression at 2420' : 120 feet of ascent
A bird's-eye view of Addacomb Hole

A beeline may be made, soon joining a track skirting the edge of the steep south face overlooking the hanging valley of Addacomb Hole. A simple final slope, all grass, curves round to the top of Wandope.

THE VIEW

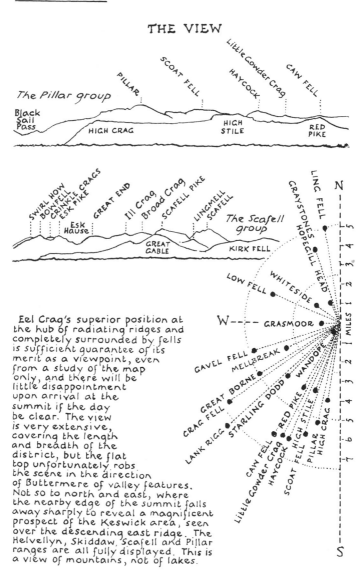

The Pillar group

Black Sail Pass · HIGH CRAG · PILLAR · SCOAT FELL · HAYCOCK · Little Cowder Crag · HIGH STILE · CAW FELL · RED PIKE

SWIRL HOW · DOWFELL · CRINKLE CRAGS · ESK PIKE · GREAT END · Esk Hause · Ill Crag · Broad Crag · SCAFELL PIKE · LINGMELL · SCAFELL · GREAT GABLE · KIRK FELL · **The Scafell group**

LING FELL · GRAYSTONES · HOPEGILL HEAD · N · LOW FELL · WHITESIDE · W --- GRASMOOR · MILES · GAVEL FELL · MELLBREAK · GREAT BORNE · WANDOPE · CRAG FELL · STARLING DODD · RED PIKE · HIGH STILE · LANK RIGG · CAW FELL · Little Cowder Crag · HAYCOCK · SCOAT FELL · HIGH CRAG · PILLAR · HIGH CRAG · S

Eel Crag's superior position at the hub of radiating ridges and completely surrounded by fells is sufficient guarantee of its merit as a viewpoint, even from a study of the map only, and there will be little disappointment upon arrival at the summit if the day be clear. The view is very extensive, covering the length and breadth of the district, but the flat top unfortunately robs the scene in the direction of Buttermere of valley features. Not so to north and east, where the nearby edge of the summit falls away sharply to reveal a magnificent prospect of the Keswick area, seen over the descending east ridge. The Helvellyn, Skiddaw, Scafell and Pillar ranges are all fully displayed. This is a view of mountains, not of lakes.

THE VIEW

Principal Fells

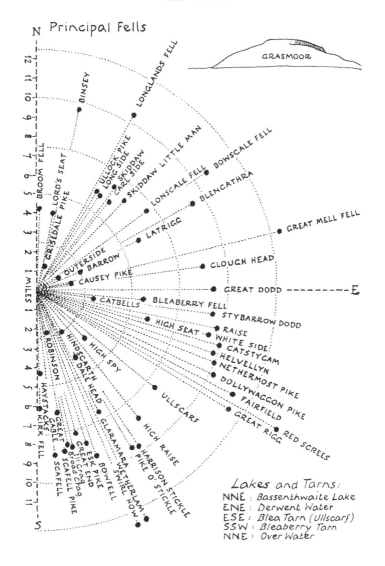

GRASMOOR

N
12 11 10 9 8 7 6 5 4 3 2 1 MILES 1 2 3 4 5 6 7 8 9 10 11
S

BINSEY
LONGLANDS FELL
ULLOCK PIKE
LONG SIDE
SKIDDAW
CARL SIDE
SKIDDAW LITTLE MAN
LONSCALE FELL
BOWSCALE FELL
BLENCATHRA
GREAT MELL FELL
LATRIGG
CLOUGH HEAD
GREAT DODD ——————— E
GREAT DODD
BROOM FELL
LITTLE FELL
LORD'S SEAT
GRISEDALE PIKE
OUTERSIDE
BARROW
CAUSEY PIKE
CATBELLS
BLEABERRY FELL
STYBARROW DODD
HIGH SEAT
RAISE
WHITE SIDE
CATSTYCAM
HELVELLYN
NETHERMOST PIKE
DOLLYWAGGON PIKE
FAIRFIELD
GREAT RIGG
RED SCREES
ROBINSON
HINDSCARTH
HIGH SPY
ULLSCARF
HIGH RAISE
HARRISON STICKLE
PIKE O'STICKLE
HAYSTACKS
KIRK FELL
GREAT GABLE
GREAT END
ESK PIKE
GILLERCOMB
BROAD CRAG
BOWFELL
GLARAMARA
WETHERLAM
SWIRL HOW
SCAFELL
SCAFELL PIKE

Lakes and Tarns:

NNE : Bassenthwaite Lake
ENE : Derwent Water
ESE : Blea Tarn (Ullscarf)
SSW : Bleaberry Tarn
NNE : Over Water

Grasmoor

2791'

from Lanthwaite Hill

NATURAL FEATURES

The culminating point of the North Western Fells occurs overlooking Crummock Water, where the massive bulk of Grasmoor towers above the threshold of the Buttermere valley, showing its full height to great advantage from the shores of the lake.   As Nature has arranged matters this particular aspect of the fell, facing west, is also the finest : a steep pyramid of rocky ribs and broken crags suspended far above the road along its base, the road that carries travellers to Buttermere — and few go this way who do not look upwards rather fearfully to the cliffs poised overhead, seeming to threaten safe passage. Yet familiarity with this monstrous monolith dispels fear and the brackeny hollows below, adjoining the unfenced road, harbour summer migrants in the shape of campers, motorists and caravanners: it is a favourite picnic and recreation ground for discerning West Cumbrians.   Apart from the two dark clefts on this face, there are no continuous courses to attract rockclimbers; the only crags of any size circle an upland combe on the north flank and rim the edge of the summit. On the south side are the most extensive scree-slopes in the district: a colourful but arid desert of stones.   Eastwards there is a high link with Eel Crag and a fine ridge descending into Newlands.   But probably most visitors to Grasmoor will remember the fell for a summit-plateau remarkable both for its extent and its luxurious carpet of mossy turf, close-cropped by the resident sheep who range these broad acres. In structure the fell assumes a simple form, the only unorthodoxy being a ramp down the middle of the south slope curving round into the heathery spur of Lad House, now known as Lad Hows. The streams bounding Grasmoor occupy the stony side-valleys of Gasgale Gill and Rannerdale Beck. It has no tarns.

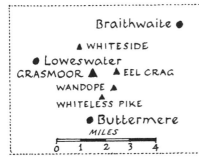

Braithwaite ●

▲ WHITESIDE

● Loweswater
GRASMOOR ▲   ▲ EEL CRAG
WANDOPE ▲
▲
WHITELESS PIKE

● Buttermere

MILES

0   1   2   3   4

The name of the fell is commonly mis-spelt as Grassmoor, even in print, by writers who would never dream of mis-spelling Grasmere Grassmere.   There is only one 's'. The gras derives from grise — wild boar — as in so many Lakeland names e.g. Grisedale.

MAP

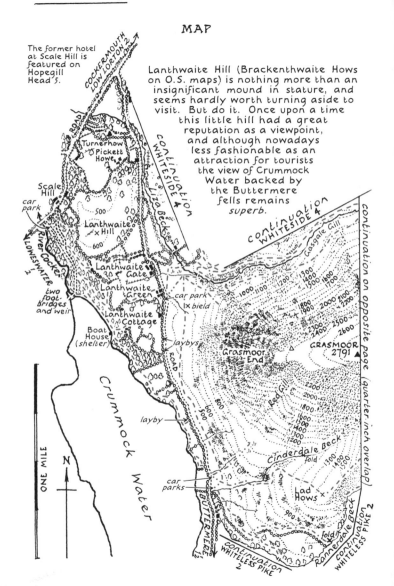

The former hotel at Scale Hill is featured on Hopegill Head 5.

Lanthwaite Hill (Brackenthwaite Hows on O.S. maps) is nothing more than an insignificant mound in stature, and seems hardly worth turning aside to visit. But do it. Once upon a time this little hill had a great reputation as a viewpoint, and although nowadays less fashionable as an attraction for tourists the view of Crummock Water backed by the Buttermere fells remains superb.

ONE MILE

N

MAP

The natural boundaries of mountains tend to be obscured by man's lines of communications. It is not the valley roads that define the limits of a mountain but the main watercourses. Here is a case in point (opposite page). The road along the bases of Whiteside and Grasmoor appears to terminate their slopes, but these fells are divided by Liza Beck (in the valley of Gasgale Gill), which, instead of completing the severance neatly by a direct cut into Crummock Water, turns north to join the River Cocker beyond the outflow of the lake and thereby claims for Grasmoor a wedge of low country that, to a casual observer, would seem to belong to Whiteside. Thus Lanthwaite Hill is Grasmoor's cub although it sits at the feet of Whiteside.

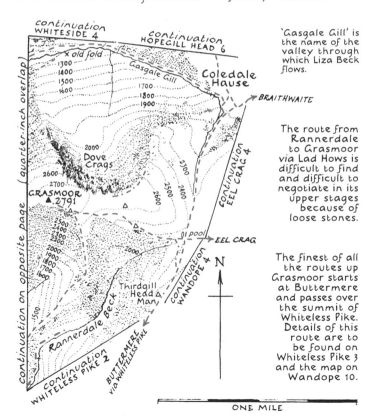

'Gasgale Gill' is the name of the valley through which Liza Beck flows.

The route from Rannerdale to Grasmoor via Lad Hows is difficult to find and difficult to negotiate in its upper stages because of loose stones.

The finest of all the routes up Grasmoor starts at Buttermere and passes over the summit of Whiteless Pike. Details of this route are to be found on Whiteless Pike 3 and the map on Wandope 10.

ONE MILE

ASCENT FROM LANTHWAITE GREEN
VIA DOVE CRAGS
2300 feet of ascent : 2 miles

GRASMOOR

Dove Crags

Grasmoor End

2700
2600 grass
2500 grass
2400
2300
2200
2100
2000
grassy basin at 1900'
1800
1700
1600
1500
1400
1300
1200
1100

grassy arete
grassy arete
rock slab
heather

One of the natural wonders of Grasmoor is the profound hollow scooped out of its north flank and encircled by Dove Crags. The floor of this amphitheatre is a grassy basin, surrounded on all sides by higher ground. It seems an obvious site for a tarn, yet is dry, although clearly all the drainage from the crags must be received there. Because of the raised edge of the hollow there is no issuing stream, nor indeed are there any watercourses within it. All this is very odd. What happens to all the water falling within the area of the combe? The explanation can only be that the screes below the crags act as soak-aways and absorb all moisture from above as it falls, releasing it to the basin so slowly that evaporation and not accumulation takes place.

During the early stages of the climb from the valley it is best to avoid the heather and keep to a pale green strip where moss is the dominant vegetation. This route is to be preferred to that described on Grasmoor 6 because it avoids the scree.

This old walkers' path on the Grasmoor side of the gill now serves only for sheep. It is rough, but still fairly clear

1000 Gasgale Gill
900
800
700
600

2 larches (1 dead)
DIRECT ROUTE

usual path to Coledale Hause

Gasgale Gill is a narrow V-shaped cutting, no wider than the bed of the stream. On the north side Whiteside rises even more steeply than Grasmoor on the south side.

bracken
falls
bracken

Nature never uses straight lines in her designs, but has come remarkably close to doing so in fashioning this arete and the approach to it from the gill along the edge of the scree. A plumb-line dropped from the summit to the valley would lie over the route almost exactly. This is very noticeable from the top of Whiteside.

600
water cut
600 grass
car park

breached weir

There are no difficulties in this ascent. The rock slab is set at an easy gradient but is greasy and needs care. The views down the crags from the arete are tremendous.

cattle grid
ROAD
Lanthwaite Green

The route can be identified from the road. Looking up the valley of Gasgale Gill, it is the skyline ridge rising smoothly to the right, the one roughness on it being the rock slab.

LORTON 3½
Lanthwaite Gate

looking south·south·east

ASCENT FROM LANTHWAITE GREEN DIRECT

2300 feet of ascent
1½ miles

GRASMOOR

grass
and mosses

2500

Grasmoor End 2400'

Upon reaching the Pinnacle (a fine vantage point) jaws drop with dismay at the sight of Grasmoor End, still distant and considerably higher. The ground between is very rough, but a curving ridge (not at first obvious) leads up to it.

2300
2200
2100

Pinnacle 2000'

The Pinnacle dominates this section of the route, forming a fine rock pyramid high above the terrace. Take to a rocky arête on the left from the terrace by way of a splintered crag (a Fat Man's Agony) and gain height by scrambling over or around a series of little cliffs.

arête
Fat Man's Agony
terrace (1600')
rake (1500:1600')

Immediately above the rock gateway turn up a green rake on the right (this reminds one of Lord's Rake — on a smaller and gentler scale). The rake leads to a terrace carrying (unexpectedly) a sheep track, but this runs horizontally both ways and is no help in the ascent.

rock gateway 1500'

rock gateway now seen directly ahead

a detached block below the first crag

Take direction from this conspicuous tongue of light-coloured scree (it is plainly in view from the road).

The tortuous crawl up the 40° slope provides opportunity for observing the flora at very close range. There are berried shrublets (cowberries), and, on the higher rocks, excellent specimens of prostrate juniper.

big gully

heather

1300
1200
1100

Go straight up (a rough, steep pull up heather and stones)

Grasmoor is a very formidable object above Lanthwaite, its tiered crags seeming almost impregnable. The direct climb, up the angle between the north and west faces, is a continuously steep and rough scramble and a severe test in route selection.
On the whole, however, the climb is probably less difficult than the North Wall of the Eiger.

heather

800

falls

bracken

A fair path through the bracken comes to an end when the first stones are reached

700

bield

600

CINDERDALE

Liza Beck

water cut

grass

car park 500

old weir

BUTTERMERE

grass

cattle grid

Lanthwaite Green

ROAD

LORTON 3½

Lanthwaite Gate

looking southeast

ASCENT FROM RANNERDALE
2430 feet of ascent : 1¼ miles

via **RED GILL**

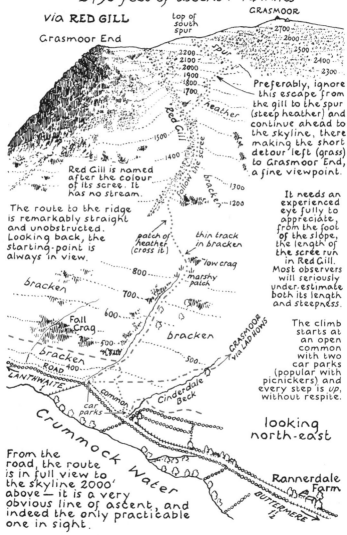

Grasmoor End

top of south spur

GRASMOOR

2700

2600

2500

2400

2300

spur

heather

Red Gill

follow the scree

bracken

2200
2100
2000
1900
1800
1700

1500

1400

1300

1200

Preferably, ignore this escape from the gill to the spur (steep heather) and continue ahead to the skyline, there making the short detour left (grass) to Grasmoor End, a fine viewpoint.

Red Gill is named after the colour of its scree. It has no stream.

The route to the ridge is remarkably straight and unobstructed. Looking back, the starting-point is always in view.

patch of heather (cross it)

thin track in bracken

low craq

marshy patch

800

700

600

500

400

Fall Crag

bracken

bracken

ROAD

LANTHWAITE

common

car parks

bracken

500

GRASMOOR via LAD HOWS

Cinderdale Beck

It needs an experienced eye fully to appreciate, from the foot of the slope, the length of the scree run in Red Gill. Most observers will seriously under-estimate both its length and steepness.

The climb starts at an open common with two car parks (popular with picnickers) and every step is *up*, without respite.

looking north-east

Crummock Water

Rannerdale Farm

BUTTERMERE 1¼

From the road, the route is in full view to the skyline 2000' above — it is a very obvious line of ascent, and indeed the only practicable one in sight.

ASCENT FROM RANNERDALE
2450 feet of ascent : 1¼ miles

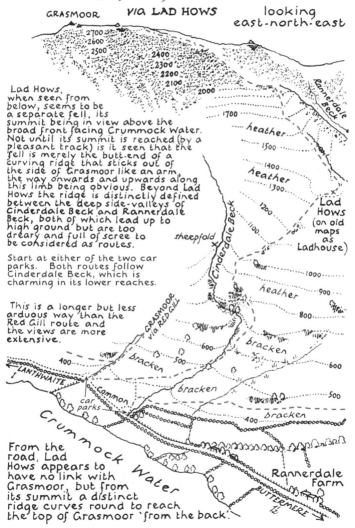

VIA LAD HOWS

looking east-north-east

GRASMOOR

2700
2600
2500
2400
2300
2200
2100
2000

Rannerdale Beck

1700

heather

1500

1400

heather

1300

1200

X
Lad Hows
(on old maps as Ladhouse)

1100

sheepfold

1000

Cinderdale Beck

900

heather

800

GRASMOOR VIA RED GILL

700

600

bracken

500

600

bracken

heather

Lad Hows, when seen from below, seems to be a separate fell, its summit being in view above the broad front facing Crummock Water. Not until its summit is reached (by a pleasant track) is it seen that the fell is merely the butt-end of a curving ridge that sticks out of the side of Grasmoor like an arm the way onwards and upwards along this limb being obvious. Beyond Lad Hows the ridge is distinctly defined between the deep side-valleys of Cinderdale Beck and Rannerdale Beck, both of which lead up to high ground but are too dreary and full of scree to be considered as routes.

Start at either of the two car parks. Both routes follow Cinderdale Beck, which is charming in its lower reaches.

This is a longer but less arduous way than the Red Gill route and the views are more extensive.

400

LANTHWAITE

Common

car parks

bracken

400

500

bracken

Crummock Water

From the road, Lad Hows appears to have no link with Grasmoor, but from its summit a distinct ridge curves round to reach the top of Grasmoor 'from the back'.

Rannerdale Farm

BUTTERMERE
½

The Scafell group

from Grasmoor

ASCENT FROM COLEDALE HAUSE
850 feet of ascent
1¼ miles

looking southeast

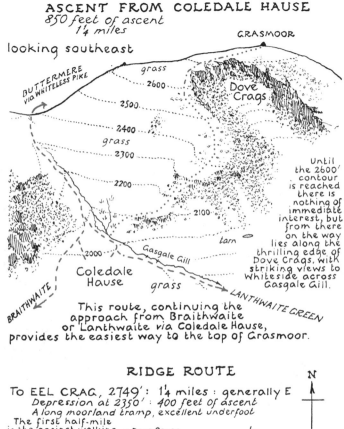

Until the 2600' contour is reached there is nothing of immediate interest, but from there on the way lies along the thrilling edge of Dove Crags, with striking views to Whiteside across Gasgale Gill.

This route, continuing the approach from Braithwaite or Lanthwaite *via* Coledale Hause, provides the easiest way to the top of Grasmoor.

RIDGE ROUTE

TO EEL CRAG, 2749': 1¼ miles: generally E
Depression at 2350': 400 feet of ascent
A long moorland tramp, excellent underfoot

The first half-mile is the easiest walking to be found anywhere; keep left for a sight of Dove Crags. After crossing the depression, bear right for a look down into Addacomb Hole. These are the only excitements.

HALF A MILE

THE SUMMIT

There are many cairns at various stations on the broad top, but no mistaking the highest of all, which is a huge heap of stones divided into shelter compartments, open to the sky, designed to give protection from wind (but not wet) coming from any direction.   Some skill and much labour has gone into its construction (where did the stones come from?) and visitors should feel a sense of responsibility for keeping it in repair.   It stands a score of yards only from the edge of the south face, and a smaller wind-shelter perched here on the brink marks a better viewpoint. The summit has a covering of shale hereabouts, but elsewhere a soft mossy turf is a pleasure to walk upon.

The top of the fell is a long plateau coming up from the east and is generally broad but midway it narrows to a waist a hundred yards wide, the north side of this section being rimmed by the top rocks of Dove Crags. This scene, and the exciting scaffold of Grasmoor End (which should be visited if time permits) are the finest topographical features of an otherwise rather dull summit.

DESCENTS: Generally, ways off lie along the plateau eastwards whatever the destination, but Red Gill is a quick and safe way down to Crummock Water for Buttermere, and the left edge of Dove Crags is a practicable route down to Gasgale for Lanthwaite and Loweswater. Grasmoor End leads only to trouble. In mist, go east for half a mile, descending very little, to the good path through the grassy hollow between Grasmoor and Eel Crag, and here turn left for Coledale Hause, right for Buttermere.

PLAN OF SUMMIT

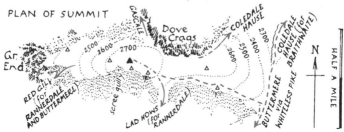

THE VIEW

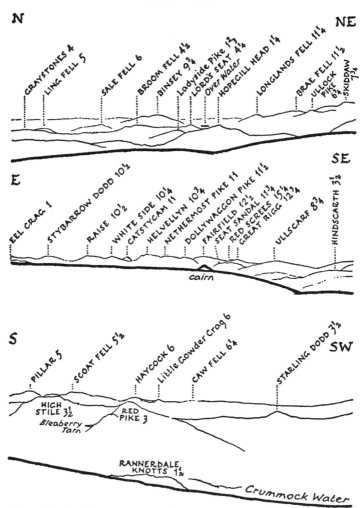

The thick line marks the visible boundaries of the summit from the cairn

THE VIEW

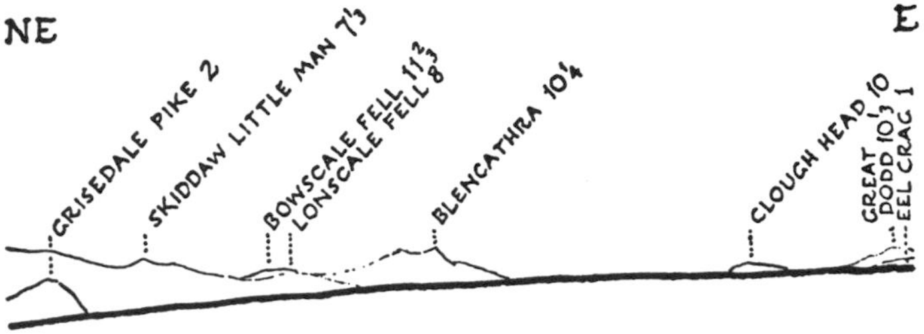
NE
E
GRISEDALE PIKE 2
SKIDDAW LITTLE MAN 7⅓
BOWSCALE FELL 11½
LONSCALE FELL 8
BLENCATHRA 10¼
CLOUGH HEAD 10
GREAT DODD 10⅓
EEL CRAG 1

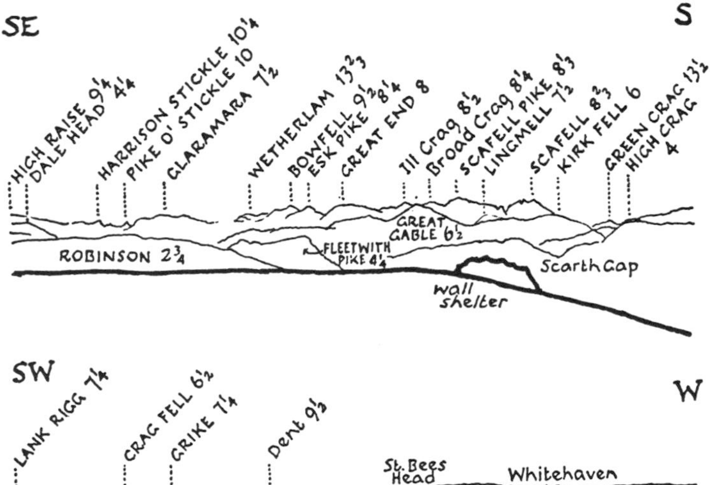
SE
S
HIGH RAISE 9¼
DALE HEAD 4¼
HARRISON STICKLE 10¼
PIKE O' STICKLE 10
GLARAMARA 7½
WETHERLAM 13⅔
BOWFELL 9½
ESK PIKE 8¾
GREAT END 8
Ill Crag 8½
Broad Crag 8¾
SCAFELL PIKE 8⅓
LINGMELL 7½
SCAFELL 8⅔
KIRK FELL 6
GREEN CRAG 13½
HIGH CRAG 4
GREAT GABLE 6½
ROBINSON 2¾
FLEETWITH PIKE 4¼
Scarth Gap
wall shelter

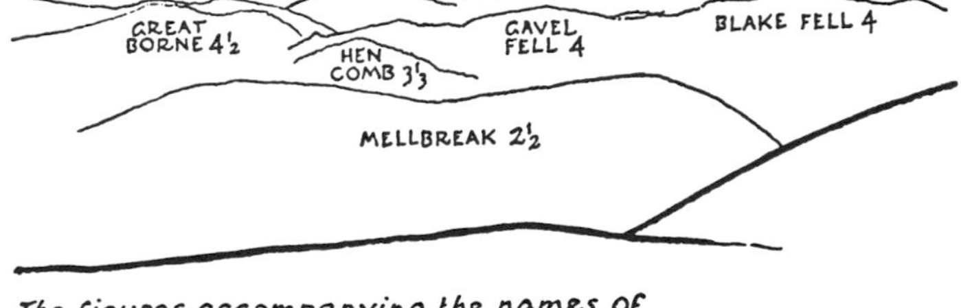
SW
W
LANK RIGG 7¼
CRAG FELL 6½
GRIKE 7¼
Dent 9⅓
St. Bees Head
Whitehaven
GREAT BORNE 4½
GAVEL FELL 4
BLAKE FELL 4
HEN COMB 3⅓
MELLBREAK 2½

The figures accompanying the names of fells indicate distances in miles

continued

THE VIEW
continued

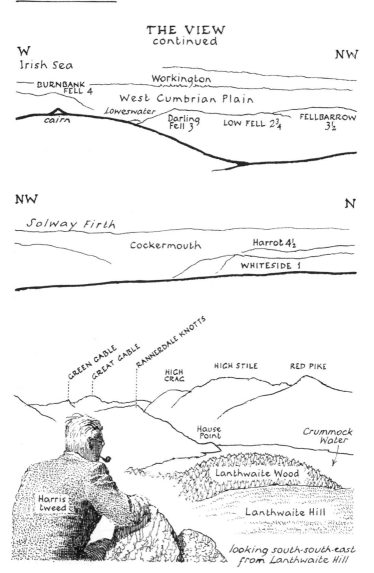

W
Irish Sea

BURNBANK
FELL 4

cairn

Workington

West Cumbrian Plain

Loweswater

Darling
Fell 3

LOW FELL 2¾

NW

FELLBARROW
3½

NW

Solway Firth

Cockermouth

Harrot 4½

WHITESIDE 1

N

GREEN GABLE
GREAT GABLE
RANNERDALE KNOTTS

HIGH
CRAG

HIGH STILE

RED PIKE

Hause
Point

Crummock
Water

Harris
tweed

Lanthwaite Wood

Lanthwaite Hill

*looking south-south-east
from Lanthwaite Hill*

Cinderdale Beck: a favourite stream, well known (but not by name) to the many motorists and campers who enjoy the freedom of the open fell alongside the road to Buttermere at the base of Grasmoor.

Dove Crags

Grasmoor End
from Crummock Water

Graystones

1476'

Cockermouth

● Wythop Mill

LING FELL ▲

GRAYSTONES ▲

Low
Lorton

▲ BROOM FELL

▲ LORD'S
SEAT

● High
Lorton

Whinlatter Pass ●

MILES

0 1 2 3 4

*from
Aiken Plantation*

NATURAL FEATURES

Graystones is the name of a summit only. The fell of which it is the highest point is Kirk Fell, rising above the western end of the motor road through the pass of Whinlatter at the head of the Vale of Lorton. This aspect of the fell is its most impressive, the declivity here being rough and steep, but northwards, facing Wythop, the slopes fall away more easily to merge in upland and undulating pastures before declining finally to the wide Embleton valley.   The western flanks too descend in simple stages to the flat land of the River Cocker, although interrupted, midway, by the small eminence of Harrot, which has a lovely view to the south. These smooth upper expanses are of grass, but the sharper eastern slope, overlooking the side valley of Aiken Beck where the long climb to Whinlatter Pass starts in earnest, is now almost completely patterned by the young evergreens and forest roads of Darling How Plantation.   At the foot of this slope, hidden in a jungle of new conifers, is a fine waterfall, Spout Force, where Aiken Beck plunges into a deep chasm before joining Whit Beck, a principal tributary of the Cocker.

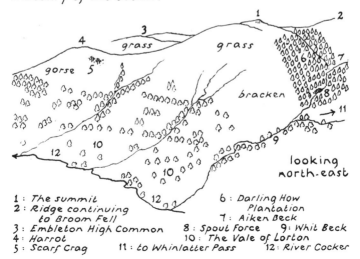

1 : The summit
2 : Ridge continuing
   to Broom Fell
3 : Embleton High Common
4 : Harrot
5 : Scarf Crag
6 : Darling How
   Plantation
7 : Aiken Beck
8 : Spout Force   9 : Whit Beck
10 : The Vale of Lorton
11 : to Whinlatter Pass   12 : River Cocker

looking north-east

MAP

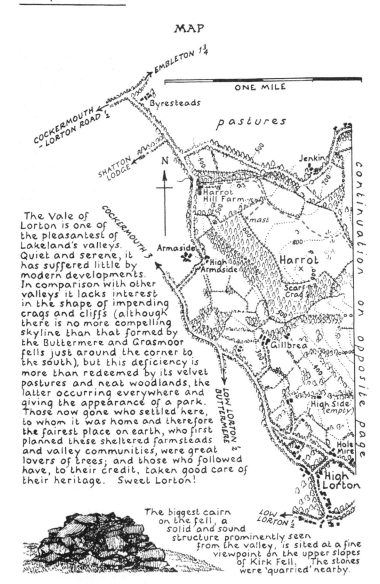

EMBLETON 1¾

ONE MILE

COCKERMOUTH - LORTON ROAD ½

Byresteads

pastures

SHATTON LODGE

N

Harrot Hill Farm

mast

Jenkin

continuation on opposite page

COCKERMOUTH 3

Armaside

High Armaside

Harrot
×

Scarf Crag

Gillbrea

LOW LORTON ½ BUTTERMERE

High Side (empty)

Hole Mire

High Lorton

LOW LORTON ½

The Vale of Lorton is one of the pleasantest of Lakeland's valleys. Quiet and serene, it has suffered little by modern developments. In comparison with other valleys it lacks interest in the shape of impending crags and cliffs (although there is no more compelling skyline than that formed by the Buttermere and Grasmoor fells just around the corner to the south), but this deficiency is more than redeemed by its velvet pastures and neat woodlands, the latter occurring everywhere and giving the appearance of a park. Those now gone who settled here, to whom it was home and therefore the fairest place on earth, who first planned these sheltered farmsteads and valley communities, were great lovers of trees; and those who followed have, to their credit, taken good care of their heritage. Sweet Lorton!

The biggest cairn on the fell, a solid and sound structure prominently seen from the valley, is sited at a fine viewpoint on the upper slopes of Kirk Fell. The stones were 'quarried' nearby.

MAP

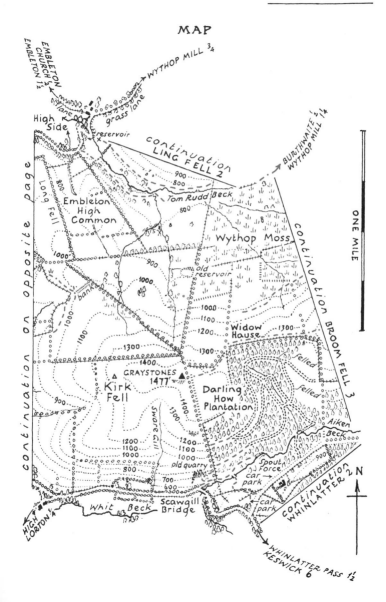

EMBLETON CHURCH 2
EMBLETON 1½

WYTHOP MILL ¾

High Side

grass lane

lane

reservoir

continuation LING FELL 2

BURTHWAITE ½
WYTHOP MILL 1¼

Long Fell

Embleton High Common

Tom Rudd Beck

Wythop Moss

continuation BROOM FELL 3

old reservoir

bank

Widow Hause

ONE MILE

GRAYSTONES 1477'

Kirk Fell

Sw016 Gill

Darling How Plantation

felled

felled

Aiken Beck

old quarry

Spout Force

car park

car park

continuation WHINLATTER 2

N

HIGH LORTON 1

Whit Beck

Scawgill Bridge

WHINLATTER PASS 1½
KESWICK 6

continuation on opposite page

ASCENT FROM EMBLETON CHURCH
1200 feet of ascent: 2½ miles

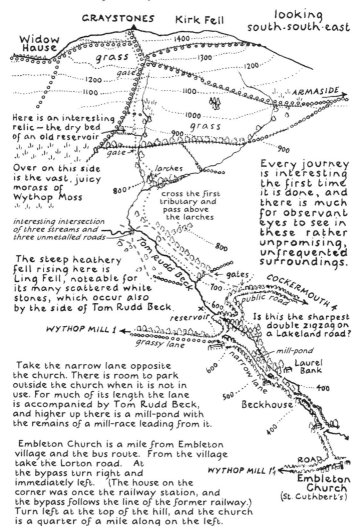

GRAYSTONES Kirk Fell

looking
south·south·east

Widow
Hause

grass

1400

1300

1200

1100

1200

1100

ARMASIDE

1000

grass

900

900

Here is an interesting
relic — the dry bed
of an old reservoir

gate

gate

larches

Over on this side
is the vast, juicy
morass of
Wythop Moss

800

cross the first
tributary and
pass above
the larches

Every journey
is interesting
the first time
it is done, and
there is much
for observant
eyes to see in
these rather
unpromising,
unfrequented
surroundings.

interesting intersection
of three streams and
three unmetalled roads

800

The steep heathery
fell rising here is
Ling Fell, noteable for
its many scattered white
stones, which occur also
by the side of Tom Rudd Beck.

Tom Rudd Beck

gates

700

COCKERMOUTH

public road

600

reservoir

WYTHOP MILL 1

grassy lane

Is this the sharpest
double zigzag on
a Lakeland road?

mill-pond

Laurel
Bank

Take the narrow lane opposite
the church. There is room to park
outside the church when it is not in
use. For much of its length the lane
is accompanied by Tom Rudd Beck, and
higher up there is a mill-pond with
the remains of a mill-race leading from it.

600

narrow lane

500

400

Beckhouse

400

Embleton Church is a mile from Embleton
village and the bus route. From the village
take the Lorton road. At
the bypass turn right and
immediately left. (The house on the
corner was once the railway station, and
the bypass follows the line of the former railway.)
Turn left at the top of the hill, and the church
is a quarter of a mile along on the left.

ROAD

WYTHOP MILL 1¼

Embleton
Church
(St. Cuthbert's)

ASCENT FROM ARMASIDE
1200 feet of ascent : 2¼ miles

looking south-east

From the young plantation it is best to climb the easy slopes straight ahead to the cairn on Kirk Fell because there is a stile in the fence here but none farther to the left. The cairn is described as a pile of stones on the Ordnance Survey map but has been rebuilt. By this route a view southwards over Lorton can be maintained to the top of Graystones.

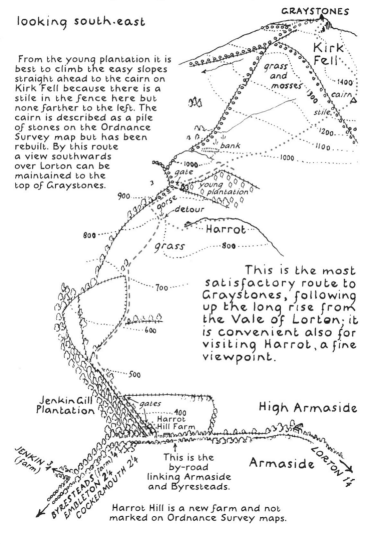

GRAYSTONES

Kirk Fell

grass and mosses

1400
cairn
stile
1200
1100

1500

1000

bank

1000

1000
gate

3

900

young plantation

gorse

detour

800

grass

Harrot

800

700

600

500

Jenkin Gill Plantation

gates
400
Harrot Hill Farm

High Armaside

This is the most satisfactory route to Graystones, following up the long rise from the Vale of Lorton; it is convenient also for visiting Harrot, a fine viewpoint.

JENKIN 3 (farm)

BYRESTEADS (farm) 2¼
EMBLETON 2¼
COCKERMOUTH 2¼

This is the by-road linking Armaside and Byresteads.

Armaside

LORTON 1¼

Harrot Hill is a new farm and not marked on Ordnance Survey maps.

ASCENT FROM SCAWGILL BRIDGE
900 feet of ascent : ¾ mile

GRAYSTONES

1400 grass

1300

1200

1100

1000

900 and

800

700

600

This ascent is short, direct and fool-proof in any conditions of weather, but it lacks excitement and is hardly worth the effort.

Darling How Plantation

bracken

gorse

old quarry

signpost

parking place

Aiken Beck

Spout Force

stile

gate

WHINLATTER PASS 1¾
KESWICK 6¼

Scawgill Bridge

COCKERMOUTH 5
HIGH LORTON 1

Whit Beck

Starting along the footpath to Spout Force, turn left ten yards before a pair of larch trees and cut across to the broken wall, which leads to the summit in a straight line. The ascent then becomes easier as height is gained; the last quarter mile, over grass, is a simple walk. If *descending* by this route keep closely to the wall to avoid the quarry.

looking north

A big bridge (still there) and a little one (gone).....

Scawgill Bridge on the Whinlatter road

Spout Force

A clearly defined gravel path leads away from Scawgill Bridge to an excellent viewpoint where the lower part of Spout Force is seen through a narrow cleft in the rocks. Things weren't always like this. When the first edition of this guide was published a signpost, inviting passers-by to use a footpath "to Spout Force only", tempted many people upstream in search of it. Only a few, grimly determined, ever saw it. The signpost, due to the effluxion of time and in particular to the habit of young spruce to add a foot a year to their height, became a bad joke. Originally it was provided by the Forestry Commission as a concession to the public, the waterfall in its rocky gorge being well worth seeing. Notwithstanding their signpost, the Commission then proceeded to plant the route with prickly young trees, which, with the passing years, encroached upon the path and obliterated it. A few yards above the stream, after painful gymnastics, a forlorn noticeboard was found in the forest, announcing the end of the path (joke no. 2). At this point an abnormally tall person could just see the upper part of the fall.

Now there is no mention of Spout Force on the signpost at Scawgill Bridge, but there is no risk of going astray. There is no longer a sign announcing the end of the public footpath either, but none is necessary: it is obvious that the path has come to an end.

Spout Force may also be reached by the Spout Force Walk. This leaves from the far end of the first car park on the road to Darling How and is provided by courtesy of the Forestry Commission.

right : The gorge

below : The force (top left corner, as seen in 1962)

END OF PUBLIC FOOTPATH

THE SUMMIT

SKIDDAW   SKIDDAW LITTLE MAN   BLENCATHRA

BROOM FELL   LORD'S SEAT

The point generally considered to be the summit lies a few yards west of the broken wall and fence crossing the top of the fell, but according to the 2½" Ordnance Survey map there is higher ground farther east.

DESCENTS : The most direct way off follows the wall straight down to Scawgill Bridge on the Whinlatter Pass road; simple at first, the ground steepens and becomes very rough near the bottom, but the roughness may be avoided by taking a path to the right below the quarry. The other routes of ascent provide pleasant walking in reverse and should give no trouble even in mist, using as guides the walls indicated on the map.

RIDGE ROUTE

To BROOM FELL, 1670' : 1½ miles : N, then ENE.

Depression at 1240' (Widow Hause) : 450 feet of ascent

A pleasant walk on grass, interest being added by the plantation.

Head east from the summit to Widow Hause, where the fence is easy to cross. Keep above the plantation, and bear left along a faint path after crossing a broken wall.

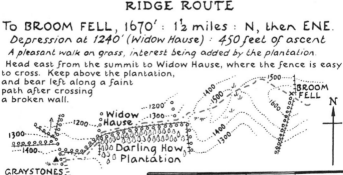

THE VIEW

A dreary foreground detracts from the view, which reveals a fine sweep of the Scottish coast with Criffell prominent, the Skiddaw group, a good section of the Helvellyn skyline and the towering Grasmoor mass across Whinlatter Pass as its best features. The Vale of Lorton, backed by the Loweswater Fells, is well seen.

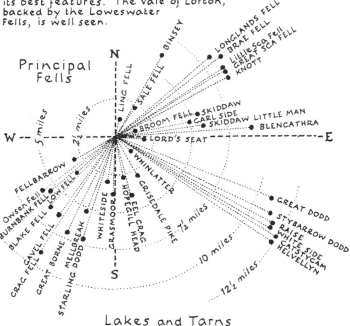

Principal Fells

LONGLANDS FELL
BRAE FELL
Little Sca Fell
GREAT SCA FELL
KNOTT
BINSEY
SALE FELL
LING FELL
SKIDDAW
CARL SIDE
SKIDDAW LITTLE MAN
BROOM FELL
BLENCATHRA
LORD'S SEAT
5 miles
2½ miles
FELLBARROW
Owsen Fell
BURNBANK FELL
BLAKE FELL
LOW FELL
WHINLATTER
GRISEDALE PIKE
HOPEGILL HEAD
EEL CRAG
WHITESIDE
GRASMOOR
GAVEL FELL
GREAT BORNE
MELLBREAK
STARLING DODD
CRAG FELL
7½ miles
GREAT DODD
STYBARROW DODD
RAISE
WHITE SIDE
CATSTYCAM
HELVELLYN
10 miles
12½ miles

N
W --- E
S

Lakes and Tarns

No lakes or tarns can be seen, but Crummock Water is brought into view by walking west to the next prominence and more of it by continuing to the subsidiary summit of Harrot, where too the Vale of Lorton appears at its best.

STARLING DODD
GREAT BORNE
GAVEL FELL
BLAKE FELL
MELLBREAK
LOW FELL

The skyline to the southwest

Crisedale Pike

2593'

from High Moss

NATURAL FEATURES

All visitors to Lakeland who come to walk on the hills turn their footsteps in due course to Grisedale Pike. It is seldom a prime objective, being a little out of the way, but the graceful peak piercing the western sky is a nagger of conscience and cannot long be ignored. Nor should it be. Conspicuously in view from the environs of Keswick, it is one of those fells that compels attention by reason of shapeliness and height.

The Pike, although of slender proportions on and towards the top, is quite broadly based, occupying the west side of Coledale through the three-mile length of the valley, from which the slopes of the fell rise steeply and unbroken for 2000 feet to a narrow crest. On this face heather and scree below the summit-rocks offer nothing to the climber but hard labour, a fact so obvious that it is virtually a no-man's-land; and the lines of approach lie along four ridges— a short one joined from Coledale Hause, and, at divergent points between north and east, three others rise from the plantations of Whinlatter, the most easterly carrying the popular route from Braithwaite. These three ridges enclose two deep valleys, partly afforested, pathless, and unfrequented, while the sombre depths of Hobcarton mark the boundary of the fell and an impressive neighbour, Hopegill Head, which are linked also at a high level, above a rim of crags, by the short ridge referred to.

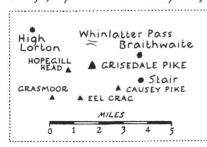

Why *Grisedale* Pike? Why not *Coledale* Pike after the valley below? Generally a mountain takes its name from a valley only if it stands *at the head*, and the rule is followed here — one of the two short valleys running north-east is named Grisedale (a fact little known), the summit of the fell being centred *exactly at the head*.

Force Crag

Coledale is straight and narrow, and without incident until, two miles up, a high barrier of rock extends across the valley like a huge dam. This is Force Crag. Over its lip pours a long cascade (Low Force) and at its foot are the buildings and the spoil-heaps of Force Crag Mine. The scene, backed by the towering skyline of Eel Crag, is magnificently wild.

Escape for the walker bound for Coledale Hause is provided by a wide path that crosses the beck and climbs round to the left of the crag. Ahead, a well-made zigzag path leads to Coledale Hause. Both above and below the zigzags faint tracks head into an amphitheatre above Force Crag, where, amazingly, the scene below is repeated. In front again now is another high wall of rock, and again a long cascade (High Force) pours over the lip. Here, too, are mine-buildings and spoil-heaps. The stream (Pudding Beck) is the same; between its two excitements it meanders quietly through this hanging valley. Force Crag is a natural formation not repeated in any other Lakeland dale and to find its unusual arrangement occurring twice, in close proximity, is remarkable.

The mine, always a rich one but not continuously worked, was used for the extraction of barytes until it finally closed down in 1991.

High Force

Force Crag

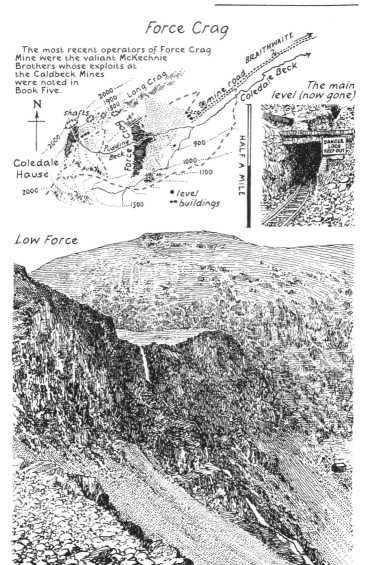

The most recent operators of Force Crag Mine were the valiant McKechnie Brothers whose exploits at the Caldbeck Mines were noted in Book Five.

N

2000
1900
1800 Long Crag
BRAITHWAITE

shafts

mine road

Coledale Beck

Coledale Hause

Pudding Beck

Force Crag

900

1000

1100

1500

2000

The main level (now gone)

DANGER
LOCO
KEEP OUT

HALF A MILE

• level
-- buildings

Low Force

MAP

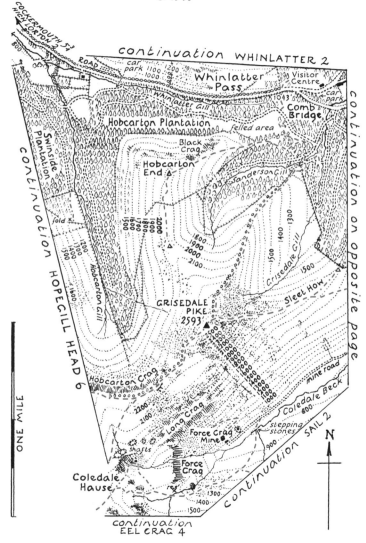

MAP

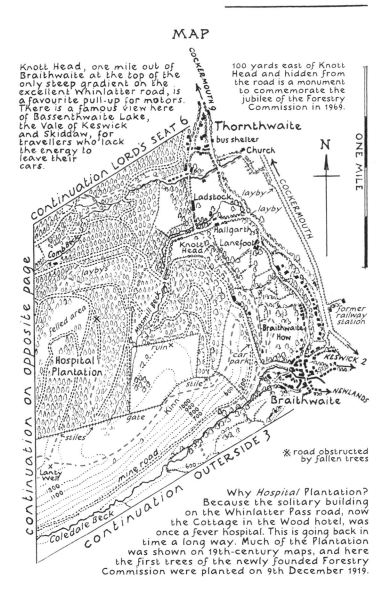

Knott Head, one mile out of Braithwaite at the top of the only steep gradient on the excellent Whinlatter road, is a favourite pull-up for motors. There is a famous view here of Bassenthwaite Lake, the Vale of Keswick and Skiddaw, for travellers who lack the energy to leave their cars.

100 yards east of Knott Head and hidden from the road is a monument to commemorate the jubilee of the Forestry Commission in 1969.

ONE MILE

N

COCKERMOUTH 9

continuation LORD'S SEAT 6

continuation on opposite page

Thornthwaite
bus shelter
Church

COCKERMOUTH

Ladstock
layby
layby
Hallgarth
Knott Head
Lanefoot
Comb Beck
laybys
Masmill Beck
felled area
ruin
Hospital Plantation
stile
gate
Kinn
stiles
Lanty Well
Coledale Beck
mine road

former railway station

Braithwaite How
car park

KESWICK 2
NEWLANDS
Braithwaite

600
800
1000
1200

※ road obstructed by fallen trees

Why *Hospital* Plantation? Because the solitary building on the Whinlatter Pass road, now the Cottage in the Wood hotel, was once a fever hospital. This is going back in time a long way. Much of the Plantation was shown on 19th-century maps, and here the first trees of the newly founded Forestry Commission were planted on 9th December 1919.

continuation OUTERSIDE 3

Grisedale Pike 7

Three Ridges

the east ridge — *the final section, from Sleet How*

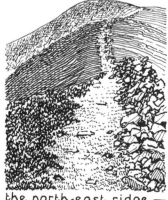

the north-east ridge —
the path by the broken wall

the north ridge —
looking from Hobcarton End

ASCENT FROM BRAITHWAITE
2400 feet of ascent : 3 miles

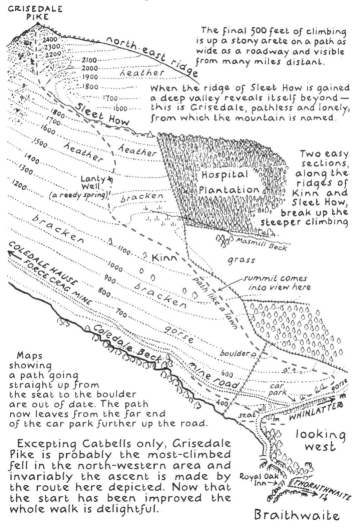

GRISEDALE PIKE

north-east ridge

2400
2300
2200
2100
2000
1900
1800
heather
1700
1600

Sleet How

1800
1700
1600
heather
heather
1500
1400
1300
1200

Lanty Well
(a reedy spring)

bracken

COLEDALE HAUSE →
← FORCE CRAG MINE

bracken

1100
Kinn
1000
900
bracken
800
700

Coledale Beck

Coledale Beck

gorse

mine road

600

path like a lawn

Hospital Plantation

Masmill Beck

grass

summit comes into view here

boulder

400

car park

seat

gorse

WHINLATTER

looking west

Royal Oak Inn →

← THORNTHWAITE 1¼

Braithwaite

The final 500 feet of climbing is up a stony arête on a path as wide as a roadway and visible from many miles distant.

When the ridge of Sleet How is gained a deep valley reveals itself beyond — this is Grisedale, pathless and lonely, from which the mountain is named.

Two easy sections, along the ridges of Kinn and Sleet How, break up the steeper climbing

Maps showing a path going straight up from the seat to the boulder are out of date. The path now leaves from the far end of the car park further up the road.

Excepting Catbells only, Grisedale Pike is probably the most-climbed fell in the north-western area and invariably the ascent is made by the route here depicted. Now that the start has been improved the whole walk is delightful.

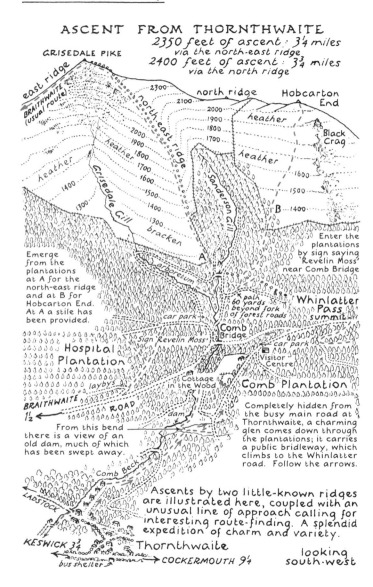

ASCENT FROM THORNTHWAITE

2350 feet of ascent : 3¼ miles
via the north-east ridge
2400 feet of ascent : 3¾ miles
via the north ridge

GRISEDALE PIKE

east ridge
BRAITHWAITE (usual route)

north ridge   Hobcarton End

2300
2100
2000
1900
1800
1700

north-east ridge

heather

Black Crag

heather

2000
1900
1800
1700
1600
1500
1400
1300

heather

1400
1300

Grisedale Gill

Sanderson Gill

1600
1500
B   1400

bracken

A

arboretum

Enter the plantations by sign saying 'Revelin Moss' near Comb Bridge

Emerge from the plantations at A for the north-east ridge and at B for Hobcarton End. At A a stile has been provided.

path 60 yards beyond fork of forest roads

car park

Whinlatter Pass summit

Comb Bridge

Hospital Plantation

Sign Revelin Moss

car park

Visitor Centre

Cottage in the Wood

laybys

Comb Plantation

BRAITHWAITE 1½ ←   ROAD

dam

From this bend there is a view of an old dam, much of which has been swept away.

Completely hidden from the busy main road at Thornthwaite, a charming glen comes down through the plantations; it carries a public bridleway, which climbs to the Whinlatter road. Follow the arrows.

Comb Beck

LADSTOCK

KESWICK 3¾   Thornthwaite
bus shelter   → COCKERMOUTH 9¼

Ascents by two little-known ridges are illustrated here, coupled with an unusual line of approach calling for interesting route-finding. A splendid expedition of charm and variety.

looking south-west

ASCENT FROM WHINLATTER PASS
1600 feet of ascent : 2¼ miles from the road

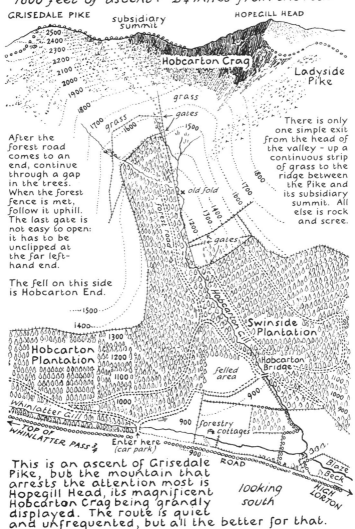

GRISEDALE PIKE
subsidiary summit
HOPEGILL HEAD

2500
2400
2300
2200
2100
2000
1900
1800

Hobcarton Crag

Ladyside Pike

grass

gates

1700   grass   1600

1500

After the forest road comes to an end, continue through a gap in the trees. When the forest fence is met, follow it uphill. The last gate is not easy to open: it has to be unclipped at the far left-hand end.

The fell on this side is Hobcarton End.

There is only one simple exit from the head of the valley – up a continuous strip of grass to the ridge between the Pike and its subsidiary summit. All else is rock and scree.

× old fold

1400
1300
1200

gates

1800
1700
1600

1500
1400

Swinside Plantation

1300

Hobcarton Plantation

1200

1100

1000

Hobcarton Bridge

felled area

900

Whinlatter Gill

TOP OF WHINLATTER PASS ¾

Enter here (car park)

900   forestry cottages

900   ROAD

Blaze Beck

HIGH LORTON

looking south

This is an ascent of Grisedale Pike, but the mountain that arrests the attention most is Hopegill Head, its magnificent Hobcarton Crag being grandly displayed. The route is quiet and unfrequented, but all the better for that.

ASCENT FROM COLEDALE HAUSE
700 feet of ascent : 1¼ miles

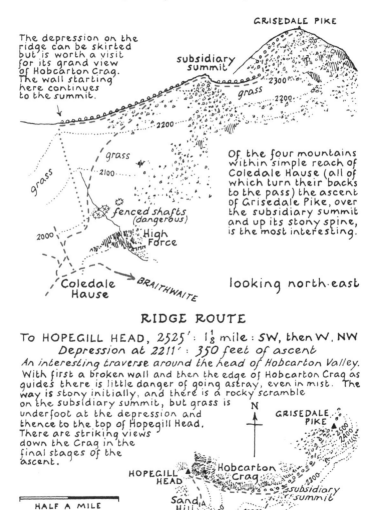

GRISEDALE PIKE

The depression on the ridge can be skirted but is worth a visit for its grand view of Hobcarton Crag. The wall starting here continues to the summit.

subsidiary summit

2300

grass

2200

grass

grass

2100

fenced shafts (dangerous)

2000

High Force

Coledale Hause

BRAITHWAITE

Of the four mountains within simple reach of Coledale Hause (all of which turn their backs to the pass) the ascent of Grisedale Pike, over the subsidiary summit and up its stony spine, is the most interesting.

looking north-east

RIDGE ROUTE

To HOPEGILL HEAD, 2525′ : 1⅛ mile : SW, then W, NW
Depression at 2211′ : 350 feet of ascent

An interesting traverse around the head of Hobcarton Valley.
With first a broken wall and then the edge of Hobcarton Crag as guides there is little danger of going astray, even in mist. The way is stony initially, and there is a rocky scramble on the subsidiary summit, but grass is underfoot at the depression and thence to the top of Hopegill Head. There are striking views down the Crag in the final stages of the ascent.

N

GRISEDALE PIKE

2200

2200

HOPEGILL HEAD

Hobcarton Crag

subsidiary summit

Sand Hill

2300

grass

HALF A MILE

THE SUMMIT

BLENCATHRA

The cairn sits upon a plinth of slate, fragments of which litter the summit thickly and add a musical tinkling to the march of boots. Much of this debris originated as a wall, now unrecognisable as such. The cairn is very small, but there is a wind-shelter 100 yards south-west of the summit and a large cairn on Sleet How ½ mile to the east.

DESCENTS : There may be initial difficulty in locating the start of the path down to Braithwaite, which is over-run by scree, but it soon becomes obvious, taking a line down the distinct ridge from the eastern corner of the summit; *in mist*, turn *right* at a pair of iron posts. A smoother alternative is provided by the north-east ridge, keeping alongside the wall down to the plantations. For Coledale Hause follow the wall along the ridge to the west and bear left just beyond the subsidiary summit, keeping *right* of the fenced shafts.

PLAN OF SUMMIT

N

NORTH-EAST RIDGE

2400
2500

PATH TO BRAITHWAITE

COLEDALE HAUSE

2400

100 YARDS

The main summit (left) from the subsidiary summit (right)

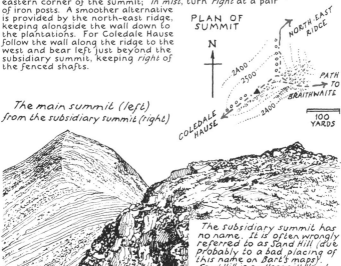

The subsidiary summit has no name. It is often wrongly referred to as Sand Hill (due probably to a bad placing of this name on Bart's maps). Sand Hill is on Hopegill Head.

THE VIEW

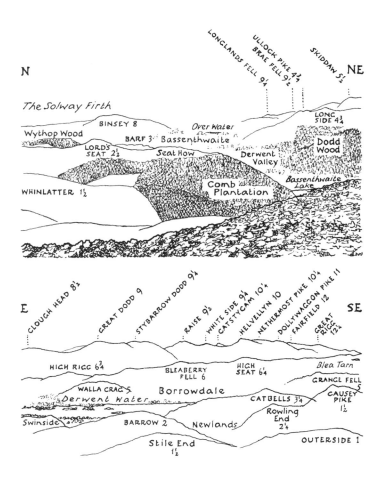

From E to S, Coledale occupies the bottom of the view

THE VIEW

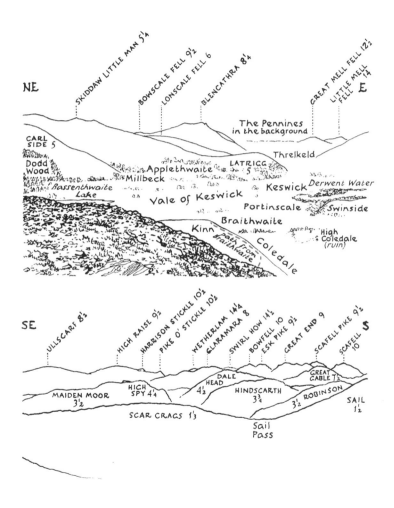

The figures accompanying the names of fells
indicate distances in miles

continued

THE VIEW

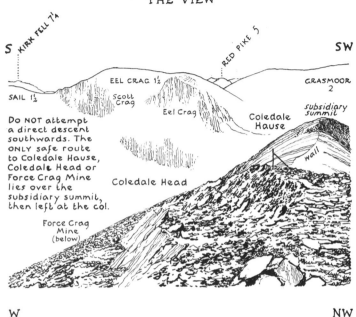

S   KIRK FELL 7½

RED PIKE 5

SW

EEL CRAG 1½

SAIL 1½

Scott Crag

Eel Crag

GRASMOOR 2

subsidiary summit

Coledale Hause

Do NOT attempt a direct descent southwards. The ONLY safe route to Coledale Hause, Coledale Head or Force Crag Mine lies over the subsidiary summit, then left at the col.

Coledale Head

wall

Force Crag Mine (below)

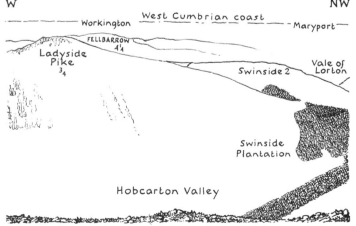

W

NW

Workington

West Cumbrian coast

Maryport

FELLBARROW 4¼

Ladyside Pike 3¼

Swinside 2

Vale of Lorton

Swinside Plantation

Hobcarton Valley

THE VIEW

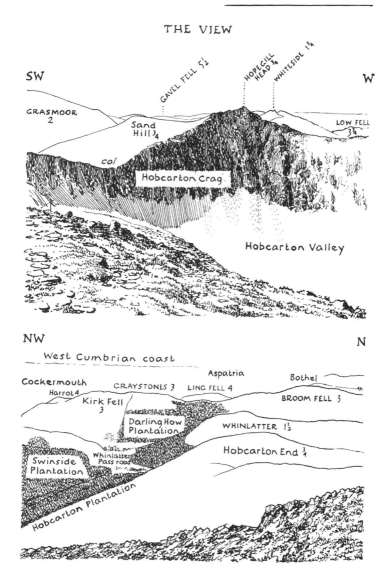

SW

GRASMOOR 2

Sand Hill 3/4

col

GAVEL FELL 5½

HOPEGILL HEAD 3/4

WHITESIDE 1¾

W

LOW FELL 3¼

Hobcarton Crag

Hobcarton Valley

NW

N

West Cumbrian coast

Cockermouth

Aspatria

Bothel

Harrot 4

CRAYSTONES 3

LING FELL 4

Kirk Fell 3

Darling How Plantation

BROOM FELL 3

WHINLATTER 1½

Whinlatter Pass road

Swinside Plantation

Hobcarton End 3/4

Hobcarton Plantation

High Spy

2143'

*also variously known as
Eel Crags, Lobstone Band
and Scawdel Fell*

from
Dalehead Tarn

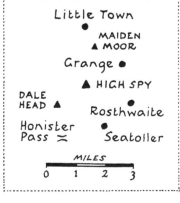

Little Town
MAIDEN
▲ MOOR
Grange ●
▲ HIGH SPY
DALE
HEAD ▲
Honister   ● Rosthwaite
Pass ≍   ● Seatoller

MILES
0   1   2   3

Hollows Farm

NATURAL FEATURES

The middle reaches of Borrowdale are bounded on the west by high fellsides, colourful and attractive side-curtains that contribute much to the beauty of the valley, yet which have never really been fully accepted by visitors as part of the lovely setting of the natural stage they come to admire. This lack of popular appeal, which is relative only to the quite unsurpassed scenery all around, is mainly because, when viewed from the valley, the rough slopes offer no obvious routes for walkers and the flat skyline promises no interesting summits above. In fact, between Catbells and Honister there is only a single breach in the four-mile wall carrying a beaten path (and *that* was beaten by quarrymen, not fellwalkers) and consequently the scenic beauties of Borrowdale are more often sought on the eastern slopes, where good paths abound.

High country can rarely be appraised properly from valley-level, however. The long skyline visible from below is not the ridge of the fell, as it appears to be, but the edge of a wide plateau where the steep rise of the slopes eases to a gentler gradient, the true spine lying well back, and it is here, along a crest, that one really enters upon fellwalkers' territory, a splendid elevated track traversing the whole length of the fell. Interest is sustained by the succession of cliffs and aretes falling away abruptly from the crest to the desolate upper Newlands valley, for on this western flank there is no wide plateau, but, in contrast, the appalling mile-long precipice known to the rock-climbing fraternity as Eel Crags. This, and the great bastion of Goat Crag above Borrowdale, are distinctive features.

The culminating point on a top of fairly uniform height is High Spy. To the south there is an easy decline to the marshy depression of Rigg Head, where many routes converge; north, the long crest descends to the level summit of Maiden Moor and continues to Catbells.

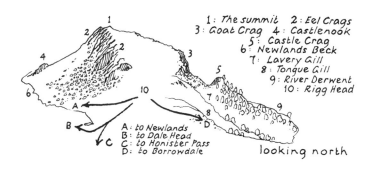

1: The summit 2: Eel Crags
3: Goat Crag 4: Castlenook
5: Castle Crag
6: Newlands Beck
7: Lavery Gill
8: Tongue Gill
9: River Derwent
10: Rigg Head

A: to Newlands
B: to Dale Head
C: to Honister Pass
D: to Borrowdale

looking north

Eel Crags

looking south from Castlenook

Red Crag

Waterfall Buttress

Miners Crag

looking north from the foot of Miners Crag

MAP

C : Castlenook Mine   R : Rigghead Quarries (both disused)

For the place-names on their maps, the Ordnance Survey rely on the information gathered over the years in their files, supplied or verified by church records, title deeds, estate books and other written sources, and often on the statements of local residents. On the Lakeland map, much reliance has been placed on spoken information volunteered locally (and in a few instances it would seem that the dialect has not been interpreted quite correctly).

The Ordnance map of the High Spy area is interesting because of the naming of the sheepfolds. This occurs elsewhere in the district, but infrequently. All sheepfolds, of course, have identifying names known to farmers and shepherds, but not normally made public. It would appear, however, that the 'tenant of the grazing on Scawdel has been unusually communicative. Thus the Ordnance map names Joe Bank's (? Banks') Fold, Robin's Fold and Wilson's Bield on 2½" and 6" editions, yet these are unremarkable structures bettered by many others elsewhere not distinguished by 'official' names.

The hinterland of Goat Crag

Joe Bank's Fold

The only frequented walkers' route on the higher parts of the fell runs along the crest of the ridge; the wide upland east of the summit, ending in a two-mile escarpment above Borrowdale, is rarely visited. This escarpment is almost continuous from Blea Crag to and beyond Goat Crag, being breached only by High White Rake and Low White Rake, both very steep passages. The upland, however, although broken by many outcrops, is good grazing ground. Getting the sheep down through the escarpment to the valley, as is necessary on occasion, is a problem that has been solved by slanting a drove-way between the top of Low White Rake and the foot of High White Rake, and this is the only route by which sheep may safely be brought down from the tops.

Immediately behind the rocky turrets of Nitting Haws and Goat Crag there is a spacious hollow, an amphitheatre, before the slope resumes its climb over the upland to the summit of High Spy, and in this hollow, where the sheep are gathered, a meandering stream finds a way down a stony ravine to the valley.

This hollow is a surprising place: it is unsuspected from the valley and is unseen from the summit-ridge. Although poised close above the busy holiday traffic of Borrowdale, it lies lonely and silent in a circle of craggy outcrops. Vegetation is lush: bracken, heather and mosses form a rich carpet of colourful pattern. Here the staghorn moss occurs profusely, covering large areas in dense mats resembling crowded nests of little green snakes, which writhe and squirm realistically under the tread of a boot.

Map labels:
Cockley How
fold
Blea Crag
H
drove way
L
A : Amphitheatre
H : High White Rake
L : Low White Rake
Nitting Haws
Eel Crags
summit ridge
2000
1900
1800
1700
Joe Bank's Fold
Minum Crag
A
Goat Crag
N
QUARTER MILE

Staghorn moss
(Common Club-moss)

ASCENT FROM GRANGE
1950 feet of ascent : 2 miles via High White Rake
2½ miles via Narrow Moor

HIGH SPY

Minum Crag — 2000

cairn (viewpoint)

Blea Crag

1900

Narrow Moor

Behind Nitting Haws is an amphitheatre of heather, bracken and mosses set amongst rocks

1800

1700 heather 1600

High White Rake — 1500

Nitting Haws →

drove road

Low White Rake

From the sheepfold the drove road may be used instead; this avoids the steepness

1900

1700
1600

1500

1300

heather — dense and floriferous and vastly more extensive than it appears from below

1100

bracken

fold

Greenup

Cockley How

boulders

900

1000

During the early stages of the walk there is a growing appreciation of the ruggedness of the great rampart of rock ahead to the left. This is a formidable barrier with only two breaches available to the walker — Low White Rake is too steep and unpromising to be considered; High White Rake becomes more obvious as it is approached and, although rough, is a practicable route to the plateau above.
Alternatively, avoiding the crags altogether, the slope may be followed up to the skyline of Narrow Moor, and the ridge-path there joined — a tedious ascent.

bracken
800

bracken

700

500

weir

gate

bracken

Swanesty How

bracken
400

HOLLOWS

waterfalls — a fine spectacle (few yards detour)

500

Ellers Beck

400

gate
stile
gate
water tank

Ellers

gate

× stone seat
Peace How

looking west

Leave Grange by the Manesty road, turning off at a gate almost opposite the Borrowdale Gates Hotel.

ROAD
gate
Hotel
Grange

ASCENT FROM SEATOLLER OR ROSTHWAITE
FROM SEATOLLER: *1800 feet of ascent: 2½ miles*
FROM ROSTHWAITE: *1900 feet; 2½ miles*

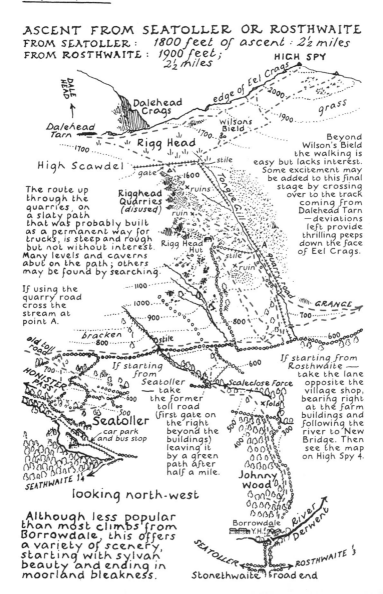

HIGH SPY

DALE HEAD

Dalehead Crags

edge of Eel Crags

2000

1900

grass

Dalehead Tarn

1700

Wilson's Bield

1700

Rigg Head

stile

High Scawdel

gate

1600

Tongue Gill

×ruins

Beyond Wilson's Bield the walking is easy but lacks interest. Some excitement may be added to this final stage by crossing over to the track coming from Dalehead Tarn — deviations left provide thrilling peeps down the face of Eel Crags.

The route up through the quarries, on a slaty path that was probably built as a permanent way for trucks, is steep and rough but not without interest. Many levels and caverns abut on the path; others may be found by searching.

Rigghead Quarries (disused)

ruin ×

Rigg Head Hut

stile

×ruin

a quarry road

1100

GRANGE

If using the quarry road cross the stream at point A.

1000

900

800

700

bracken 800

stile

600

600

old toll road

700

If starting from Seatoller — take the former toll road (first gate on the right beyond the buildings) leaving it by a green path after half a mile.

HONISTER PASS

600

500

Seatoller
car park and bus stop

Scaleclose Force

×fold

500

400

300

If starting from Rosthwaite — take the lane opposite the village shop, bearing right at the farm buildings and following the river to New Bridge. Then see the map on High Spy 4.

SEATHWAITE 1¼

looking north-west

Johnny Wood

Borrowdale
Y.H.

River Derwent

Although less popular than most climbs from Borrowdale, this offers a variety of scenery, starting with sylvan beauty and ending in moorland bleakness.

SEATOLLER

ROSTHWAITE 1¼

Stonethwaite ¾ broad end

ASCENT FROM LITTLE TOWN
1650 feet of ascent : 4 miles

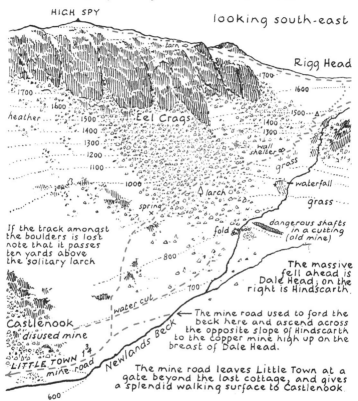

HIGH SPY

looking south-east

tarn

Rigg Head

1700

1600

1700

1600

heather

1500

Eel Crags

1500

1400

1400

1300

1300

1200

wall shelter

1100

grass

1000

waterfall

spring

larch

grass

If the track amongst
the boulders is lost
note that it passes
ten yards above
the solitary larch

fold

dangerous shafts
in a cutting
(old mine)

800

The massive
fell ahead is
Dale Head; on the
right is Hindscarth

100

Castlenook
disused mine

water cut

LITTLE TOWN 1¾
mine road

Newlands Beck

600

← The mine road used to ford the
beck here and ascend across
the opposite slope of Hindscarth
to the copper mine high up on the
breast of Dale Head.

The mine road leaves Little Town at a
gate beyond the last cottage, and gives
a splendid walking surface to Castlenook.

The first thing to note about this route (which may also be used
for crossing from Newlands to Borrowdale or Honister) is that the
old path, closely following the side of the beck, has largely gone
to seed. Instead, a popular track now turns off the mine road just
around the corner from the old workings at Castlenook, and at
once starts climbing to swing round across the screes of Eel Crags,
finally joining the original zigzags. Note the dried-up water cut,
which can be followed (left) to Castlenook Mine.

The upper reaches of the Newlands valley are wild and
secluded, with many evidences of man's searches for
its precious minerals, and this route gives an excellent
opportunity of seeing its features at close quarters.

THE SUMMIT

Bassenthwaite Lake

SKIDDAW

SKIDDAW LITTLE MAN

   The top of the fell undulates without much variation in height over a considerable distance, and although the ultimate point is not in doubt the rough ground above Blea Crag, half a mile from the summit-cairn, is little inferior in elevation. Between the two is a simple promenade, easy walking among many small outcrops, but sustained excitement may be added to the journey by keeping to the fringe of the precipice of Eel Crags, which extends unbroken along the Newlands edge in a bewildering array of aretes, gullies and cliffs. The summit cairn is a solid, well-built structure, the result of diligent toil: a memorial to its unknown builders.

DESCENTS: Leave the fell by the ridge, either south to Rigg Head or north to Hause Gate before turning off. The easy slope down towards Borrowdale is tempting, but ends in crags; and a direct descent unscathed into Newlands is palpably impossible.

The summit, looking south

GREAT END

SCAFELL PIKE

SCAFELL

GREAT GABLE

DALE HEAD

Dalehead Tarn

THE VIEW

The view is extensive and generally good, the main interest being centred in the south, where the Scafell group captures attention and Great Gable is especially prominent. The long ten-mile wall of the Helvellyn range forms the limit of view eastwards, and Skiddaw and Blencathra stand up well in the north. As a viewpoint, the cairn is a little too far from the edge of the precipice to add drama to the scene, but there are several places nearby where profound glimpses down into the wild recesses of upper Newlands may be obtained.

Principal Fells

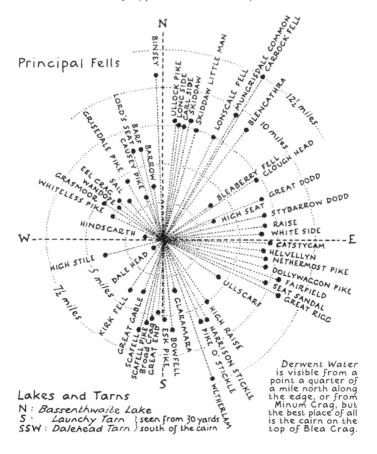

Lakes and Tarns

N : Bassenthwaite Lake
S :   Launchy Tarn   } seen from 30 yards
SSW: Dalehead Tarn } south of the cairn

Derwent Water is visible from a point a quarter of a mile north along the edge, or from Minum Crag, but the best place of all is the cairn on the top of Blea Crag.

RIDGE ROUTES

To MAIDEN MOOR, 1887′: 1½ miles : N

Depression at 1860′: 100 feet of ascent

Half-an-hour's pleasant, straightforward walking.

Easy walking on a sketchy track along the undulating top leads to a long incline down to Narrow Moor, the path hereabouts being excellent. Continue with a steep fall on the left to the indefinite top of Maiden Moor. A detour to the Blea Crag cairn is recommended.

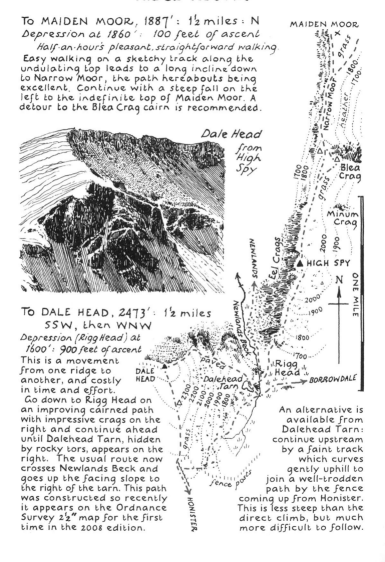

Dale Head from High Spy

To DALE HEAD, 2473′: 1½ miles SSW, then WNW

Depression (Rigg Head) at 1600′: 900 feet of ascent

This is a movement from one ridge to another, and costly in time and effort.

Go down to Rigg Head on an improving cairned path with impressive crags on the right and continue ahead until Dalehead Tarn, hidden by rocky tors, appears on the right. The usual route now crosses Newlands Beck and goes up the facing slope to the right of the tarn. This path was constructed so recently it appears on the Ordnance Survey 2½″ map for the first time in the 2008 edition.

An alternative is available from Dalehead Tarn: continue upstream by a faint track which curves gently uphill to join a well-trodden path by the fence coming up from Honister. This is less steep than the direct climb, but much more difficult to follow.

Goat (or Gate) Crag
from Castle Crag

Hindscarth

2385'

from High Snab Bank

Little Town ●

⤙ Newlands Hause
ROBINSON ▲
▲ HINDSCARTH
Buttermere ●
DALE HEAD ▲
Seatoller ●

Honister Pass ⤙

MILES

0 1 2 3 4

NATURAL FEATURES

Only a minority of the walkers who traverse the fine ridge between Dale Head and Robinson turn aside for a visit to the intermediate summit of Hindscarth, this lying half a mile off the direct course across a simple but uninteresting plateau.   Comparatively few, too, climb the fell for its own sake; those who do invariably ascend from Newlands along the only natural line of approach, the ridge of Scope End. Steep-sided and narrow-crested, and richly carpeted in heather, this ridge is a beauty.

Hindscarth is a twin to Robinson. Both were created in the same upheaval and sculptured in the same mould. They turn broad backs to the Buttermere valley and go hand-in-hand together down to Newlands, their ridges reaching the valley at the beautiful watersmeet near the little church. Between them is the upland hollow of Little Dale, much of it a bog, but having an interesting feature in a rocky gorge where waterfalls leap to lower levels beneath the near-vertical acclivity of Scope End; further down an old reservoir has served its purpose and become a charming pool. Mining operations have left a few scars on Scope End, and some open shafts, levels and fractures that invite attention. Gold has been won here, giving Hindscarth its greatest distinction — but walkers who halt in their travels to search the spoilheaps for discarded nuggets will be wasting their time, the area having already been thoroughly combed by the author — also without success. Those who carry their search into the long-abandoned workings are unlikely to return.

The eastern flank of Hindscarth falls very roughly and steeply into the upper Newlands valley, draining to the fell's main watercourse, Newlands Beck, which goes on to join the Derwent. A few feeble streams flow south to Gatesgarthdale and unexpectedly become subterranean at the 500' contour.

1 : The summit
2 : Ridge continuing to Robinson
3 : High Crags
4 : Scope End

grass

grass

waterfalls

reservoir

pastures

5 : Little Dale
6 : Scope Beck
7 : Newlands Beck
8 : Step Gill

looking south

Newlands is exceptionally well-favoured by its circle of exciting mountain peaks and wide choice of ascents, and is an ideal centre for fellwalking. Among many striking outlines, Scope End in particular arrests one's attention, assuming, when seen from Little Town, the shape of a narrow-crested ridge with three turrets — an aspect illustrated above. In this view Hindscarth (on the left) appears to be quite detached from Scope End, but they are connected by a simple rising ridge.

Newlands Church

MAP

The area of the two levels to the north-west of Scope End is confusing. If walking from Low Snab to the reservoir it is necessary to find a way from the path below the levels to the path above the levels.

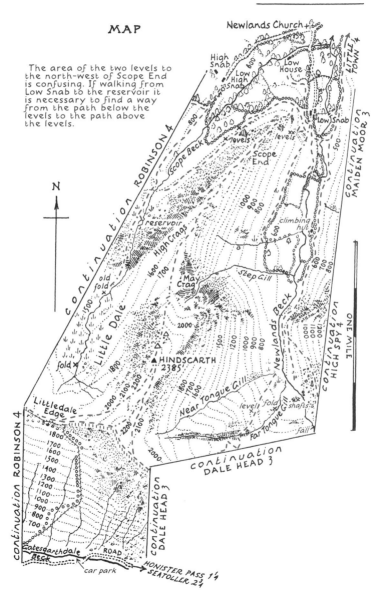

Goldscope Mine

Goldscope Mine was abandoned in 1864 after intermittent operation over a period of six centuries. One of the oldest mines in the district, it was also the most important in output, having rich veins of lead and copper. Silver and gold, too, have been extracted. Its early development, on a large scale, was undertaken by Germans, and its long history has been marked by many adventures and much litigation.

Upper Pan Holes

External evidence of the mine is indicated mainly by spoil-heaps on the Newlands Beck side of Scope End: immediately above is the main adit of Lower Pan Holes (from which a stream issues) with a second opening a few yards higher, under a tree. Further up the fellside is a curious slanting gash in a rockface — the Upper Pan Holes. On the other (Scope Beck) flank of the ridge are several levels.

Scope End is therefore pierced from both sides and the main level runs into the fell for such a considerable distance (over 300 yards) before becoming impassable, due to roof-falls, that it is reasonable to suppose that in the later years of operation it would be possible to walk right through the heart of it. In the darkness of these inner workings is a great shaft, which was sunk to such a depth ultimately that the pumping of water from it became too costly — this, not exhaustion of the minerals, was the reason for closure.

Lower Pan Holes

ASCENT FROM NEWLANDS CHURCH
2000 feet of ascent
2½ miles

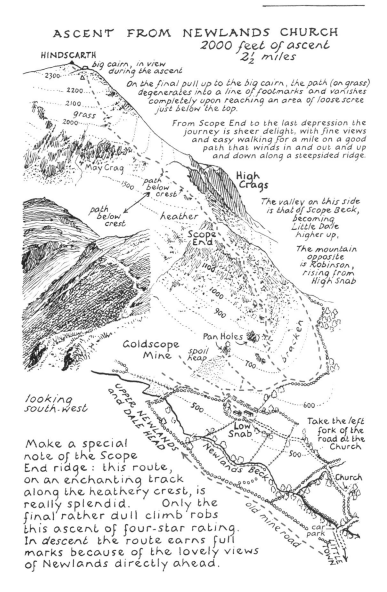

HINDSCARTH

big cairn, in view during the ascent

On the final pull up to the big cairn, the path (on grass) degenerates into a line of footmarks and vanishes completely upon reaching an area of loose scree just below the top.

From Scope End to the last depression the journey is sheer delight, with fine views and easy walking for a mile on a good path that winds in and out and up and down along a steepsided ridge.

2300
2200
2100
grass
2000

May Crag

1500

High Crags

path below crest

path below crest

heather

Scope End

The valley on this side is that of Scope Beck, becoming Little Dale higher up.

The mountain opposite is Robinson, rising from High Snab

1100

1000

900

Pan Holes

bracken

Goldscope Mine

spoil heap

700

looking south-west

UPPER NEWLANDS and DALE HEAD

500

600

Low Snab

Take the left fork of the road at the Church

Newlands Beck

500

Church

old mine road

car park

LITTLE TOWN

Make a special note of the Scope End ridge: this route, on an enchanting track along the heathery crest, is really splendid.   Only the final rather dull climb robs this ascent of four-star rating. In descent the route earns full marks because of the lovely views of Newlands directly ahead.

ASCENT FROM GATESGARTH

2050 feet of ascent
3 miles

HINDSCARTH

looking north-east

Hindscarth Edge

The summit is two-fifths of a mile beyond the ridge-fence on a lateral spur, and is easily reached over gravelly turf

grass

ROBINSON Edge

Littledale Edge

DALE HEAD

heather

ROUTE A: Incline half-left at the bend in the stream, keeping above the bracken but below the main scree to a wall, which leads to the depression between Robinson and Hindscarth. Here join the track leading to the right.

ROUTE B: Above the bend, the stream emerges from a narrow gully, green and mossy at first but a scree-channel later. There is no difficulty in following this to the ridge, but much pleasanter is the arête bordering the gully, reached by an obvious rake just beyond the first rocks on the right and before the gully narrows. The steeper final tower on the arête can be avoided by a traverse to the gully. The old ridge-fence (a few posts only remaining) is reached at the lowest part of the depression between Hindscarth and Dale Head. Turn left.

Hindscarth is usually visited after first passing over Robinson or Dale Head, to which there are popular paths from Buttermere and Honister Pass, but here illustrated is a direct climb, from the road between, that avoids the preliminary adjoining summits. The route is straightforward and easier than it appears from below.

At this point, with the gully narrowing ahead and the ground around becoming rougher and steeper, two routes are available: A is a simple walk, B a scramble.

The stream is subterranean during much of its course and at its foot.

stream sinks   boulder

TOP OF HONISTER PASS 18

ROAD   parking place

BUTTERMERE 2   car park   Gatesgarthdale Beck   it is an easy mile from Gatesgarth to the bridge

Gatesgarth

As the climb proceeds it is interesting to measure progress by comparison with the craggy steeps of Fleetwith Pike (2126') immediately opposite just across the Pass.

THE SUMMIT

1 : BOWFELL
2 : ESK PIKE
3 : GREAT END
4 : Ill Crag
5 : Broad Crag
6 : SCAFELL PIKE
7 : GREAT GABLE
8 : GREEN GABLE
9 : BRANDRETH
10 : GREY KNOTTS

The top of Hindscarth is a full half-mile in length, the contours gently building up to the highest point, near the north-east end, where a large and untidy pile of stones stands amongst embedded rocks.   Elsewhere the summit is grassy, with patches of gravel.

Continuing the line of the ridge and 200 paces away, on the edge of the north-east declivity, there is a big circular cairn of some antiquity, the Ordnance Survey maps formerly giving it distinction by the use of the lettering reserved for objects of historic interest. This is the cairn prominently seen from Newlands, and it commands the finest view from the mountain.   The interior is hollowed out to provide a wind-shelter with its entrance facing north-west. The main cairn has also been made into a wind-shelter.

DESCENTS : The summit is pathless, but simple in design and uncomplicated in structure. Ways off are along the axis, which runs NNE and SSW. Both flanks are scarped.

For Newlands, go down by the big cairn, keeping the long ridge of Scope End in front and descending to it. A track soon materialises. *In mist* it is important to find it; the start is marked by a well-sited cairn.

Go SSW to the fence for Buttermere or Honister. *Leftwards* the fence climbs over Dale Head (which can NOT be by-passed) before going down to Honister Pass. *Rightwards,* from the first depression a safe descent may be made down an easy slope to Gatesgarthdale.

"A .....cairn of some antiquity"

THE VIEW

There is a good all-round panorama, especially pleasing over Newlands to the Vale of Keswick and Skiddaw — the big north cairn is a better place for photographs in this direction — with, in contrast, a rugged skyline forming the southern horizon. The familiar shape of Scafell is missing from the scene, hidden behind Great Gable.

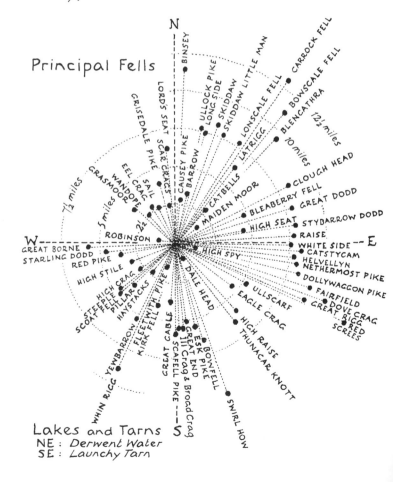

Principal Fells

Lakes and Tarns
NE : Derwent Water
SE : Launchy Tarn

RIDGE ROUTES

To ROBINSON, 2417': 1½ miles: SSW, WNW and N.
Depression at 1880': 550 feet of ascent
A simple circuit around the head of Little Dale

Hindscarth and Robinson are lateral spurs springing from the main fenced ridge of the north wall of Gatesgarthdale. A beeline between the two summits is

out of the question and the ridge must be used to pass from one to the other. The depression midway is considerable. An interest can be added to the climb therefrom by a short detour over the fence to look at the strange formation known as Hackney Holes.

To DALE HEAD, 2473': 1¼ miles: SSW, then ESE
Depression at 2156': 330 feet of ascent
Increasing interest and excellent views

The path to the SSW from Hindscarth to the main ridge is going out of use, and nowadays it is more usual to cut off the corner. The main ridge from here onwards is very good, although not as exciting as it promises to be. Buttermere comes into view when the ridge narrows. The fence-posts are too far apart to follow in mist.

Briefly and inadequately glimpsed from the ridge to Dale Head, down on the left, is the strange ravine of Far Tongue Gill. For half a mile this huge cut in the side of Hindscarth, a remarkable chasm out of all proportion to the stream it accommodates, is walled by great pale slabs of slate. Remote from usual walkers tracks, the best view of it from a distance is seen along the ridge of High Spy.

The ravine of Far Tongue Gill

Hopegill Head

2525'

also known as
Hobcarton Pike

from Scar Crags

NATURAL FEATURES

A high mountain ridge leaps like a rainbow
from the woods and fields of Brackenthwaite
and arcs through the sky for five miles to the
east, where the descending curve comes down
to the village of Braithwaite.   This ridge has
three main summits, of which the central one
(and the finest, but not the highest) is known
locally as Hobcarton Pike and to mapmakers
as Hopegill Head. The supporting fell stretches
far to the north, having roots in Whinlatter and
the Vale of Lorton, whence the heathery flanks
of Swinside rise to form the main ridge to the top
peak, passing over the subsidiary Ladyside Pike
(formerly Lady's Seat).   Scarped edges join the
two neighbouring fells of Grisedale Pike, east,
and Whiteside, west, while a short slope, halted
by the rounded hump of Sand Hill, falls easily to
Coledale Hause southwards. But it is the aspect
to the north that invests the mountain with its
special character.   Here, Swinside is bounded,
on both sides, by deep valleys :   sterile Hope Gill
and afforested Hobcarton.   The latter, now a
coniferous jungle, leads up to a great semicircle
of cliffs around the valley-head: this is a nature
stronghold, Hobcarton Crag.   The valley of Hope
Gill is rarely visited and has little of interest; it
seems rather surprising that this valley, and not
the other, has given its name to the fell —— until
one stands on the shapely summit and sees Hope
Gill winding away directly below, while the valley
of Hobcarton is obscured
by the north ridge. Then
the choice of name of the
cartographers cannot be
questioned.   'Hopegill
Head' is right.

1 : The summit
2 : Ridge continuing to
    Grisedale Pike
3 : Ridge continuing to Whiteside
4 : Ladyside Pike   5 : Swinside
6 : Hobcarton Crag   7 : Swinside Plantation
8 : Hobcarton Plantation
9 : Hobcarton Gill   10 : Hope Gill

looking
south

Hobcarton Crag

Hobcarton Crag is the property of the National Trust, and no ordinary cliff. Its size is impressive — 500 feet in height above the scree along a half-mile curve — but the rocks are broken and interspersed with lush bilberry meadows, so that the appeal of the crag is not related to climbing: indeed, the rock is unsuitable for exploration.

This is Skiddaw slate, fracturing and splintering easily, yet it has a special attraction nevertheless, obvious to all who observe as they walk: where natural weathering has taken place and erosion is absent there is a very high degree of contortion and striation, evidence of the severe pressures to which it was subjected during formation.

A greater fame, although also within a specialist field of study, is attributable to the rare species of flora in the two main gullies; in particular, here is the only known habitat in England of the red alpine catchfly (*Viscaria alpina*). The National Trust were largely influenced in their acquisition of the Crag by its great botanical interest (and partly by a desire to limit the afforestation of the valley-head below).

The Crag is a haven of quiet solitude, within sight but out of reach of a popular walking route.   In summer sunlight there is pleasant colour, the bilberry — greenest of greens — making a luxuriant velvety patchwork among the grey and silver rocks. In shadow, the scene is sombre and forbidding. The silence is interrupted only by the croaking of the resident ravens and the occasional thud of a falling botanist.

This is a place to look at and leave alone.

A feature of the northern rim of Hobcarton Crag is a curious break in the curtain of rocks forming the sharp arete below the summit: here, a steep scree gully falls from a square cleft in the vertical wall of crag. A name is needed for this strange place and The Notch fits it well.

The lower picture shows the arete rising above the Notch to the summit. An arrow at the side indicates the direction of a groove or fault in the slabs, and this is advised for ascent or descent if the rocks are icy or greasy. In the foreground is a platform of rock — a perfect spot for a sunbathe but not for slumber, the unprotected edge here falling away sheer.

The Notch,
Hobcarton Crag

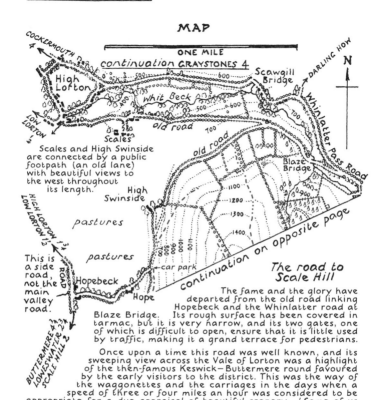

MAP

ONE MILE

continuation GRAYSTONES 4

N

Scales and High Swinside are connected by a public footpath (an old lane) with beautiful views to the west throughout its length.

This is a side road, not the main valley road.

continuation on opposite page

The road to Scale Hill

The fame and the glory have departed from the old road linking Hopebeck and the Whinlatter road at Blaze Bridge. Its rough surface has been covered in tarmac, but it is very narrow, and its two gates, one of which is difficult to open, ensure that it is little used by traffic, making it a grand terrace for pedestrians.

Once upon a time this road was well known, and its sweeping view across the Vale of Lorton was a highlight of the then-famous Keswick—Buttermere round favoured by the early visitors to the district. This was the way of the waggonettes and the carriages in the days when a speed of three or four miles an hour was considered to be appropriate for a due appraisal of beautiful scenery. (Some of us still think so.) Eyes were more appreciative then and minds more receptive. Not one of the passengers along this highway would give a thought to nuclear bombs. Not one would be in a hurry. Those were the days of the artists and poets. The good days.

The coaching-house in the valley was the Scale Hill Inn, a hostelry of renown and good reputation, the accepted centre for visitors to western Lakeland. Today there is still a Scale Hill Inn, no less favourably situated in one of the most delectable corners of a lovely landscape, but it has been converted into holiday cottages, and its significance in the itinerary of tourists has gone. Langdale and Borrowdale are in current fashion. Most visitors have never heard of Scale Hill, and anyway would consider the place too remote, too quiet, off today's beaten tracks.

Half a century ago it gave old-timers a certain nostalgic pleasure to note that the signpost at the junction with the Whinlatter road still pointed to 'Scale Hill', a name that thrilled Victorian and Edwardian hearts, but meant nothing to the Elizabethan lunatics rattling past at 60 m.p.h. This old signpost was a link with the days of sanity. It has now gone (but old-timers may take comfort that the name of Scale Hill still appears on the signpost at Hopebeck).

MAP

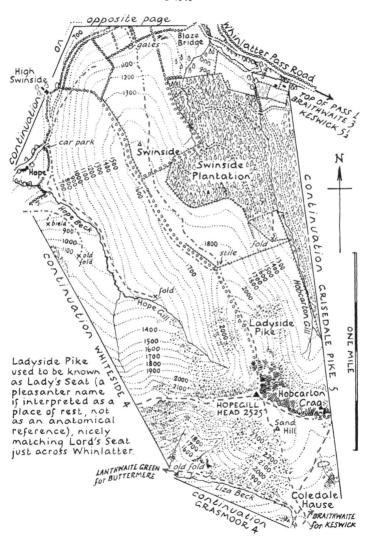

on opposite page

700

Blaze Bridge

gates

Whinlatter Pass Road

1100
1200
1300

High Swinside

continuation

car park

Hope

Swinside

Swinside Plantation

TOP OF PASS 1
BRAITHWAITE 3
KESWICK 5½

N

1500
1300
1400
1000
1100
1200
900
800

Hope Beck

x biela

900

1000

1100

x old fold

fold

Hope Gill

1800

stile

fold

1700

1400
1500
1600

1400
1500
1600
1700
1800
1900

2000

Ladyside Pike

Hobcarton Gill

continuation
CRUSEDALE PIKE 5

2000
2100

Ladyside Pike used to be known as Lady's Seat (a pleasanter name if interpreted as a place of rest, not as an anatomical reference), nicely matching Lord's Seat just across Whinlatter.

continuation
WHITESIDE 4

ONE MILE

Hobcarton Crag

HOPEGILL HEAD 2525

Sand Hill

1800
1600

1700
1600

old fold

LANTHWAITE GREEN
for BUTTERMERE

Liza Beck

2100
2000
1900

2200

2100
2000

Coledale Hause

continuation
GRASMOOR 4

BRAITHWAITE
for KESWICK

Hobcarton

Viscaria
alpina

Hobcarton Valley and Crag —
the only English home of Viscaria alpina

ASCENT FROM COLEDALE HAUSE
600 feet of ascent : ¾ mile

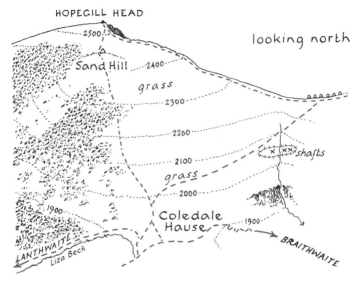

HOPEGILL HEAD

looking north

2500!

Sand Hill — 2400

grass

2300

2200

2100 — ×× shafts
×

grass

2000

Coledale Hause — 1900

1900

LANTHWAITE

Liza Beck

BRAITHWAITE

On the direct route the summit remains concealed until the cairn on Sand Hill is reached. The path from Coledale Hause to Sand Hill is easy at first, but for much of its length it is on loose scree; a better plan is to take the path on the right past the fenced mine shafts and up the edge of Hobcarton Crag.

The summit of Hopegill Head, from the cairn on Sand Hill

ASCENT FROM WHINLATTER PASS
1850 feet of ascent : 2½ miles from the road

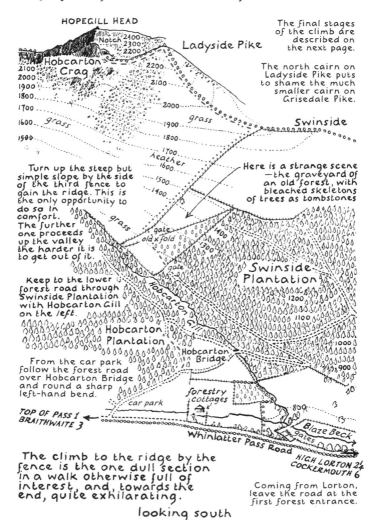

HOPEGILL HEAD

Notch 2400 2300 2200

Ladyside Pike

Hobcarton Crag

2100 2000 1900 1800 1700

2200

2100

2000

1600 grass

1900

grass

1500

1800

Swinside

1700 heather 1600

1500

1400

The final stages of the climb are described on the next page.

The north cairn on Ladyside Pike puts to shame the much smaller cairn on Grisedale Pike.

Here is a strange scene —the graveyard of an old forest, with bleached skeletons of trees as tombstones

Turn up the steep but simple slope by the side of the third fence to gain the ridge. This is the only opportunity to do so in comfort.
The further one proceeds up the valley the harder it is to get out of it.

grass

gate old x fold

1400

1300

gate

Swinside Plantation

1200

Keep to the lower forest road through Swinside Plantation with Hobcarton Gill on the left.

Hobcarton Gill

1100

Hobcarton Plantation

Hobcarton Bridge

1000

900

From the car park follow the forest road over Hobcarton Bridge and round a sharp left-hand bend.

forestry cottages

car park

800

Blaze Beck

TOP OF PASS 1 BRAITHWAITE 3

Whinlatter Pass Road

gates

HIGH LORTON 2½ COCKERMOUTH 6

The climb to the ridge by the fence is the one dull section in a walk otherwise full of interest, and, towards the end, quite exhilarating.

Coming from Lorton, leave the road at the first forest entrance.

looking south

ASCENT FROM HIGH LORTON
2450 feet of ascent : 3¾ miles

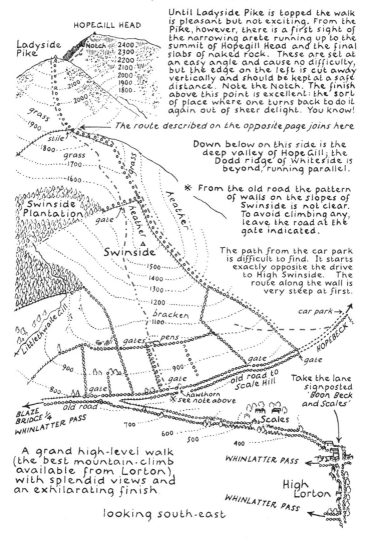

HOPEGILL HEAD

Ladyside Pike

Notch 2400 2300 2200 2100 2000 1900 1800

grass 1900

stile 1800

grass 1700

1600

Swinside Plantation

gate

Swinside

grass

heather

heather

Littlethwaite Gill

1500

1400

1300

1200

bracken
1100

gates   pens

900   900

gate

gate

old road to Scale Hill

800   gate

hawthorn
X see note above

old road

BLAZE BRIDGE ¼
WHINLATTER PASS

700

600

500

400

Scales

car park →

HOPEBECK

gate   gate

Take the lane signposted 'Boon Beck and Scales'

WHINLATTER PASS

High Lorton

WHINLATTER PASS

Until Ladyside Pike is topped the walk is pleasant but not exciting. From the Pike, however, there is a first sight of the narrowing arête running up to the summit of Hopegill Head and the final slabs of naked rock. These are set at an easy angle and cause no difficulty, but the edge on the left is cut away vertically and should be kept at a safe distance. Note the Notch. The finish above this point is excellent: the sort of place where one turns back to do it again out of sheer delight. You know!

The route described on the opposite page joins here

Down below on this side is the deep valley of Hope Gill; the Dodd ridge of Whiteside is beyond, running parallel.

※ From the old road the pattern of walls on the slopes of Swinside is not clear. To avoid climbing any, leave the road at the gate indicated.

The path from the car park is difficult to find. It starts exactly opposite the drive to High Swinside. The route along the wall is very steep at first.

A grand high-level walk (the best mountain-climb available from Lorton) with splendid views and an exhilarating finish.

looking south-east

ASCENT FROM HOPEBECK
2150 feet of ascent : 2½ miles

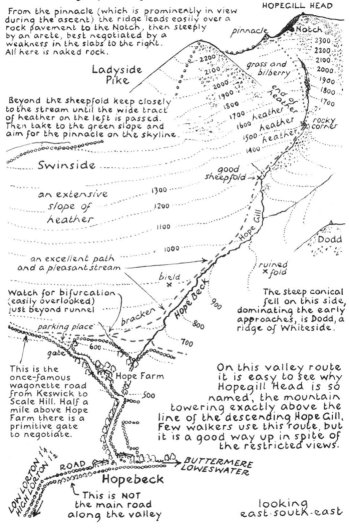

HOPEGILL HEAD

From the pinnacle (which is prominently in view during the ascent) the ridge leads easily over a rock pavement to the Notch, then steeply by an arete, best negotiated by a weakness in the slabs to the right. All here is naked rock.

pinnacle   Notch

Ladyside Pike

2300
2200
2100
2000
1900
1800
1700

2200
2100
2000
1900
1800
1700
1600
1500
1400

grass and bilberry

end of heather

heather

heather

rocky corner

Beyond the sheepfold keep closely to the stream until the wide tract of heather on the left is passed. Then take to the green slope and aim for the pinnacle on the skyline.

Swinside

good sheepfold →

an extensive slope of heather

1300
1200
1100
1000

Hope Gill

Dodd

an excellent path and a pleasant stream

ruined × fold

bield ×

The steep conical fell on this side, dominating the early approaches, is Dodd, a ridge of Whiteside.

Watch for bifurcation (easily overlooked) just beyond runnel

bracken

Hope Beck

900

800

700

parking place

600

gate

Hope Farm

500

This is the once-famous wagonette road from Keswick to Scale Hill. Half a mile above Hope Farm there is a primitive gate to negotiate.

On this valley route it is easy to see why Hopegill Head is so named, the mountain towering exactly above the line of the descending Hope Gill. Few walkers use this route, but it is a good way up in spite of the restricted views.

LOW LORTON 1¼
HIGH LORTON 1½

ROAD

BUTTERMERE
LOWESWATER

Hopebeck

↑ This is NOT the main road along the valley

looking east·south·east

THE SUMMIT

The culmination of the rising lines of the fell occurs where the slender ridge coming up from Whiteside quite suddenly collapses in the contorted rocks of Hobcarton Crag, exactly at the point of junction of routes ascending the two flanks of the precipice to its apex. Thus, in the space of a few feet, is formed a small, neat summit, a true peak poised above a profound abyss, its delicate proportions uncharacteristic of the general expansiveness of the fell. It is a delightful top, fashioned for the accommodation of solitary walkers: large parties here are an intrusion. Slate debris litters the ground and visitors occasionally scrape a little together to make an insignificant cairn.

The summit is a favourite haunt of birds, which have quick selective eyes for good vantage points. The Hobcarton ravens make a fine sight as they soar and spiral above the gullies and rock battlements, often alighting on the narrow top to survey the domain of which they are undisputed overlords; and particular mention must be made of the regular summer visitations of swifts, which have a liking for steep cliffs and airy summits, and here dart and swoop through the air in an ecstatic and erratic highspeed flight, their whirring wings creating a commotion of vibrating sound.

This summit is a generous reward for the effort of reaching it.

BOWSCALE FELL   BLENCATHRA   GRISEDALE PIKE   GREAT MELL FELL   CLOUGH HEAD

DESCENTS: For High Lorton, Hopebeck or Whinlatter Pass, reverse the routes of ascent: they have a common start down the north slabs. Use a fault or groove away from the edge for safer foothold. In mist, this initial section looks intimidating, but step bravely into the void and go cautiously. Anybody who finds himself falling through space will have missed the route.

PLAN OF SUMMIT

HIGH LORTON   WHINLATTER   HOPEBECK

N

100 YARDS

2300

WHITESIDE   2400   COLEDALE HAUSE   GRISEDALE PIKE

Coledale Hause is quickly reached by following the natural slope down from the protuberance of Sand Hill, taking patches of scree in the stride. In mist, be on guard against two hazards, dangerous because unexpected: the fenced mine-shafts and the crag-edge of High Force; keep well to the right if these appear out of the gloom.

THE VIEW

The view is less comprehensive than the diagram suggests, the best part of the Lakeland skyline, to the south, being concealed by Grasmoor and Eel Crag, but in other directions, particularly west (across the Solway Firth) and east (to the Helvellyn range) the panorama is unrestricted. There is a satisfactory grouping of the Scafells just left of Wandope, however, and a quaint glimpse of Pike o' Stickle — a remarkable outline — between Sail and Eel Crag.

Principal Fells

N

BINSEY
LONGLANDS FELL
BRAE FELL
Little Sca Fell
BROOM FELL
SALE FELL
LORD'S SEAT
LING FELL
GRAYSTONES
ULLOCK PIKE
LONG SIDE
DODD
SKIDDAW
Horrot
Swinside
SKIDDAW LITTLE MAN
BOWSCALE FELL
LONSCALE FELL
BLENCATHRA
5 miles
FELLBARROW
2½
CRISEDALE PIKE
GREAT MELL FELL
LITTLE MELL FELL
LOW FELL
W
CLOUGH HEAD
E
HIGH RIGG
WHITESIDE
GREAT DODD
BURNBANK FELL
CAUSEY PIKE
BLEABERRY FELL
STYBARROW DODD
BLAKE FELL
SCAR CRAGS
HIGH SEAT
RAISE
GAVEL FELL
GRASMOOR
SAIL
WHITE SIDE
Dent
MELLBREAK
CATSTYCAM
HEN COMB
EEL CRAG
HELVELLYN
WANDOPE
DALE
HEAD
NETHERMOST PIKE
GRIKE
DOLLYWAGGON PIKE
CRAG FELL
GREAT BORNE
HIGH SPY
FAIRFIELD
7½ miles
HIGH CRAG
ULLSCARF
GREAT RIGG
KIRK FELL
10 miles
GREAT GABLE
GLARAMARA
HIGH RAISE
HERON PIKE
SCAFELL PIKE
12½ miles
SCAFELL
PIKE O' STICKLE
S

Lakes and Tarns
NNE : Over Water
SE : Blea Tarn (Ullscarf)
WSW : Crummock Water

RIDGE ROUTES

To GRISEDALE PIKE, 2593′ : 1⅛ mile : SE, then E, NE
Depression at 2211′ : 400 feet of ascent

An interesting traverse around the head of Hobcarton Valley.
With the precipice close on the left hand, but not too close, go
down to the grassy depression south-eastwards, where a broken
wall is joined and followed upwards, first over a minor summit
and then on to the main top. The well-defined rim of crags on the
left throughout, plus the wall, makes the crossing safe in mist.

To WHITESIDE, 2317′ : 1⅛ mile : Generally W, then SW
Main depression at 2200′ : 150 feet of ascent

A splendid high-level walk with striking views of Gasgale Gill.
The way leads down the straight and narrow grassy west ridge,
becoming rough and rocky as it descends to a pronounced hollow
bridged by a heathery crest : this is the best section of the journey.
Beyond, easy rocks are climbed, or skirted on the right, and the
ridge widens although continuing sharply defined along the left
edge. In mist, the east top may be mistaken for the main top.

The ridge to Whiteside

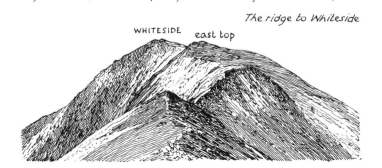

WHITESIDE   east top

Knott Rigg

from Buttermere

Keskadale is the long arm of Newlands extending southwest and providing the only outlet for vehicles from the head of the valley. The road is accommodated for two long miles along the side of a narrow and steepsided ridge of moderate height before climbing over a pass, Newlands Hause, formed by the gentle termination of the ridge; lovely Buttermere is beyond. This ridge has two distinct summits: the higher, overlooking Newlands, is Ard Crags; the lower, overlooking Buttermere, is Knott Rigg.

Sail Beck, coming down from the Eel Crag massif, of which Knott Rigg is an offshooting spur, very sharply marks the western boundary of the fell.

EEL CRAG ▲

Rigg Beck ●

▲ ARD CRAGS

● Keskadale

▲ KNOTT RIGG

⚡ Newlands Hause

● Buttermere

MILES
0   1   2   3

MAP

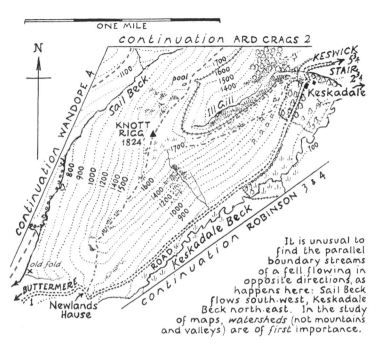

ONE MILE

N

continuation ARD CRAGS 2

continuation WANDOPE 4

Sail Beck

pool

1100

700
1600
1500
1400

Ill Gill

KESWICK 5¼
STAIR 2¾
Keskadale

Keskadale

KNOTT RIGG 1824

1700

1400

1500

1600

1400
1200
1100
900

700

ROAD

Keskadale Beck

continuation ROBINSON 3 & 4

800
900
1000
1200
1500
1600

old fold

BUTTERMERE 1

Newlands Hause

It is unusual to find the parallel boundary streams of a fell flowing in opposite directions, as happens here: Sail Beck flows south-west, Keskadale Beck north-east. In the study of maps, *watersheds* (not mountains and valleys) are of *first* importance.

looking down to the Buttermere valley from the south end of the ridge, with High Stile and Red Pike in the background and the Newlands road descending across the side of Robinson in the middle distance

ASCENT FROM NEWLANDS HAUSE
720 feet of ascent : 1 mile

Upon reaching the ridge there is at once a fine view down the other side to Sail Beck and across it to the tremendous scarred wall of Wandope, Eel Crag and Sail.

Beyond the last outcrop the excellent turf of the ridge gives place to tougher grass, the summit being reached across a marshy plateau.

An advantage of solitary travel on the fells, greatly appreciated by all lone walkers, is the freedom to perform a certain function as and where one wishes, without any of the consultations and subterfuges necessitated by party travel. The narrow crest of the Knott Rigg ridge is no place for indulging the practice, however, whether alone or accompanied, walkers here being clearly outlined against the sky and in full view from two valleys. This comment is intended for males particularly. Women (according to an informant) have a different way of doing it.

Newlands Hause is commonly but wrongly referred to as Buttermere Hause

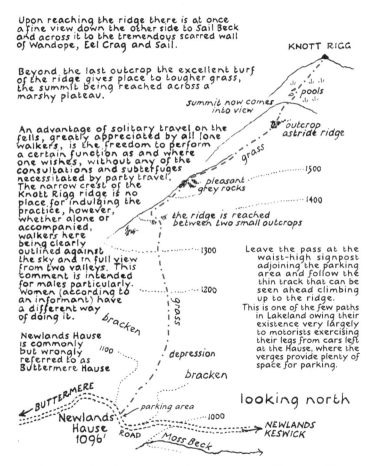

KNOTT RIGG

pools

summit now comes into view

outcrop astride ridge

grass

1500

pleasant grey rocks

1400

the ridge is reached between two small outcrops

1300

1200

grass

1100

depression

bracken

Leave the pass at the waist-high signpost adjoining the parking area and follow the thin track that can be seen ahead climbing up to the ridge.

This is one of the few paths in Lakeland owing their existence very largely to motorists exercising their legs from cars left at the Hause, where the verges provide plenty of space for parking.

bracken

looking north

BUTTERMERE

parking area

Newlands Hause 1096'

ROAD

1000

Moss Beck

NEWLANDS KESWICK

This is a simple and straightforward climb on the sunny side of the Hause, requiring an absence of one hour only from a car parked there. It affords a pleasant exercise, very suitable for persons up to 7 years of age or over 70.

ASCENT FROM KESKADALE
1000 feet of ascent : 1¼ miles

Upland *marshes* occur on almost all fells : on flat summits and plateaux, in hollows and on grassy shelves. They act as reservoirs for the streams, draining very slowly and holding back moisture to ensure continuous supplies independent of present prevailing weather. It is because of the marshes that the streams seldom lack water. They are safe to walk upon and cause little discomfort.
Bogs are not functional. They are infrequent in Lakeland; there are no places bad enough to trap walkers, but some are a danger to sheep.

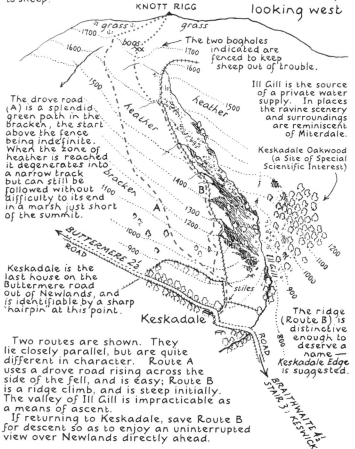

KNOTT RIGG

looking west

grass ↓↓ grass

1700

bogs ···

1600 ← The two bogholes indicated are fenced to keep sheep out of trouble.

1700

1600

Ill Gill is the source of a private water supply. In places the ravine scenery and surroundings are reminiscent of Miterdale.

The drove road (A) is a splendid green path in the bracken, the start above the fence being indefinite. When the zone of heather is reached it degenerates into a narrow track but can still be followed without difficulty to its end in a marsh just short of the summit.

heather

heather

1500

Keskadale Oakwood (a Site of Special Scientific Interest)

1500

bracken

1400

B

1300

1200

A

1100

1000

900

BUTTERMERE 2½ ROAD

Keskadale is the last house on the Buttermere road out of Newlands, and is identifiable by a sharp hairpin at this point.

Keskadale

1200

1100

1000

Ill Gill

900

stiles

800

The ridge (Route B) is distinctive enough to deserve a name — *Keskadale Edge* is suggested.

ROAD

BRAITHWAITE 4½ STAIR 3; KESWICK 6

Two routes are shown. They lie closely parallel, but are quite different in character. Route A uses a drove road rising across the side of the fell, and is easy; Route B is a ridge climb, and is steep initially. The valley of Ill Gill is impracticable as a means of ascent.
If returning to Keskadale, save Route B for descent so as to enjoy an uninterrupted view over Newlands directly ahead.

THE SUMMIT

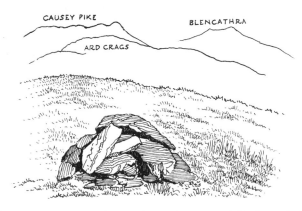

There are two summits at about the same altitude and about thirty yards apart. The more southerly has two tiny cairns.

DESCENTS :
The simplest way off the fell is south to Newlands Hause, and the finest is via Keskadale Edge, but between these routes (assuming they cannot be located in mist) there should not be any trouble in going straight down to the road at the base of the fell. Sail Beck is rougher to approach and saves nothing.

Considering that it is clearly in view to travellers along the Buttermere road and conveniently near, the side valley of Ill Gill is rarely entered. It has many charming features beyond its rather hostile portals and is worth a visit as far as a waterslide a quarter-mile in.

Keskadale Edge and Ill Gill

THE VIEW

Knott Rigg is so tightly sandwiched between the impending masses of Robinson and the Eel Crag range that an extensive view is not to be expected. The distant scene is not completely restricted, however, and eastwards there is a glorious outlook across the valley of Newlands to the lofty skyline of Helvellyn and the Dodds.

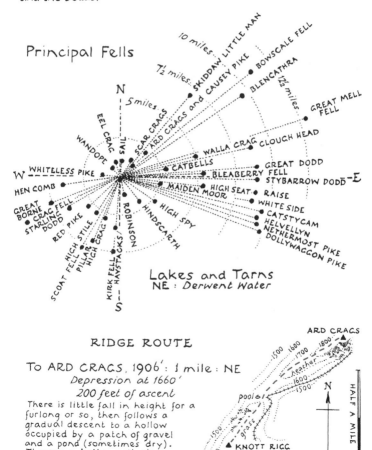

Principal Fells

Lakes and Tarns
NE : Derwent Water

RIDGE ROUTE

To ARD CRAGS, 1906': 1 mile: NE

Depression at 1660'
200 feet of ascent

There is little fall in height for a furlong or so, then follows a gradual descent to a hollow occupied by a patch of gravel and a pond (sometimes dry). Thereon a better path rises through heather to Ard Crags.

Ling Fell

1224'

from Sale Fell

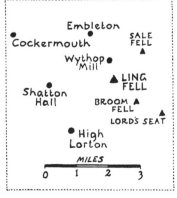

Embleton

Cockermouth

SALE
FELL ▲

Wythop
Mill ●

▲ LING
FELL

Shatton
Hall ●

BROOM ▲
FELL

LORD'S SEAT ▲

● High
Lorton

MILES

0   1   2   3

One of the many
speckled boulders
in the valley of
Tom Rudd Beck

NATURAL FEATURES

Ling Fell is an isolated rounded hill on the northwest perimeter of Lakeland, its unattractive appearance on all sides being accentuated by a dark covering of heather that makes it look gloomy and sulky even on the sunniest of days. Its lack of visual appeal, however, is somewhat misleading and belies its nature, for the easy slopes and commodious top are extremely pleasant to wander upon, heather, bracken, incipient gorse and grass alternating underfoot in colourful patches but never so densely as to impede progress.

The fell is one of the portals of the quiet Wythop dale, which lies alongside and behind, hidden and unsuspected, but is overshadowed by the higher western ridge of Kirk Fell coming down from Lord's Seat. In spite of its inferior height the Ordnance Survey have recognised its worth as a triangulation station and erected a stone column on the summit. This is almost the only feature of note, although the attention of geologists may be directed to a scattering of handsome white stones on the steeper southwest flank overlooking the little valley of Tom Rudd Beck, which has the function of draining the morass of Wythop Moss, a job it performs ineffectively. An insignificant spring on this side rejoices in the name of Bladder Keld — which is more than it deserves.

MAP

N

Green Lonning is a grass lane, with many holly trees. Other roads on this map are surfaced.

ONE MILE

EMBLETON 1

COCKERMOUTH 3½

PHEASANT INN 1½

continuation SALE FELL 7

Wythop Mill

Wythop Beck

Eskin

WYTHOP HALL 1

EMBLETON CHURCH 2

Green Lonning

Burthwaite

700

800

900

1000

800

LING FELL 1224

1100

1200

800

900

continuation BROOM FELL 3

1000

Bladder Keld

Wythop Moss

1100

600

continuation GRAYSTONES 4

Tom Rudd Beck

continuation BROOM FELL 3

ASCENT FROM WYTHOP MILL
850 feet of ascent : 1½ miles

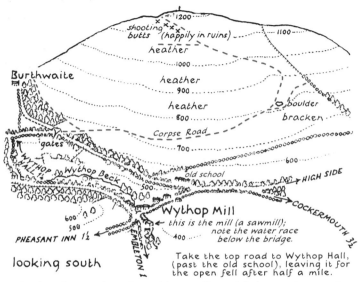

looking south

Take the top road to Wythop Hall,
(past the old school), leaving it for
the open fell after half a mile.

A simple and enjoyable walk, which ought to be,
but isn't, a popular ramble for Cockermouth folk.

THE SUMMIT

The Ordnance surveyors have selected the highest point in this
sea of heather as a trigonometrical station.   Five indistinct
paths radiate from the column, and 30 yards south-east of it is
a cairn at about the same altitude.

THE VIEW

Broom Fell, rising just across Wythop Moss, severely circumscribes the view inland, but the Skiddaw group is impressive and the skyline of the Grasmoor fells is good —otherwise this is not a favourable station for viewing the hills of Lakeland and the main interest is found by looking away from it, to Criffell and the Galloway hills.

Ling Fell, however, is the best Lakeland height for seeing the town of Cockermouth.

Principal Fells

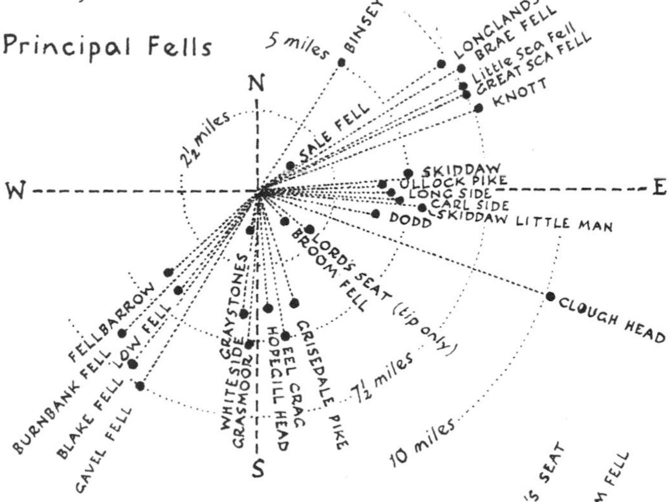

5 miles

BINSEY

LONGLANDS FELL
BRAE FELL
Little Sca Fell
GREAT SCA FELL
KNOTT

2½ miles

SALE FELL

N

W — — — — — — — — — — — — — — — — E

SKIDDAW
ULLOCK PIKE
LONG SIDE
CARL SIDE
DODD SKIDDAW LITTLE MAN

LORDS SEAT
BROOM FELL

CLOUGH HEAD

FELLBARROW
BURNBANK FELL
LOW FELL
BLAKE FELL
GAVEL FELL
WHITESIDE
GRASMOOR
GRAYTONES
HOPEGILL HEAD
EEL CRAG
CRISEDALE PIKE
BROOM FELL (tip only)

7½ miles

10 miles

S

Lakes and Tarns
NE: *Bassenthwaite Lake (foot of)*

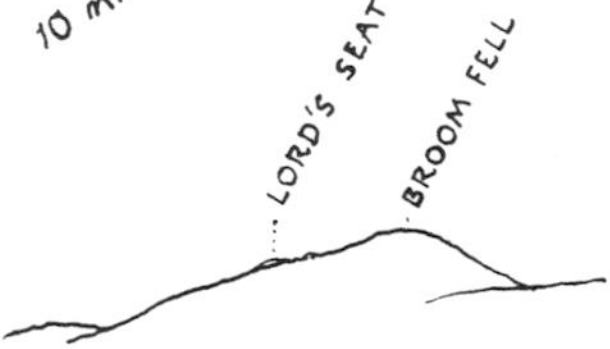

RIDGE ROUTES

Ling Fell is dome-shaped, like the top of a Christmas pudding. A Christmas pudding, in its pristine state, has no ridges. Neither has Ling Fell.

LORD'S SEAT

BROOM FELL

looking southeast

Lord's Seat

1811'

BROOM
FELL
▲

BARF
▲   Powter
LORD'S ▲   • How
SEAT   Thornthwaite

• High
Lorton

Whinlatter
Pass

• Braithwaite

MILES

0   1   2   3   4

from a forest road
in Comb Plantation

NATURAL FEATURES

Some mountains have better names than they deserve and some deserve better names than they have. Lord's Seat is a fine title for any ultimate peak amongst the clouds, and while the modest Lakeland fell of this name hardly aspires to the nobility it suggests it is a pleasing recognition of the commanding position and superior height of this central point in the distinctive group of hills comprising Thornthwaite Forest, between Bassenthwaite Lake and Whinlatter Pass. It is the pivot of this upland area, having four ridges radiating from the summit that enclose streams flowing north, south, east and west — all of which join later in the Derwent. Within the last eighty years the fell has been given a dark overcoat of timber by the Forestry Commission, an operation that has detracted from its native appearance, but added to its interest. Since the creation of the Whinlatter Forest Park, Lord's Seat has become a popular climb — and the heathery top is a pleasant lunching-place, retaining the indefinable charm of Lakeland in spite of the advancing march of the Norwegian and American spruces in all directions.

Two elevations on the descending ridges, Barf and Seat How, overlook the Vale of Keswick and are excellent viewpoints.

1 : The summit
2 : Barf
3 : Seat How
4 : Whinlatter Pass
5 : Comb Beck
6 : Comb Gill
7 : Chapel Beck
8 : River Derwent
9 : Beckstones Gill
10 : Bassenthwaite Lake
11 : Thornthwaite

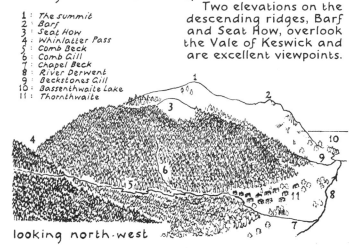

looking north-west

Lord's Seat 3

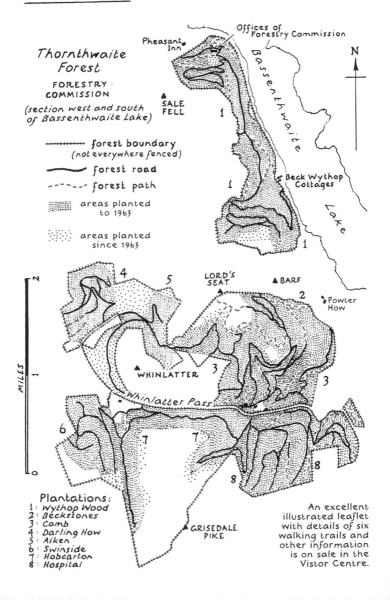

Thornthwaite Forest

FORESTRY COMMISSION

(section west and south of Bassenthwaite Lake)

++++++++ forest boundary (not everywhere fenced)

——— forest road

– – – – forest path

▦ areas planted to 1963

⠐⠂ areas planted since 1963

Pheasant Inn

Offices of Forestry Commission

Bassenthwaite Lake

N

▲ SALE FELL

1

1

Beck Wythop Cottages

1

MILES

2

1

0

4

5

LORD'S SEAT

▲ BARF

2

Powter How

▲ WHINLATTER

3

3

Whinlatter Pass

6

7

7

8

8

8

▲ GRISEDALE PIKE

Plantations:
1: Wythop Wood
2: Beckstones
3: Comb
4: Darling How
5: Aiken
6: Swinside
7: Hobcarton
8: Hospital

An excellent illustrated leaflet with details of six walking trails and other information is on sale in the Visitor Centre.

Lord's Seat cannot be ascended from any direction without an increasing awareness of the vast areas of this and neighbouring fells now under timber as a result of the operations

Thornthwaite Forest

of the Forestry Commission. Lord's Seat is the geographical centre of their activities south of Bassenthwaite Lake; on all sides there are plantations. Except for the slopes of Barf the full length of this side of the lake is now afforested, the old-established Wythop Wood being adopted and extended to a new forest fence along the top of the declivity, and further south the Beckstones and Comb Plantations cover the flanks of Lord's Seat, while round to the west the new Darling How and Aiken Plantations are creeping up to the skyline. Over Whinlatter Pass the Hobcarton and Hospital Plantations are firmly entrenched on the northern slopes of Grisedale Pike, and Swinside Plantation clothes the foothills of Hopegill Head. It is interesting to note that the tops of both Lord's Seat and Grisedale Pike are reached by the forest boundary, but not yet planted. All this wealth of timber is, for administrative purposes, known as Thornthwaite Forest, the name including also Dodd Wood across Bassenthwaite Lake and plantations nearer Cockermouth.

The newer plantings are coniferous, spruce predominating, and dense on the ground to promote upright growth. Approach to all parts of the forest, and removal of the timber harvest, is facilitated by a well-planned network of forest roads. The roads generally have a good dry surface and are excellent to walk upon, but one's sense of direction is soon at fault in these dark cuttings, which 'hairpin' and spiral considerably to gain height. The author's map on the opposite page — the result of a score of expeditions in the forest (without meeting a soul) — was compiled before the forest roads were shown on Ordnance Survey maps. For this edition, roads and paths made since the end of 1961 have been added.

A forest road Comb Plantation

THE WHINLATTER FOREST PARK:
   This comprises all the plantations shown on the opposite page south of Lord's Seat, plus Dodd Wood.

THE LAKE DISTRICT OSPREY PROJECT:
   In 1998 an artificial platform was set up at the top of a tree in Wythop Wood in the hope that it would be chosen as a nest site. Incredibly, this was successful, and chicks have been raised there every year from 2001 to 2007. Since 2003 it has been possible to watch the nest site from the Visitor Centre using closed circuit television, and in 2004 the project won the Tourism Team of the Year Award. This is the first time ospreys have bred in England since 1842. In 2008 the birds moved across the lake but they can still be seen on C.C.T.V.

MAP

Thornthwaite Mine

It is hard to believe, looking at the green pastures between the old road and the A66 north of the village of Thornthwaite, that until recently much of this area was covered by spoil from the valuable and extensive Thornthwaite Mine. The head of the engine-shaft, which went down about 500 feet, well below sea-level, and served several long galleries at different depths, is amongst trees by the roadside further north. Other shafts and adits at higher points on the side of the fell have been engulfed by the Beckstones and Comb Plantations. The mine workings were far-reaching, following the line of mineral veins up to Seat How and beyond, and they were in use, with few interruptions, for hundreds of years until the early decades of the twentieth century. A variety of ores was extracted, but the mine was usually referred to as a *lead* mine.

A Forest Walk

It may be noted from the map that the farm of Darling How is connected to the Visitor Centre by a continuous forest road, which may be used by the public, but not in vehicles. The road wanders through the forest for three and a half miles, reaching a maximum height of 1500 feet. This is a route of exceptional interest for walkers.

The main part of the forest is the subject of a remarkably accurate map published by the West Cumberland Orienteering Club and on sale in the Visitor Centre. It is on a larger scale than the maps on these pages, and shows paths in greater detail.

The prohibition on forest roads of unauthorised traffic does not apply to bicycles or horses. Consequently these roads offer a perfect parade, undisturbed and quiet, for cyclists and horse riders. The forest is also used for orienteering, and near the Visitor Centre will be found an adventure playground and a big artificial badger sett.

MAP

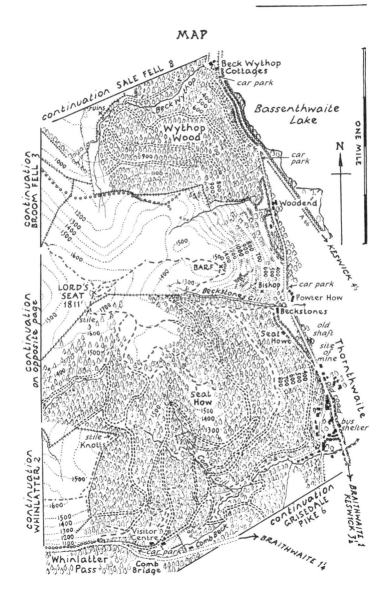

continuation SALE FELL 8
continuation BROOM FELL 3
continuation on opposite page
continuation WHINLATTER 2
continuation GRISEDALE PIKE 6

Beck Wythop Cottages
car park
Beck Wythop
Bassenthwaite Lake
Wythop Wood
car park
ONE MILE
N
Woodend
A 66
KESWICK 4½
ruins
BARF
Bishop
car park
Powter How
Beckstone Gill
Beckstones
LORD'S SEAT 1811'
stile
old shaft
Seal Howe
site of mine
Thornthwaite
Seal How
old road
bus shelter
stile
Knotts
Comb Gill
BRAITHWAITE 1
KESWICK 3½
Visitor Centre
car park
Comb Beck
BRAITHWAITE 1¼
Whinlatter Pass
Comb Bridge

ASCENT FROM THORNTHWAITE
1550 feet of ascent : 2½ miles

The public footpath climbing through Beckstones Plantation is of long standing and is frequently used for the combined ascent of Lord's Seat and Barf.   It may also be used for a direct ascent of Lord's Seat.   Although the fence indicates a possible route for the later section of the climb, trees and thick heather on one side and a swamp on the other make it desirable to use one or other of the forest roads (it doesn't matter which) to gain another that doubles back at a higher level through the trees. The road eventually becomes a path and passes through areas that are a mixture of spruce and heather. The mix is more attractive than either on its own. Here the Forestry Commission has improved upon nature.

looking west

LORD'S SEAT

- 1700

heather

- 1600

heather

forest fence

- 1500

- 1400

forest road

A well-made gravel path rises to the forest fence, where a stile is provided.

1300

forest road

felled

BARF

1300

1200

The bumpy summit across here is BARF

1100

falls

1200

Beckstones

900

Plantation

800

Here scrambling is necessary in order to negotiate a small rockface. Aim for the post.

900

old forest road

800

this road has been out of use for so long that its surface is covered in moss

Beckstones Gill

The Bishop

600

An enjoyable climb, full of interest all the way, and made easier by a gravel path through the heather towards the end.

Take the path rising through the wood

500

400

stile

500

400

Beckstones

BUS ROUTE

PHEASANT INN 3¾
COCKERMOUTH 8½

THORNTHWAITE ½
KESWICK 4¼

bus stop and car park

Powter How
Bus route X5 (Keswick – Workington)
(The bus stop is called Old Swan Hotel)

car park

ASCENT FROM HIGH LORTON
1550 feet of ascent : 4 miles

looking east-north-east

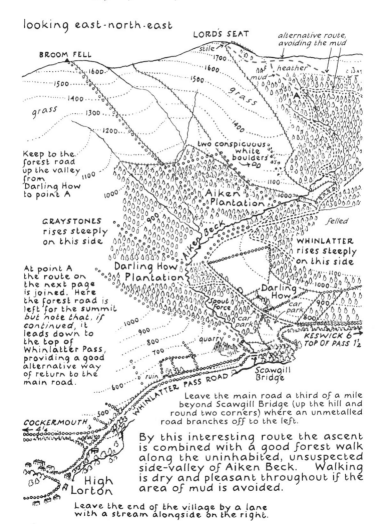

LORD'S SEAT

alternative route, avoiding the mud

BROOM FELL

stile

1700

1600

heather

mud

1600

1500

1400

grass

1500

1300

1400

grass

1200

A

1100

Keep to the forest road up the valley from Darling How to point A

two conspicuous white boulders

1100

1000

Aiken Plantation

GRAYSTONES rises steeply on this side

felled

WHINLATTER rises steeply on this side

At point A the route on the next page is joined. Here the forest road is left for the summit but note that, if continued, it leads down to the top of Whinlatter Pass, providing a good alternative way of return to the main road.

Darling How Plantation

Darling How

car park

1100

1000

900

800

Spout Force

car park

1000

900

quarry

800

700

KESWICK 6 →
TOP OF PASS 1½

600

ruin

WHINLATTER PASS ROAD

Scawgill Bridge

500

COCKERMOUTH
← 4¼

Leave the main road a third of a mile beyond Scawgill Bridge (up the hill and round two corners) where an unmetalled road branches off to the left.

High Lorton

By this interesting route the ascent is combined with a good forest walk along the uninhabited, unsuspected side-valley of Aiken Beck. Walking is dry and pleasant throughout if the area of mud is avoided.

Leave the end of the village by a lane with a stream alongside on the right.

ASCENT FROM WHINLATTER PASS
800 feet of ascent : 2 miles

LORD'S SEAT

forest fence

SEAT HOW

1700

mud

1600

heather   A   heather   B

1500

1400

1300

DARLING HOW for LORTON

summit now in view

1500

1400

1300

1200

1100

100

1400

1300

1200

Horsebox Crossroads

VISITOR CENTRE

parking place

young

top of Whinlatter Pass 1043'

LORTON 3

BRAITHWAITE 2

Route B is preferable to Route A since it avoids the mud. The path is surfaced with gravel all the way to the forest fence.

Leave the surfaced road after crossing a beck, doubling back along a cut path to the ridge.

This is one of the oddest fell climbs of all, five-sixths of the distance being along forest roads engulfed in dense plantations, walking 'blind' and with little sense of direction until, at a thinning, the summit is seen ahead. Avoid all roads branching off the 'through' routes shown.

A delightfully easy ascent — but silent gloomy forests aren't everybody's cup of tea!

looking nor'nor'east

The path leaves the road at the top of the pass where the mature conifers give way to younger trees. If starting at the Visitor Centre follow the 'trails' signposts and then the green-banded posts to the Horsebox Crossroads.

THE SUMMIT

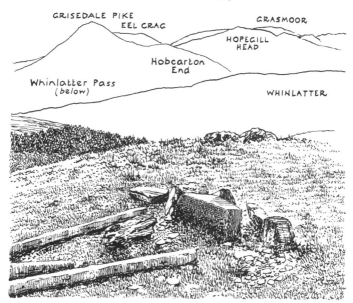

GRISEDALE PIKE
EEL CRAG
GRASMOOR
HOPEGILL HEAD
Hobcarton End
Whinlatter Pass (below)
WHINLATTER

The summit is bare and open to the sky, refreshingly so if the ascent has been made through the plantations. An iron post on the highest point and another one a hundred yards to the north-east are the remains of three fences that once met at the summit. They have been superseded by the forest fence, which, out of deference for the freedom of the summit, crosses the top of the fell a hundred yards distant.

It is said that the name of the fell derives from a natural rock seat just below the top on the north-west side — but anyone who spends time trying to identify the place will question the legend, for not even the commonest commoner could instal himself in any of the few rocky recesses hereabouts with the standard of comfort his lordship would surely have demanded.

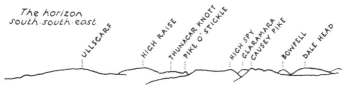

The horizon south-south-east

ULLSCARF
HIGH RAISE
THUNACAR KNOTT
PIKE O' STICKLE
HIGH SPY
GLARAMARA
CAUSEY PIKE
BOWFELL
DALE HEAD

THE VIEW

The pleasantest scene is eastward, where there is a view down to the Vale of Keswick and beyond, in the distance, the far Pennines, with Cross Fell appearing on the skyline between Blencathra and Great Mell Fell. Southeast is the long line of the Helvellyn range; the little green oasis and white farmhouse seen in this direction is Askness Farm. But note especially the nearby Wythop valley, north-west, rising as a green shelf and then plunging suddenly down a wooded declivity to Bassenthwaite Lake: an unusual geographical arrangement; above and beyond is an excellent view of the Solway Firth and Criffell. The Grasmoor fells conceal many of the central heights, which are revealed only in unfamiliar fragments above the skyline of Scar Crags.

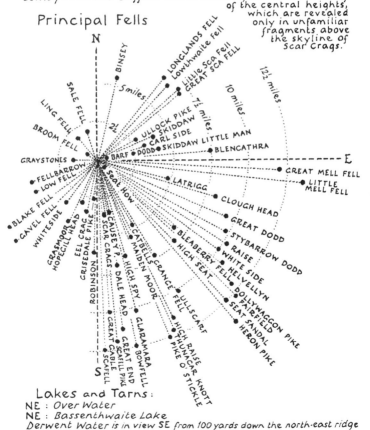

Principal Fells

Lakes and Tarns:
NE : Over Water
NE : Bassenthwaite Lake
Derwent Water is in view SE from 100 yards down the north-east ridge

RIDGE ROUTES

To BROOM FELL, 1670': ⁷⁄₈ mile : NW
Depression at 1586': 120 feet of ascent
Easy, uninteresting walking on a wide ridge

Unless it's misty, the column on Broom Fell is plainly visible, and the route is never in doubt. Go down north-west from Lord's Seat to the obvious connecting ridge, which is marshy in patches, wide, and gently undulating for half a mile, without any definite col, before rising to the flat top of Broom Fell. A curiosity is a number of small fenced enclosures, some of them in ruins.

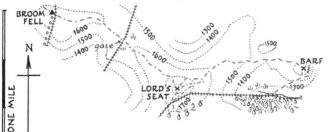

To BARF, 1536': ¾ mile : ENE, then E
Depression at 1400': 150 feet of ascent
Rough walking; best left alone in mist

There is a path, but the point where it leaves the ridge is not clear. There are patches of heather, which are easy to avoid. Note that the far side of Barf's summit is craggy, and leave it by a path on the south flank.

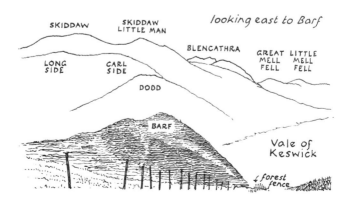

looking east to Barf

Maiden Moor 1887'

from Rigg Beck

Stair
▲ CATBELLS
● Little Town
▲ MAIDEN MOOR
● Grange
▲ HIGH SPY
Rosthwaite

MILES

| 0 | 1 | 2 | 3 |

from Scope End

NATURAL FEATURES

From mid-Newlands, Maiden Moor is seen to rise in three tiers: the lowest, rock-crowned, behind the hamlet of Little Town; the second, also craggy, above but some distance back; and finally the summit, set at the edge of a steep fall to the upper reaches of the valley. To the left of these successive steps is the wide hollow of Yewthwaite Comb, formerly a scene of mining activity but now a quiet sheep-pasture, below the slow decline of the summit-slope eastwards across a tilted plateau.

On the opposite side of the fell is the parallel valley of Borrowdale, to which Maiden Moor presents a steep slope of undistinguished appearance and a high level skyline, this being not the ridge but the plateau edge, the summit itself being out of sight.

Maiden Moor is the middle section of a very popular fellwalk, starting with Catbells and ending at Honister, along the spine of the ridge forming the Newlands and Borrowdale watershed. Both flanks are scarped — that facing Newlands almost continuously — so that, while the walk along the top is simple and pleasant, on grass, direct access from either valley is possible only in a few places without encountering rock.

The streams are small and insignificant; they drain into the River Derwent to the east and Newlands Beck to the west, joining, however, in the flat country before Bassenthwaite Lake.

1: The Summit
2: High Crags
3: Knott End
4: Yewthwaite Comb
5: Yewthwaite Mine
6: Newlands Beck
7: Yewthwaite Gill
8: High Spy
9: slope of Catbells

looking south

The entrance to Little Mine — one of two small mines opened on the lower slopes above Newlands, in view from the old road leading up the valley.

MAP

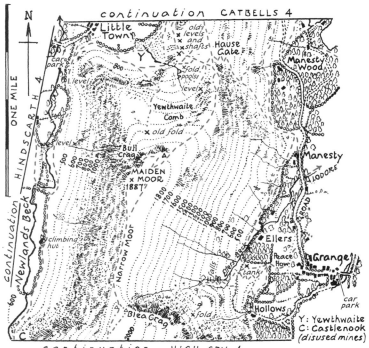

continuation CATBELLS 4

Little Town

old levels and shafts

Hause Gate

Manesty Wood

Y

fold pools

car park

level

level

Yewthwaite Comb

old fold

ONE MILE

HINDSCARTH 4

continuation Newlands Beck

level

Bull Crag

MAIDEN MOOR 1887'

Manesty

LODORE

climbing hut

Narrow Moor

ROAD

Ellers

Grange

Peace How

tank

car park

Blea Crag

fold

Hollows

Y: Yewthwaite
C: Castlenook
(disused mines)

continuation HIGH SPY 4

In the vicinity of Ellers.......

Peace How

Ellers Beck flows alongside the grounds of Ellers, a natural boundary being provided by a long wall of rock bordering the stream. The cave illustrated (right) – evidence of old mining activity – was in the rock-face directly behind the house of Ellers. In 2008 it could not be found.

Bedecked with rhododendrons and watered by a sweet stream, this was Lakeland's most exotic cave.

ASCENTS FROM GRANGE
via MANESTY
1600 feet of ascent
2½ miles

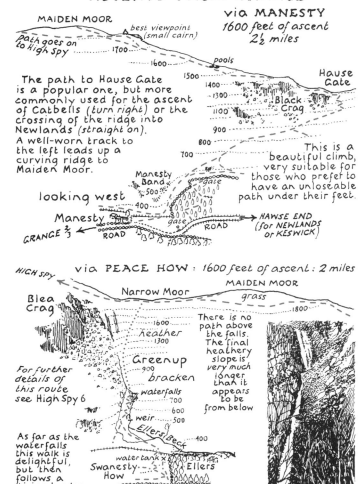

MAIDEN MOOR

best viewpoint (small cairn)

path goes on to High Spy 1700

...... 1600

pools

...... 1500

Hause Gate

1400

1300 — Black
1100 — Crag

900

800

700

The path to Hause Gate is a popular one, but more commonly used for the ascent of Catbells (turn right) or the crossing of the ridge into Newlands (straight on).
A well-worn track to the left leads up a curving ridge to Maiden Moor.

This is a beautiful climb, very suitable for those who prefer to have an unloseable path under their feet.

Manesty Band
......500
......400

gate

gate

looking west

Manesty

ROAD

gate

ROAD

HAWSE END (for NEWLANDS or KESWICK)

GRANGE ¾ ← ROAD

via PEACE HOW : 1600 feet of ascent : 2 miles

HIGH SPY

MAIDEN MOOR

Narrow Moor

grass

Blea Crag

...... 1800

...... 1600

heather
1300

There is no path above the falls. The final heathery slope is very much longer than it appears to be from below

Greenup

900

bracken

For further details of this route see High Spy 6

waterfalls
700
600
weir 500

Ellers Beck

400

As far as the waterfalls this walk is delightful, but then follows a tiring trudge up a steepening, uninteresting slope.

water tank x

Ellers

Swanesty How

x seat Peace How

Grange

MANESTY

ROAD

Hotel

looking west

Waterfalls above Ellers Beck

ASCENT FROM LITTLE TOWN
1250 feet of ascent: 1½ or 2 miles

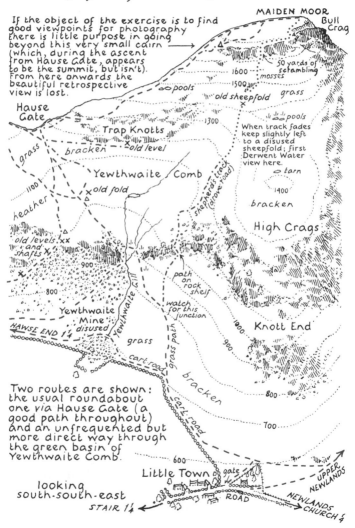

MAIDEN MOOR

Bull Crag

If the object of the exercise is to find good viewpoints for photography there is little purpose in going beyond this very small cairn (which, during the ascent from Hause Gate, appears to be the summit, but isn't). From here onwards the beautiful retrospective view is lost.

50 yards of scrambling mosses

1600

1500

grass

old sheepfold

Hause Gate

pools

Trap Knotts

1300

When track fades keep slightly left to a disused sheepfold; first Derwent Water view here.

bracken — old level

Yewthwaite Comb

grass

pools

1100

old fold

tarn

1400

heather

bracken

High Crags

old levels and shafts

shepherd's track (drove road)

900

path on rock shelf

800

watch for this junction

Knott End

Yewthwaite Mine disused

HAWSE END 1¼

grass

900

cart road

800

700

grass path

Two routes are shown: the usual roundabout one via Hause Gate (a good path throughout) and an unfrequented but more direct way through the green basin of Yewthwaite Comb.

cart road

bracken

600

Little Town

gate

UPPER NEWLANDS

looking south-south-east

STAIR 1¼

ROAD

NEWLANDS CHURCH ¾

THE SUMMIT

Short of lying down with eyes at ground level and taking a few elementary perspectives, there is no way by which a layman can determine the highest point of the fell — and although the Ordnance Survey have been on the spot with instruments and arrived at their own expert conclusions they have left no sign of their visit, and there is no cairn. The actual top could be anywhere within a twenty-yard radius. All is grassy and uninteresting here, without as much as a stone to sit on or an outcrop to recline against, but those who feel the ascent has merited a rest can take their reward on the edge of the steep drop into Newlands, just west of whatever is decided as the summit. A track follows this edge, but the main path across the moor runs some 200 yards to the east.

DESCENTS : Join the path referred to (you can't miss it, even in mist: it stands out from the grass as a dark grey ribbon of gravel) and follow it left down to Hause Gate for Newlands, left, or Borrowdale, right.

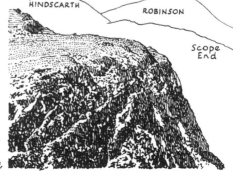

Bull Crag is bull-nosed, i.e. in profile it appears as a rounded overhang

The Newlands edge from the top of Bull Crag, looking south-west

THE VIEW

A dreary foreground detracts from the view and unfortunately hides Borrowdale and most of Derwent Water. In other respects the scene is satisfactory, and especially good looking north. A tiny cairn on the edge of the plateau to the north-east commands a much more beautiful though less extensive view.

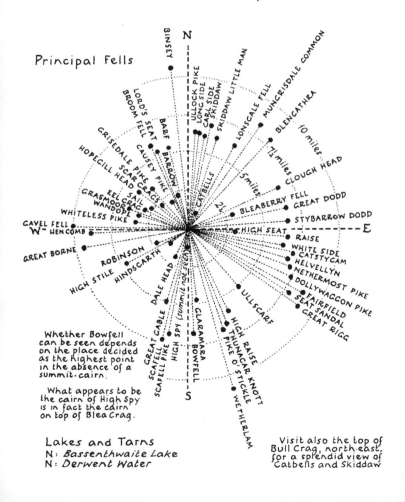

Principal Fells

Whether Bowfell can be seen depends on the place decided as the highest point in the absence of a summit-cairn.

What appears to be the cairn of High Spy is in fact the cairn on top of Blea Crag.

Lakes and Tarns
N: *Bassenthwaite Lake*
N: *Derwent Water*

Visit also the top of Bull Crag, north-east, for a splendid view of Catbells and Skiddaw

RIDGE ROUTES

TO CATBELLS, 1481′ : 1½ miles : N.E, then N.
Depression (Hause Gate) at 1180′ : 310 feet of ascent

It must be something like this in Heaven

Cross to the cairn on the north-east edge of the plateau (this is a notable viewpoint), reaching this preferably by keeping to the rim of the crags. A well-worn path now goes down in a curve to Hause Gate, whence a broad grass path leads easily upwards to Catbells. Beautiful views.

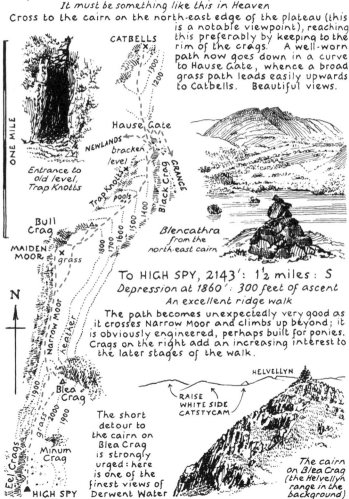

CATBELLS
×
1300
1200

Hause Gate

NEWLANDS
bracken
level

GRANGE

Black Crag

Entrance to old level, Trap Knotts

Trap Knotts
×
pools
1400
1500
1600
1700
1800

ONE MILE

Bull Crag

MAIDEN MOOR × grass

Blencathra from the north-east cairn

N

Narrow Moor

Aealker

TO HIGH SPY, 2143′ : 1½ miles : S
Depression at 1860′ : 300 feet of ascent

An excellent ridge walk

The path becomes unexpectedly very good as it crosses Narrow Moor and climbs up beyond; it is obviously engineered, perhaps built for ponies. Crags on the right add an increasing interest to the later stages of the walk.

Blea Crag

1900
grass
2000
1900
grass

Eel Crags

Minum Crag

▲ HIGH SPY

HELVELLYN

RAISE
WHITE SIDE
CATSTYCAM

The short detour to the cairn on Blea Crag is strongly urged: here is one of the finest views of Derwent Water

The cairn on Blea Crag (the Helvellyn range in the background)

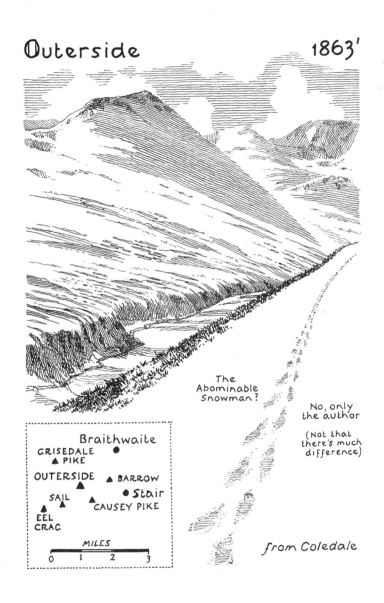

Outerside

1863'

The
Abominable
Snowman?

No, only
the author

(Not that
there's much
difference)

Braithwaite ●

GRISEDALE
▲ PIKE

OUTERSIDE ▲ ▲ BARROW

SAIL ● Stair

▲ ▲
EEL   CAUSEY PIKE
CRAG

MILES

0   1   2   3

from Coledale

NATURAL FEATURES

The valley of Coledale, coming down straight as an arrow to Braithwaite, is deeply enclosed by a continuous horseshoe rim of high summits, from Causey Pike round to Grisedale Pike, but while the latter descends uncompromisingly in a very steep and unbroken slope, the opposite ridge of Causey Pike is accompanied by a lower and parallel ridge like an inner balcony, the fall to the valley being thereby interrupted. The main eminence on this subsidiary ridge is the abrupt summit of Outerside, and its position is such that it looks *down* into the vast pit of the head of Coledale and *up* to the exciting skyline of the surrounding ring of peaks. This secondary ridge ends in Barrow, overlooking Newlands, and above a thousand feet has a rich heather cover, which gives to the upper expanses a gloomy and forbidding appearance that is belied by a close acquaintance. Between Outerside and Barrow, but out of alignment like a dog's back leg, rises the lesser height of Stile End, which, seen from the Braithwaite approach, forms a noble pyramid.

Outerside springs quite steeply from the abyss of Coledale, and in a less distinctive company it would attract much attention. As it is, visitors rarely tread its pleasant summit.

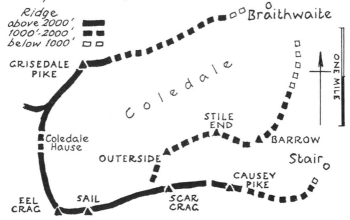

MAP

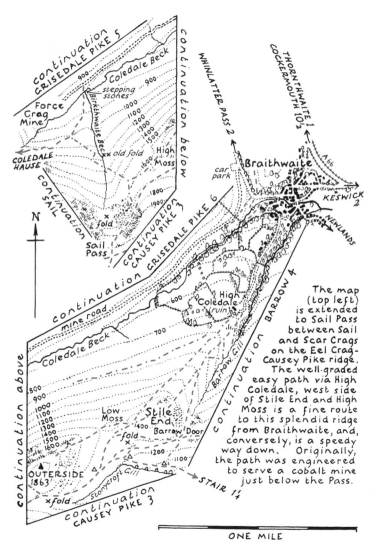

The map (top left) is extended to Sail Pass between Sail and Scar Crags on the Eel Crag-Causey Pike ridge. The well-graded easy route via High Coledale, west side of Stile End and High Moss is a fine route to this splendid ridge from Braithwaite, and, conversely, is a speedy way down. Originally, the path was engineered to serve a cobalt mine just below the Pass.

ONE MILE

ASCENT FROM STAIR
1550 feet of ascent · 2¼ miles

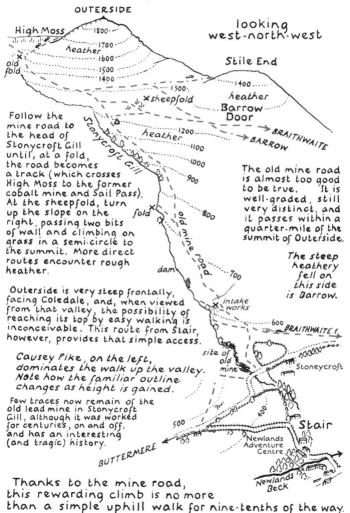

OUTERSIDE

looking
west·north·west

High Moss

1800
heather
1700
1600
1500
1400

old
fold

Stile End

1300

×sheepfold

1400
heather
Barrow
Door

Stonycroft Gill

heather
1200
1100
1000
900

BRAITHWAITE
BARROW

Follow the mine road to the head of Stonycroft Gill until, at a fold, the road becomes a track (which crosses High Moss to the former cobalt mine and Sail Pass). At the sheepfold, turn up the slope on the right, passing two bits of wall and climbing on grass in a semi-circle to the summit. More direct routes encounter rough heather.

fold ×
old mine road
800

The old mine road is almost too good to be true. It is well-graded, still very distinct, and it passes within a quarter-mile of the summit of Outerside.

The steep heathery fell on this side is Barrow.

dam
700

Outerside is very steep frontally, facing Coledale, and, when viewed from that valley, the possibility of reaching its top by easy walking is inconceivable. This route from Stair, however, provides that simple access.

×intake works

600 BRAITHWAITE 1

Causey Pike, on the left, dominates the walk up the valley. Note how the familiar outline changes as height is gained.

site of old mine

Stoneycroft

Few traces now remain of the old lead mine in Stonycroft Gill, although it was worked for centuries, on and off, and has an interesting (and tragic) history.

500

400

Stair

Newlands
Adventure
Centre

BUTTERMERE

Newlands
Beck

Thanks to the mine road, this rewarding climb is no more than a simple uphill walk for nine-tenths of the way.

ASCENT FROM BRAITHWAITE
1650 feet of ascent : 2½ miles

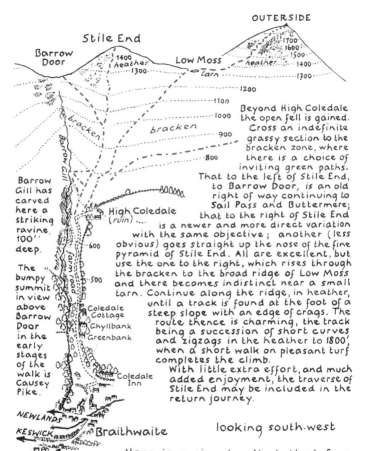

OUTERSIDE

Stile End

Barrow Door

1400 heather 1300

Low Moss

heather 1700 1600 1500 1400

1300

1200

1100

1000

900

800

Barrow Gill

bracken

bracken

Barrow Gill has carved here a striking ravine, 100' deep.

High Coledale (ruin)

600

The bumpy summit in view above Barrow Door in the early stages of the walk is Causey Pike.

500

farm road

Coledale Cottage

Chyllbank

Greenbank

Coledale Inn

NEWLANDS

KESWICK

Braithwaite

bus shelter

Beyond High Coledale the open fell is gained. Cross an indefinite grassy section to the bracken zone, where there is a choice of inviting green paths. That to the left of Stile End, to Barrow Door, is an old right of way continuing to Sail Pass and Buttermere; that to the right of Stile End is a newer and more direct variation with the same objective; another (less obvious) goes straight up the nose of the fine pyramid of Stile End. All are excellent, but use the one to the right, which rises through the bracken to the broad ridge of Low Moss and there becomes indistinct near a small tarn. Continue along the ridge, in heather, until a track is found at the foot of a steep slope with an edge of crags. The route thence is charming, the track being a succession of short curves and zigzags in the heather to 1800', when a short walk on pleasant turf completes the climb.

With little extra effort, and much added enjoyment, the traverse of Stile End may be included in the return journey.

looking south-west

Here is a simple climb that few walkers ever bother to do; and by this omission they deny themselves a lot of pleasure and a rewarding introduction to the grand circle of hills around Coledale.

THE SUMMIT

From the east the highest point is reached at the end of a gradual incline; from the west it appears abruptly at the top of a rising pavement of embedded rocks: here a few loose stones form a small cairn. The Coledale edge is close by, falling away sharply in an escarpment, and in mist this edge may be followed as a guide to a track down the eastern ridge, the only path off the top.

DESCENTS: The escarpment can be negotiated, with care, on initially steep ground if a direct way down into Coledale is desired, but there is little point in this since Coledale leads only to Braithwaite, which is more quickly and attractively reached by the eastern ridge (watch for a track in the heather) and then by a good path slanting down to the left below the rise to Stile End. For Stair, too, the eastern ridge is best, turning down to the right at the depression to join the Stonycroft mine road.

Sail Pass (left), Sail and Eel Crag
from Outerside

THE VIEW

Outerside is severely circumscribed by the mountains around Coledale, which maintain a consistently higher skyline, and only between north and south-east is there an open prospect. The view lacks charm, but its intimate detail of the tremendous declivities amongst which the head of Coledale is so deeply inurned — a fine mountain scene — is very impressive.

Who dare tackle Grisedale Pike direct from the beck after seeing its 2000 feet of near-verticality from this viewpoint? Only the brave!

Principal Fells

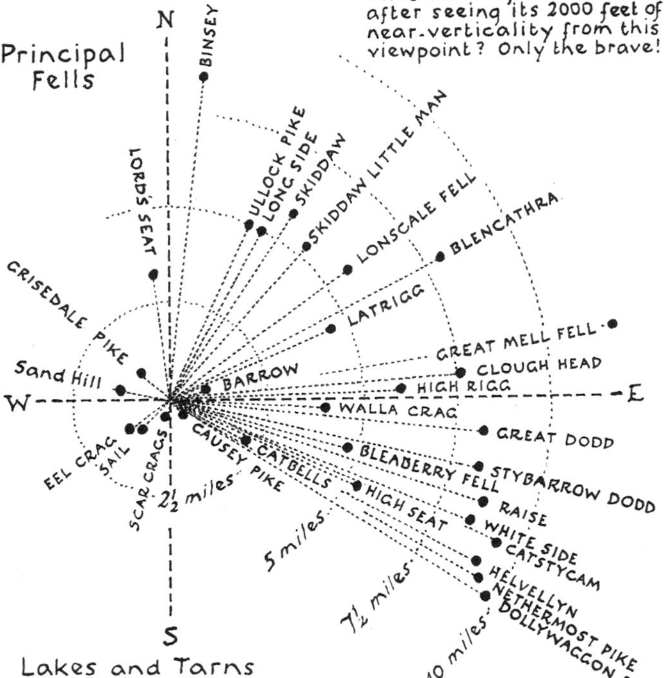

N

BINSEY

ULLOCK PIKE
LONG SIDE
SKIDDAW
SKIDDAW LITTLE MAN
LONSCALE FELL
BLENCATHRA
LATRIGG
GREAT MELL FELL
CLOUGH HEAD
HIGH RIGG — E
WALLA CRAG
GREAT DODD
BARROW
BLEABERRY FELL
STYBARROW DODD
RAISE
HIGH SEAT
WHITE SIDE
CATSTYCAM
HELVELLYN
NETHERMOST PIKE
DOLLYWAGGON PIKE

LORD'S SEAT

GRISEDALE PIKE

Sand Hill

W —

EEL CRAG
SAIL
SCAR CRAGS
CAUSEY PIKE
CATBELLS

2½ miles

5 miles

7½ miles

10 miles

S

Lakes and Tarns
N: Bassenthwaite Lake
E: Derwent Water

Stile End, as seen on the approach from Braithwaite, with Barrow Door on the left and Causey Pike beyond

RIDGE ROUTE

To BARROW, 1494': 1¼ miles : ENE, then SE and ENE
Depressions at 1380' and 1270'
400 feet of ascent
Rough walking in heather. Avoid Stile End in mist.
If the ridge is to be followed conscientiously, the traverse of
Stile End must be included in this walk, although this middle
height can more easily be bypassed
between Low Moss and Barrow Door.
Starting down the eastern ridge,
keep always to the highest
ground ahead; on Stile End
this means a sharp turn
to the right.

Outerside from Stile End

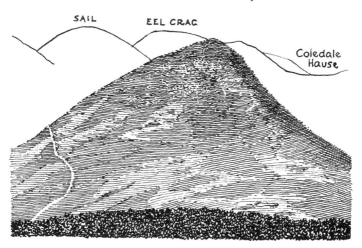

Rannerdale Knotts 1165'

• Rannerdale
▲ RANNERDALE KNOTTS
• Buttermere

ONE MILE

from High Rannerdale

Rannerdale is seen by most visitors to Buttermere — but only as a farm and a cottage and a patchwork of fields on the shore of Crummock Water: a pleasant green oasis in the lap of shaggy fells, but unremarkable.   Passers-by sometimes tarry in the limpid coves of Crummock, or stroll along convenient paths in the bracken, but most hurry past, to or from Buttermere, unsuspecting that these few acres, now peaceful pastures, were once a scene of violent strife. Rannerdale has a lasting place in history as the setting of a fierce battle in which the Norman invaders were ambushed and routed by the English in the years after the Conquest.

Alongside the fields, and thrusting as a headland into the lake, is the abrupt and rugged end of a low fell that extends south-east for a mile, gradually declining to Sail Beck. All the excitement is concentrated in the dark tower of rock above the lake. Behind, a quiet valley isolates the fell from the greater heights in the rear.

This is Rannerdale Knotts, a mountain in miniature, and a proud one. Not even Gable has witnessed a real battle! And, what's more, our side won!!

MAP

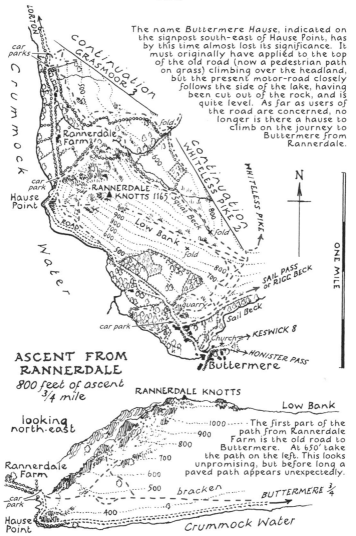

The name *Buttermere Hause*, indicated on the signpost south-east of Hause Point, has by this time almost lost its significance. It must originally have applied to the top of the old road (now a pedestrian path on grass) climbing over the headland, but the present motor-road closely follows the side of the lake, having been cut out of the rock, and is quite level. As far as users of the road are concerned, no longer is there a hause to climb on the journey to Buttermere from Rannerdale.

ASCENT FROM RANNERDALE
800 feet of ascent
3/4 mile

looking north-east

RANNERDALE KNOTTS

Low Bank

The first part of the path from Rannerdale Farm is the old road to Buttermere. At 650' take the path on the left. This looks unpromising, but before long a paved path appears unexpectedly.

BUTTERMERE 3/4

Crummock Water

ASCENT FROM BUTTERMERE
850 feet of ascent : 1½ miles

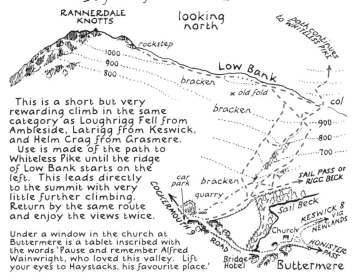

RANNERDALE KNOTTS   looking north   path continues to WHITELESS PIKE

rockstep
1000
900
800   Low Bank
bracken   × old fold
bracken   col
900
800
700
car park   bracken   SAIL PASS or RIGG BECK
quarry
Sail Beck   KESWICK 8 VIA NEWLANDS
Church
HONISTER PASS
Bridge Hotel   Buttermere

COCKERMOUTH ROAD

This is a short but very rewarding climb in the same category as Loughrigg Fell from Ambleside, Latrigg from Keswick, and Helm Crag from Grasmere.
Use is made of the path to Whiteless Pike until the ridge of Low Bank starts on the left. This leads directly to the summit with very little further climbing. Return by the same route and enjoy the views twice.

Under a window in the church at Buttermere is a tablet inscribed with the words 'Pause and remember Alfred Wainwright, who loved this valley. Lift your eyes to Haystacks, his favourite place.'

THE SUMMIT

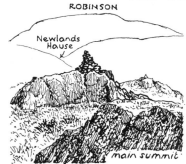

ROBINSON

Newlands Hause

main summit

second summit

A succession of rocky tors athwart the narrow crest gives a fine distinction to this modest fell. Glorious views in addition make this a place for leisurely exploration. Rock formations and striations are interesting.

DESCENTS : The best way off is along the ridge of the fell, Low Bank, to Buttermere, and, after an initial rockstep just beyond the second summit, is a very easy stroll indeed. In mist, the road may be safely reached by a straight descent to Crummock Water from the depression between the two summits, but not elsewhere.

THE VIEW

The view is confined to a distance of a few miles only, but makes up in charm what it lacks in extensiveness; indeed the scene southeast, over Buttermere, is of classical beauty. Crummock Water is much better viewed from a rocky tower 80 yards west, beyond a natural dyke. A feature of interest is the 'hidden' upper course of Rannerdale Beck, directly opposite, the four bends greatly accentuated by foreshortening.

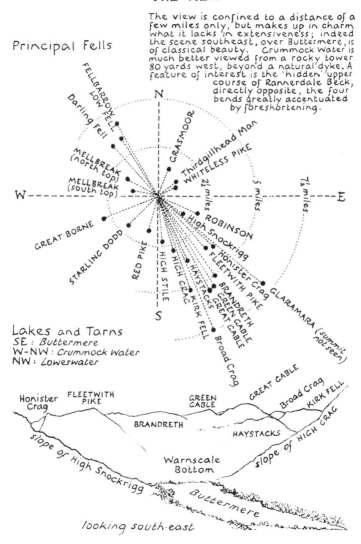

Principal Fells

FELLBARROW
LOW FELL
Darling Fell
MELLBREAK (north top)
MELLBREAK (south top)
GREAT BORNE
STARLING DODD
RED PIKE
HIGH STILE
HIGH CRAG
KIRK FELL
Broad Crag
GREAT GABLE
GREEN GABLE
HAYSTACKS
BRANDRETH
FLEETWITH PIKE
Honister Crag
High Snockrigg
ROBINSON
WHITELESS PIKE
Thirdgillhead Man
GRASMOOR
GLARAMARA (summit not seen)

N
W
E
S

2½ miles
5 miles
7½ miles

Lakes and Tarns
SE : Buttermere
W-NW : Crummock Water
NW : Loweswater

Honister Crag
FLEETWITH PIKE
BRANDRETH
GREEN GABLE
GREAT GABLE
Broad Crag
KIRK FELL
HAYSTACKS
slope of High Snockrigg
Warnscale Bottom
slope of HIGH CRAG
Buttermere

looking south-east

Robinson

2417'

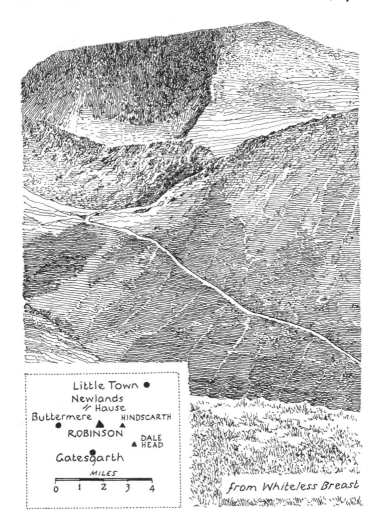

Little Town ●
Newlands
↟ Hause
Buttermere ● HINDSCARTH ▲
ROBINSON ▲
DALE
HEAD ▲
Gatesgarth ●

MILES

0   1   2   3   4

from Whiteless Breast

NATURAL FEATURES

This fell with the prosaic name is, to look at, the least attractive of the group around Buttermere, a defect largely due to its position on the sunny side of the valley. Lack of shadow always reduces the visual appeal of mountain scenery, and on Robinson the steep slopes rise blandly to the sky with nothing in particular to attract the eye, nothing to exercise curiosity and imagination — in complete contrast to the darkly mysterious and more challenging heights across the lake. Robinson's summit lies back, out of sight, beyond a wide shelf at mid-height that serves as an effective gathering ground for Keskadale Beck: this wet expanse is Buttermere Moss, a bad place for walkers. Except for the neat apex of a lower summit, High Snockrigg, and a rough cleft above the woods of Hassness, Robinson contributes little to the scenic value of the Buttermere picture, and one must see it from Newlands to appreciate its distinctive skyline and the long ridge that characterises this aspect, its finest; while from Newlands Hause, too, where passing motorists are excited by a close view of Moss Force, it is strongly in evidence, here fringed by the half-mile precipice of Robinson Crags.

Robinson descends to Newlands in the close company of Hindscarth, which is almost a twin, and between them is the unfrequented valley of Little Dale, which tumbles to a lower level in a gorge thunderous with waterfalls that put many better-known ones to shame; here, too, is a small reservoir, built for mining operations long ceased and now a quiet pool. Streams join the Cocker, and the Derwent via Newlands Beck.

1 : The summit
2 : Ridge continuing to Hindscarth
3 : Robinson Crags
4 : Buttermere Moss
5 : Moss Force
6 : Newlands Hause
7 : High Snab Bank
8 : Keskadale Beck
9 : Scope Beck
10 : Newlands Beck

grass

waterfalls

bracken

reservoir

bracken

pastures

looking south

It's a pity about the name, which derives from a Richard Robinson who purchased estates, including this unnamed fell, at Buttermere in the 16th century; thereafter it was known as 'Robinson's Fell'. But it could have been worse: this early land speculator might have been a Smith or a Jones or a Wainwright.

MAP

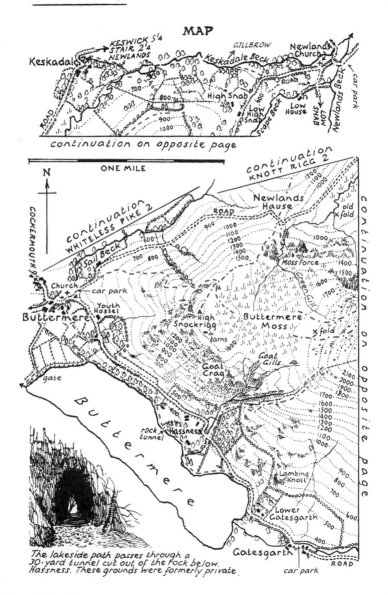

Keskadale · Keswick 5¼ STAIR 2¼ NEWLANDS · GILLBROW · Keskadale Beck · Newlands Church · car park · ROAD · High Snab · Low High Snab · Scope Beck · Low House · LOW SNAB · Newlands Beck · 700 · 800 · 900 · 1000

continuation on opposite page

continuation KNOTT RIGG 2

continuation WHITELESS PIKE 2

N · ONE MILE

COCKERMOUTH 9 · Sail Beck 3 · Church · car park · Youth Hostel · Buttermere · gate · Buttermere · rock tunnel · Hassness · ROAD · Newlands Hause · old X fold · Moss Force · Green Gill · High Snockrigg · tarns · Buttermere Moss · X fold · Goat Crag · Goat Gills · Lambing Knott · Lower Gatesgarth · Gatesgarth · car park · ROAD · 600 · 700 · 800 · 900 · 1000 · 1100 · 1200 · 1300 · 1400 · 1500 · 1600 · 1700 · 1800 · 1900 · 2000 · 2100 · 400 · 500

continuation on opposite page

The lakeside path passes through a
30-yard tunnel cut out of the rock below
Hassness. These grounds were formerly private.

MAP

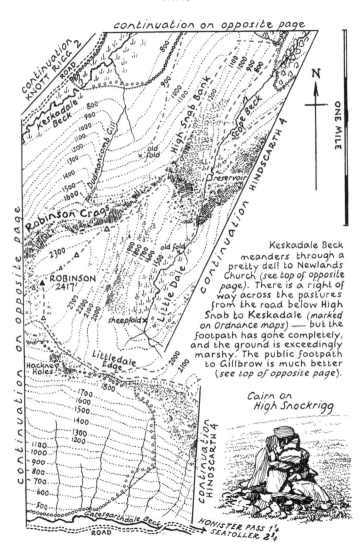

continuation on opposite page

continuation KNOTT RIGG 2

continuation HINDSCARTH 4

ROAD

Keskadale Beck

High Snab Bank

Scope Beck

N

ONE MILE

old fold

reservoir

Robinson Crags

Little Dale

old fold

ROBINSON 2417'

sheepfold

Littledale Edge

Hackney Holes

continuation HINDSCARTH 4

Gatesgarthdale Beck

ROAD

HONISTER PASS 1¼
SEATOLLER 2¼

Keskadale Beck meanders through a pretty dell to Newlands Church (see top of opposite page). There is a right of way across the pastures from the road below High Snab to Keskadale (marked on Ordnance maps) — but the footpath has gone completely, and the ground is exceedingly marshy. The public footpath to Gillbrow is much better (see top of opposite page).

Cairn on High Snockrigg

ASCENT FROM NEWLANDS CHURCH

2000 feet of ascent
3 miles

ROBINSON

looking
south-west

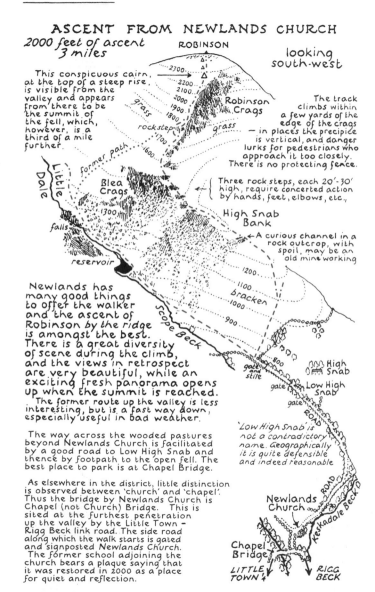

This conspicuous cairn, at the top of a steep rise, is visible from the valley and appears from there to be the summit of the fell, which, however, is a third of a mile further.

2300
2200
2100
2000
1900
1800
grass
rock step
1700
1600
former path

Robinson Crags
grass

The track climbs within a few yards of the edge of the crags — in places the precipice is vertical, and danger lurks for pedestrians who approach it too closely. There is no protecting fence.

Little
Dale

Blea Crags
1300

falls

reservoir

Three rock steps, each 20'-30' high, require concerted action by hands, feet, elbows, etc.,

High Snab Bank

←A curious channel in a rock outcrop, with spoil, may be an old mine working

1200
1100
1000
900
bracken

Scope Beck

gate and stile
gate
gate

800

High Snab
Low High Snab

ROAD

Newlands has many good things to offer the walker and the ascent of Robinson by the ridge is amongst the best. There is a great diversity of scene during the climb, and the views in retrospect are very beautiful, while an exciting fresh panorama opens up when the summit is reached.
The former route up the valley is less interesting, but is a fast way down, especially useful in bad weather.

The way across the wooded pastures beyond Newlands Church is facilitated by a good road to Low High Snab and thence by footpath to the open fell. The best place to park is at Chapel Bridge.

'Low High Snab' is not a contradictory name. Geographically it is quite defensible and indeed reasonable

Newlands Church

Keskadale Beck

ROAD

As elsewhere in the district, little distinction is observed between 'church' and 'chapel'. Thus the bridge by Newlands Church is Chapel (not Church) Bridge. This is sited at the furthest penetration up the valley by the Little Town - Rigg Beck link road. The side road along which the walk starts is gated and signposted *Newlands Church*. The former school adjoining the church bears a plaque saying that it was restored in 2000 as a place for quiet and reflection.

Chapel Bridge

LITTLE TOWN 4

RIGG BECK

ASCENT FROM NEWLANDS HAUSE
1400 feet of ascent : 1¼ miles

Except for two short sections, the full length of the route is clearly in view from the Hause. *The wife, left in the car, will be watching every move!*

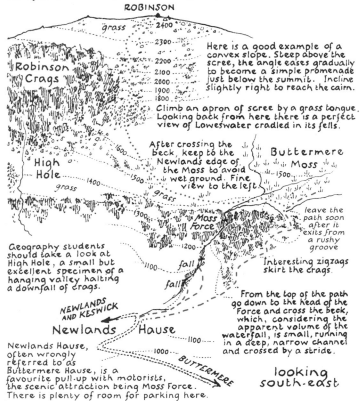

ROBINSON

grass   2400

2300

Robinson
Crags

2200
2100
2000
1900
1800

Here is a good example of a convex slope. Steep above the scree, the angle eases gradually to become a simple promenade just below the summit. Incline slightly right to reach the cairn.

Climb an apron of scree by a grass tongue. Looking back from here there is a perfect view of Loweswater cradled in its fells.

1600

High
Hole

grass   1400

After crossing the beck, keep to the Newlands edge of the Moss to avoid wet ground. Fine view to the left.

1500

Buttermere
Moss

1500

grass

1300   Moss
Force

leave the path soon after it exits from a rushy groove

Geography students should take a look at High Hole, a small but excellent specimen of a hanging valley halting a downfall of crags.

1200

1100   fall

fall

Interesting zigzags skirt the crags.

NEWLANDS
AND KESWICK

Newlands — Hause

Newlands Hause, often wrongly referred to as Buttermere Hause, is a favourite pull-up with motorists, the scenic attraction being Moss Force. There is plenty of room for parking here.

1100

1000

BUTTERMERE

From the top of the path go down to the head of the Force and cross the beck, which, considering the apparent volume of the waterfall, is small, running in a deep, narrow channel and crossed by a stride.

looking
south-east

Motorists, having less energy than walkers, may be attracted by this opportunity of starting 1100 feet up and so shortening the climb. The ascent does not live up to its early promise, however, becoming very dreary at the level of the Moss. Wet ground cannot be avoided entirely, but the walk is generally better in this respect than the direct route from Buttermere across the Moss. Try to do it in one hour.

ASCENT FROM BUTTERMERE
2100 feet of ascent
2½ miles

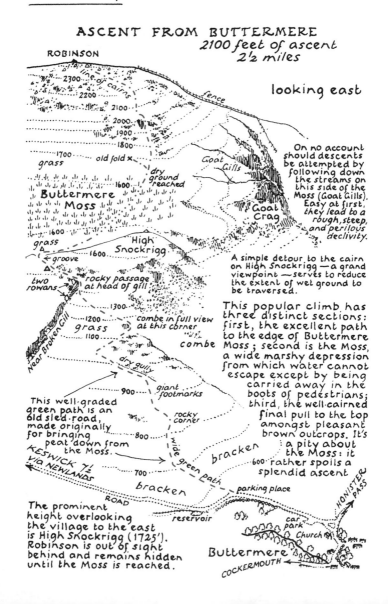

ROBINSON

2300 — line of cairns
2200
2100
2000
1900
1800
1700
grass   old fold ×
dry ground reached
1600
Buttermere Moss
Goat Gills
1600
grass   High Snockrigg
groove   1600
two rowans   rocky passage at head of gill
1300
1200   combe in full view at this corner
grass   1100
combe
Near Broken Gill
dry gully
900   giant footmarks
This well-graded green path is an old sled-road, made originally for bringing peat down from the Moss.
rocky corner
800
wide green path
KESWICK 7½ VIA NEWLANDS
700
bracken
ROAD
bracken   parking place
The prominent height overlooking the village to the east is High Snockrigg (1725'). Robinson is out of sight behind and remains hidden until the Moss is reached.
reservoir
car park   Church
Buttermere
COCKERMOUTH ←
HONISTER PASS
600

looking east

On no account should descents be attempted by following down the streams on this side of the Moss (Goat Gills). Easy at first, they lead to a rough, steep, and perilous declivity.

Goat Crag

A simple detour to the cairn on High Snockrigg — a grand viewpoint — serves to reduce the extent of wet ground to be traversed.

This popular climb has three distinct sections: first, the excellent path to the edge of Buttermere Moss; second is the Moss, a wide marshy depression from which water cannot escape except by being carried away in the boots of pedestrians; third, the well-cairned final pull to the top amongst pleasant brown outcrops. It's a pity about the Moss: it rather spoils a splendid ascent

ASCENT FROM HASSNESS
1900 feet of ascent : 1½ miles

ROBINSON

This approach was little used until it was shown as a right of way on the footpath map at Buttermere (and later on Ordnance Survey maps); now there is a path most of the way, and stiles have been provided where necessary.

looking north-east

2300
cairns grass
2200
route from Buttermere
2100
outcrops grass
2000
1900
1800

Buttermere Moss

The fence continues almost to the summit but to avoid wet ground ahead cross it here and ascend by a line of pleasant rocks. At the top of these a short traverse to the left leads to the usual cairned route from Buttermere.

stile
1700
grass
1600

1500
Goat Gills
1400
fall

Here the steepness ends and there is an open view ahead to the top.

1500

When the first edition of this book was prepared in 1964, the author noted that a young rowan tree had secured a precarious root-hold on this crag. He asked readers to let him know if it survived, and many did so. It became known as 'Wainwright's Rowan' and was still there in 2008.

1500
1400
1300
1200
1100
1000
900
800
700

Goat Crag

heather

weir

stile
1100
900
800
700

There are striking views here of the tremendous ravines of Goat Gills.

600

ROAD
Hassnesshow Beck
BUTTERMERE

In the first section the path follows the wall. Then the upper end of the wall is rounded, and the path doubles back to the left.

stile
500

A kissing gate at the point where fence and wall meet indicates the place to leave the road.

layby

lake **Hassness** → GATESGARTH ¾; HONISTER PASS

ASCENT FROM GATESGARTH
2050 feet of ascent : 3 miles

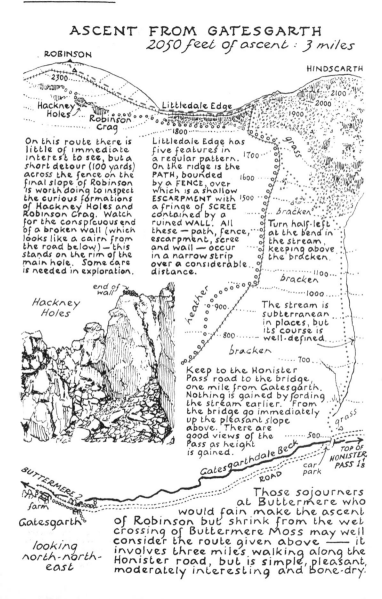

ROBINSON

2300

Hackney
Holes

Robinson
Crag

HINDSCARTH

Littledale Edge

2100
2000
1900

1800

1700

1600

1500

grass

bracken

On this route there is
little of immediate
interest to see, but a
short detour (100 yards)
across the fence on the
final slope of Robinson
is worth doing to inspect
the curious formations
of Hackney Holes and
Robinson Crag. Watch
for the conspicuous end
of a broken wall (which
looks like a cairn from
the road below) — this
stands on the rim of the
main hole. Some care
is needed in exploration.

Littledale Edge has
five features in
a regular pattern.
On the ridge is the
PATH, bounded
by a FENCE, over
which is a shallow
ESCARPMENT with
a fringe of SCREE
contained by a
ruined WALL. All
these — path, fence,
escarpment, scree
and wall — occur
in a narrow strip
over a considerable
distance.

Turn half-left
at the bend in
the stream,
keeping above
the bracken

1100
1000

bracken

Hackney
Holes

end of
wall

heather

900

800

bracken

700

The stream is
subterranean
in places, but
its course is
well-defined

Keep to the Honister
Pass road to the bridge,
one mile from Gatesgarth.
Nothing is gained by fording
the stream earlier. From
the bridge go immediately
up the pleasant slope
above. There are
good views of the
Pass as height
is gained.

grass

500

BUTTERMERE 2

farm

Gatesgarth

looking
north-north-
east

Gatesgarthdale Beck

car
park

ROAD

TOP OF
HONISTER
PASS 1⅛

Those sojourners
at Buttermere who
would fain make the ascent
of Robinson but shrink from the wet
crossing of Buttermere Moss may well
consider the route given above —— it
involves three miles walking along the
Honister road, but is simple, pleasant,
moderately interesting and bone-dry.

THE SUMMIT

Two long low outcrops of rock run parallel across the summit, the width of a road apart, almost like natural kerbstones or parapets — the westerly is slightly the higher and has the main cairn. The 'road' between is surfaced with loose stones. The top of the fell is a broad plateau with nothing of interest and no hazards.

DESCENTS : The descent to Newlands heads northeast, passing between two small tarns; after a third of a mile the ground steepens suddenly beyond a superior cairn. The Buttermere (direct) route goes off southwest: a cairn on a subsidiary summit indicates the direction to be taken.

In mist, the top is confusing and bad conditions may make it advisable to find the ridge-fence as a preliminary to descent. For Newlands, go left alongside the fence to the first depression, where turn down left into Little Dale. For Buttermere, if the usual track cannot be located, the fence is a good guide to the intake wall above Hassness, the last part being very steep and slippery, and having dangerous ground immediately to the right.

Moss Force,
Newlands Hause

Goat Gills, Hassness

THE VIEW

The broad, nearly-flat summit detracts from the quality of the view, but although the valleys are hidden the surround of fells is excellent. Honister Pass, with the motor road snaking over it, is an interesting feature. It is odd to find Scafell Pike's towering summit for once missing from a view, especially as all its satellites are there in force : the Pike is exactly covered by the top of Great Gable, but its south-west slope going down to the gap of Mickledore is clearly visible. Robinson is one of the few fells that has the shy Floutern Tarn in its sights.

Principal Fells

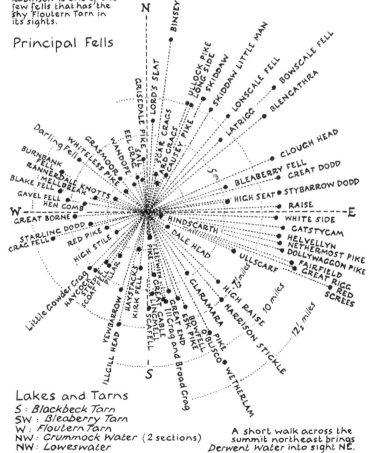

Lakes and Tarns

S : *Blackbeck Tarn*
SW : *Bleaberry Tarn*
W : *Floutern Tarn*
NW : *Crummock Water* (2 sections)
NW : *Loweswater*

A short walk across the summit northeast brings *Derwent Water* into sight NE.

RIDGE ROUTE

To HINDSCARTH, 2385′: 1½ miles: S, ESE and NNE
Depression at 1880′: 520 feet of ascent
A linking of two lateral spurs

Little Dale lies deeply between the two summits and can only be circumvented by using the fenced ridge to the south. It is customary to bear left in the depression and cut across to the summit. An alternative is to remain on the ridge beyond the depression and turn left at the top of the rise.

The north-east ridge of Robinson, from Scope End

Sail

2536'

Braithwaite
CRISEDALE ▲ PIKE
                                    Stair
GRASMOOR   SAIL
         ▲   ▲   CAUSEY
         EEL   PIKE
         CRAG   ▲
                 ARD CRAGS

● Buttermere

MILES
0   1   2   3   4

from Sail Beck

NATURAL FEATURES

Sail is the least obtrusive of the 2500-footers, being completely dominated by its vaster and more rugged neighbour, Eel Crag, and an absence of attractive or interesting features adds to its inferiority complex.

Sail is, however, an unavoidable obstacle on the way to or from the bigger fell by the fine east ridge rooted in Newlands, and the well-trodden path to its summit is invariably used for this purpose and not with Sail as the main object of the walk; indeed, the path does not even trouble to visit the cairn. The flanks of the fell are steep, excessively so to the south, above Sail Beck, with much scree and heather; northwards they fall more gently to Coledale, where, low down, they are traversed by the rising path from Force Crag Mine.

MAP

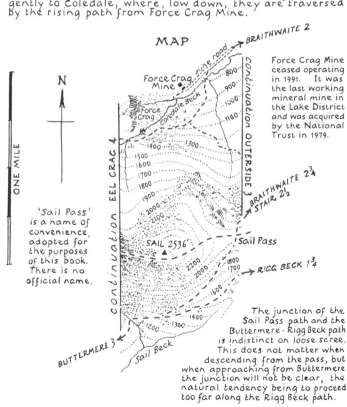

Force Crag Mine ceased operating in 1991. It was the last working mineral mine in the Lake District and was acquired by the National Trust in 1979.

'Sail Pass' is a name of convenience, adopted for the purposes of this book. There is no official name.

ONE MILE

N

The junction of the Sail Pass path and the Buttermere-Rigg Beck path is indistinct on loose scree. This does not matter when descending from the pass, but when approaching from Buttermere the junction will not be clear, the natural tendency being to proceed too far along the Rigg Beck path.

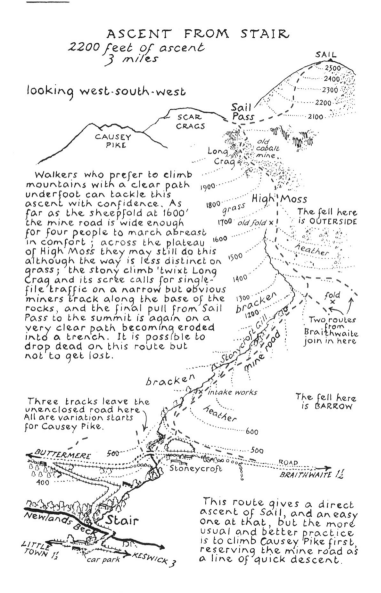

ASCENT FROM STAIR
2200 feet of ascent
3 miles

looking west·south·west

SAIL
2500
2400
2300
2200
2100

Sail Pass

SCAR CRAGS

CAUSEY PIKE

Long Crag

old cobalt mine

High Moss

Walkers who prefer to climb mountains with a clear path underfoot can tackle this ascent with confidence. As far as the sheepfold at 1600' the mine road is wide enough for four people to march abreast in comfort; across the plateau of High Moss they may still do this although the way is less distinct on grass; the stony climb 'twixt Long Crag and its scree calls for single-file traffic on a narrow but obvious miners track along the base of the rocks, and the final pull from Sail Pass to the summit is again on a very clear path becoming eroded into a trench. It is possible to drop dead on this route but not to get lost.

1900
1800 grass
1700 old fold x
1600
1500
1400
1300 bracken
1200

The fell here is OUTSIDE

heather

fold x

Two routes from Braithwaite join in here

Stonycroft Gill

mine road

bracken

intake works

heather

The fell here is BARROW

Three tracks leave the unenclosed road here All are variation starts for Causey Pike.

600
500

BUTTERMERE 500

400

Stoneycroft

ROAD

BRAITHWAITE 1½

Newlands Beck

Stair

LITTLE TOWN 1½   car park   KESWICK 3

This route gives a direct ascent of Sail, and an easy one at that, but the more usual and better practice is to climb Causey Pike first, reserving the mine road as a line of quick descent.

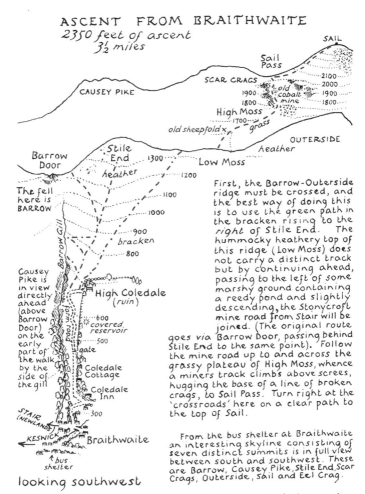

ASCENT FROM BRAITHWAITE
2350 feet of ascent
3½ miles

SAIL

Sail Pass

SCAR CRAGS — old cobalt mine — 2100 / 2000 / 1900 / 1800

CAUSEY PIKE — 1900 / 1800

High Moss — 1700 — grass

old sheepfold ×

OUTERSIDE — heather

Barrow Door

Stile End — 1300 — Low Moss

heather — 1200

The fell here is BARROW — 1100

1000

900 — bracken

800

Barrow Gill

Causey Pike is in view directly ahead (above Barrow Door) on the early part of the walk by the side of the gill

High Coledale (ruin)

600 — covered reservoir

500 — gate

Coledale Cottage

Coledale Inn

STAIR (NEWLANDS)

300

KESWICK

Braithwaite

↑ bus shelter

looking southwest

First, the Barrow-Outerside ridge must be crossed, and the best way of doing this is to use the green path in the bracken rising to the *right* of Stile End. The hummocky heathery top of this ridge (Low Moss) does not carry a distinct track but by continuing ahead, passing to the left of some marshy ground containing a reedy pond and slightly descending, the Stonycroft mine road from Stair will be joined. (The original route goes via Barrow Door, passing behind Stile End to the same point). Follow the mine road up to and across the grassy plateau of High Moss, whence a miners track climbs above screes, hugging the base of a line of broken crags, to Sail Pass. Turn right at the 'crossroads' here on a clear path to the top of Sail.

From the bus shelter at Braithwaite an interesting skyline consisting of seven distinct summits is in full view between south and southwest. These are Barrow, Causey Pike, Stile End, Scar Crags, Outerside, Sail and Eel Crag.

This route coincides with that from Stair beyond a subsidiary ridge linking Barrow and Outerside, but is more attractive initially, being easier to the feet and having wider views. All gradients are moderate and this is the simplest way of getting a high footing on the Coledale 'horse-shoe' from Braithwaite.

THE SUMMIT

SWIRL HOW • BOWFELL • ESK PIKE • GREAT END • ILL Crag • Broad Crag • SCAFELL PIKE • SCAFELL

Esk Hause • GREAT GABLE • ROBINSON

Robinson Crags

The summit, a rounded dome of heather and mosses, has nothing of immediate interest, and the much-trodden path across the top does not even trouble to visit the small cairn 25 yards distant.

DESCENTS: Join the path and go down to Sail Pass, where either continue over Scar Crags and on to Causey Pike, or turn left along the mine road, for Stair, Newlands.

RIDGE ROUTES

The ridge to Eel Crag

To EEL CRAG, 2749': ⅔ mile : W
Depression at 2430'
320 feet of ascent

An easy drop of 100' to the connecting depression (which is not a pass) is the prelude to an exhilarating climb up a narrow crest with two rocky rises, to the broad top of Eel Crag. Here the path (which has been clear throughout) fades away, but the summit is close at hand and reached by bearing half-right.

To SCAR CRAGS, 2205': ¾ mile : ENE
Depression (Sail Pass) at 2046'
160 feet of ascent

A long swinging downhill walk on a path so well-worn that it can be seen distinctly from Keswick leads to Sail Pass (right for Buttermere, left for Stair and Braithwaite) whence the long flat top of Scar Crags is quickly reached up the opposite slope.

EEL CRAG ▲△ — 2300 — SAIL ▲△ — 2100 — Sail Pass — 2100 — SCAR CRAGS ▲△ — 2000

N

ONE MILE

THE VIEW

Few walkers will hesitate long over this panorama, with the better viewpoint of Eel Crag so near (or just visited), but those who cannot go a step further without a rest may settle down to enjoy what is really a very fine prospect, although unbalanced by the disproportionate bulk of Eel Crag filling the western sky.

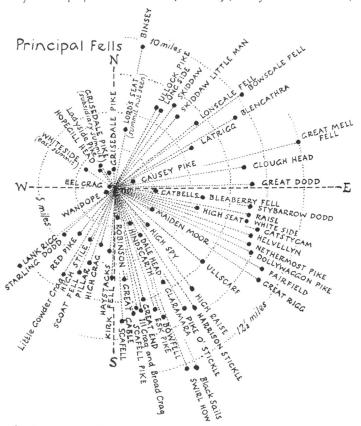

Principal Fells

Lakes and Tarns
NNE: *Bassenthwaite Lake* and *Over Water*
ENE: *Derwent Water* } in view 10 yards from the cairn.
SSW: *Buttermere*
SSW: *Bleaberry Tarn*   EE: *Blea Tarn (Ullscarf)*

Sale Fell

1178'

from the Wythop valley

Embleton
●

Dubwath
●

Wythop
Mill ●

▲ SALE FELL

LING ▲
FELL

● Beck
Wythop

BROOM ▲
FELL

▲ LORD'S
SEAT

● High
Lorton

Thornthwaite ●

MILES

0   1   2   3

NATURAL FEATURES

Sale Fell is the extreme corner-stone of the North Western Fells, with an outlook ranging far across the west Cumbrian plain to the Scottish coast. It is a familiar sight on the busy Keswick-Workington road, of which it has an oversight for several miles; going west along this road, Sale Fell marks the end of Lakeland.

It is a pleasant eminence of low altitude, not remarkable in itself (although of some interest to geologists) and its main attraction to walkers will be as an easy promenade providing an aerial survey of the hidden Wythop valley. The fell is grassy, with bracken, but the eastern slopes, going down sharply to Bassenthwaite Lake, are within the boundary of Thornthwaite Forest, and thickly planted. This is an old part of the forest, long known as Wythop Wood, and there is a welcome blend of its natural growth of deciduous trees with the more-favoured evergreens introduced commercially in the twentieth century.

There is a significance in the name of the olde hostelry, the Pheasant Inn, at the foot of the fell. At one time this neighbourhood was actively engaged in the rearing of game birds and there were pheasantries at Lothwaite Side and in the Wood itself.

One very delightful feature of Wythop Wood is the presence of the lovely little roe deer, shyest of creatures. The new plantations are fenced off against them, but they have freedom to roam in the older woodlands, and the men of the Forestry Commission deserve a very good mark for tolerating and harbouring these gentle animals in their preserves.

Baby roe deer

born to be free? or to be hunted and snared and shot by brave sportsmen?

Roe buck

The Wythop Valley

The name is pronounced *With-up* locally. This quiet valley, almost unknown to Lakeland's visitors, is unique, not moulded at all to the usual pattern, a geographical freak.

The opening into it at Wythop Mill, between Sale Fell and Ling Fell, is so narrow and so embowered in trees that it might well pass without notice but for a signpost indicating a byway to Wythop Hall. Following this through a richly-wooded dell, the view up the valley opens suddenly beyond the farm of Eskin to reveal a lofty mountain directly ahead a few miles distant — a sight to stop explorers in their tracks. Of course all valleys run up into hills ..... but what can this towering height be ?.... Hearts quicken .... have we discovered an unknown 3000' peak? Wainwright's map on page 8 indicates no mountain ahead.... Get out a *decent* map, the Ordnance Survey one-inch — and the truth slowly dawns ..... why, of course ....it's dear old Skiddaw, of course, not immediately recognisable from this angle ...... But how odd! What an illusion! The valley certainly *appears* to lead directly to the mountain, *but*, completely out of sight and unsuspected from this viewpoint, the wide trench containing Bassenthwaite Lake profoundly interrupts the rising contours in the line of vision. The fact is that the Wythop valley, like all others, has hills along both sides, but instead of the normal steepening of ground at its head there occurs a sharp declivity to another (and major) valley system, the Derwent, occupied here by the unseen lake with Skiddaw rising from its far shore. The Wythop valley, elevated 600 feet above that of the Derwent, drains *away* from it, and the unobtrusive watershed (a meeting of green pastures and dark forest) may therefore be likened to a pass. The whole arrangement is unusual and remarkable.

SALE FELL · Wythop Wood · line of sight · SKIDDAW · the floor of the valley · Bassenthwaite Lake

Having described the valley as a freak, it is important to say also, and emphasise, that its scenery is in no way freakish. *Here is a charming and secluded natural sanctuary in an idyllic setting, a place of calm,* where a peaceful farming community husband the good earth now as for centuries past. Every rod, pole and perch of it is delightful and unspoilt. Motorcars can penetrate as far as Wythop Hall but happily are unaware of this. The valley is undisturbed and quiet; red squirrels can still be seen. There are five scattered farmsteads and, at the head, Wythop Hall, rich in story and legend. In days gone by the valley maintained a larger population and a church.

The Wythop Valley

The Great Illusion
(see opposite page)

Looking up the Wythop Valley to Skiddaw, from the slopes of Ling Fell. The furthest line of trees marks the end of the valley and Skiddaw rises beyond the unseen Bass Lake.

In this view from Lord's Seat, the Wythop Valley is seen sloping up gently from the left to the plantations of Wythop Wood, which fall steeply to Bass Lake. The distant hill on the right is Binsey.

Ladies Table

In Wythop Wood

Ladies Table is a little peak at the head of the Wythop Valley above the declivity to Bassenthwaite Lake and within the forest boundary. Now wooded to the top at 950', it has lost its former reputation as a viewpoint. A flat boulder, probably used by Victorian picnickers, may have given the place its name, but more likely it is a gentle parody on Lord's Seat nearby.

All the paths in this area are completely overgrown or blocked by trees, and a visit is not recommended. The place is forgotten and only the name remains.

In the woodlands to the west of Ladies Table are numbered nesting boxes and life-size models of deer and peacocks.

The Walton Memorial

Perched on the edge of a crag in the heart of the forest, with a splendid vista of Skiddaw, is a memorial seat in native green stone, with a tablet inscribed " Thornthwaite Forest. In memory of WILFRED WALTON, Head Forester 1948-1959. In appreciation."

looking southwest

Putting out pipes and cigarettes, follow the forest paths from the cottages as indicated, watching for the first turn left in 250 yards. Don't let the children go on ahead : DANGER!

Looking across the Wythop Valley to Lord's Seat, from Lothwaite

Lothwaite is the eastern shoulder of Sale Fell. A grassy alp, it is a pleasant sheep pasture and in summer is a floral garden. Apart from a solitary boulder it is featureless. It gives its name to the farmstead of Lothwaite Side. The suffix 'thwaite' is unusual for an open upland.

MAP

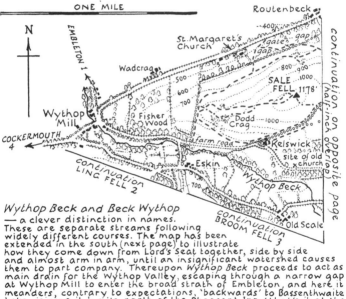

At the side of a public bridleway beyond Kelswick is the crumbled masonry of a small building that would be passed without notice but for a tablet inscribed SITE OF WYTHOP OLD CHURCH against the inner wall. (On Ordnance maps it is indicated by 'Chapel — Remains of'.)

This old church has been replaced by a new one — St. Margarets — on the road between Wythop Mill and Routenbeck, but once a year a public service (necessarily open-air) is held in or near the ruins.

St. Margarets

Wythop Beck and Beck Wythop

— a clever distinction in names. These are separate streams following widely different courses. The map has been extended in the south (next page) to illustrate how they come down from Lord's Seat together, side by side and almost arm in arm, until an insignificant watershed causes them to part company. Thereupon *Wythop Beck* proceeds to act as main drain for the Wythop Valley, escaping through a narrow gap at Wythop Mill to enter the broad strath of Embleton, and here it meanders, contrary to expectations, 'backwards' to Bassenthwaite Lake, joining it ¼ mile north of the Pheasant Inn (that's it at the top of the map, next page) after a circular tour around the base of Sale Fell. *Beck Wythop* has a much briefer passage, falling rapidly in its wooded gorge to join Bass Lake at Beck Wythop cottages.

Failure of an Enterprise

There is a story behind the ruins on the edge of the wood (south of Wythop Hall, map next page). Here are substantial foundations of buildings, and it is a great surprise to find them in so remote a place and in such rural surroundings. In the 1930's modern plant was installed here for the manufacture of silica bricks, a mineral railway laid, the road to Wythop Hall improved and re-routed and scores of workmen engaged. The product was not of sufficiently good quality. The buildings and plant were dismantled and taken away, the men dismissed and the site vacated. Today only the road-extension to Wythop Hall remains in use.

MAP

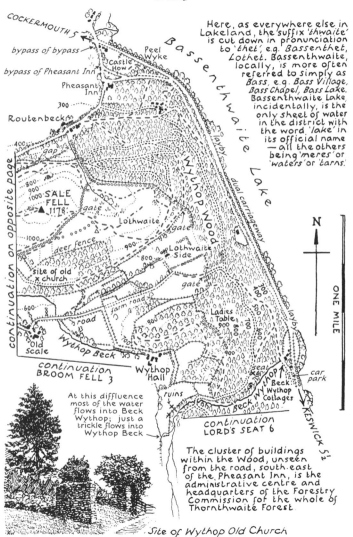

COCKERMOUTH 5

bypass of bypass

bypass of Pheasant Inn

Pheasant Inn

300

Routenbeck

400

gap

800
900
1000
SALE FELL 1178

gate

Lothwaite

1000

deer fence

site of old church

600

Old scale

road

farm road

Wythop Beck

continuation BROOM FELL 3

Wythop Hall

ruins

At this diffluence most of the water flows into Beck Wythop; just a trickle flows into Wythop Beck

Peel Wyke

Castle How

Bassenthwaite Lake

Wythop Wood

layby

dual carriageway

gate

Lothwaite Side

800
900

gate

Ladies Table
900

800

700

seat

300

700
600
900

layby

Beck Wythop Cottages

car park

N

ONE MILE

KESWICK 5½

continuation LORD'S SEAT 6

Here, as everywhere else in Lakeland, the suffix 'thwaite' is cut down in pronunciation to 'thet', e.g. Bassenthet, Lothet. Bassenthwaite, locally, is more often referred to simply as Bass, e.g. Bass Village, Bass Chapel, Bass Lake. Bassenthwaite Lake, incidentally, is the only sheet of water in the district with the word 'lake' in its official name — all the others being 'meres' or 'waters' or 'tarns'.

continuation on opposite page

The cluster of buildings within the Wood, unseen from the road, south-east of the Pheasant Inn, is the administrative centre and headquarters of the Forestry Commission for the whole of Thornthwaite Forest.

Site of Wythop Old Church

ASCENT FROM THE PHEASANT INN
930 feet of ascent : 2 miles

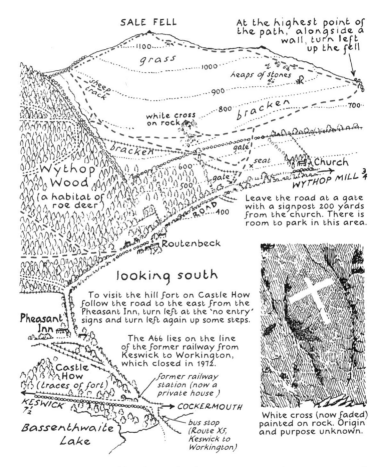

SALE FELL

At the highest point of the path, alongside a wall, turn left up the fell

1100

grass

1000

heaps of stones

sheep track

900

white cross on rock

800

bracken

700

bracken

Wythop Wood
(a habitat of roe deer)

gate

seat

Church

600

gate

WYTHOP MILL ¾

500

Leave the road at a gate with a signpost 200 yards from the church. There is room to park in this area.

ROAD

400

Routenbeck

looking south

To visit the hill fort on Castle How follow the road to the east from the Pheasant Inn, turn left at the 'no entry' signs and turn left again up some steps.

Pheasant Inn

The A66 lies on the line of the former railway from Keswick to Workington, which closed in 1972.

Castle How
(traces of fort)

former railway station (now a private house)

KESWICK 7½

← COCKERMOUTH

Bassenthwaite Lake

bus stop (Route X5, Keswick to Workington)

White cross (now faded) painted on rock. Origin and purpose unknown.

A pleasant little climb. Make a traverse of the fell by using both routes; preferably that on the left for ascent, that on the right as a way down. The round journey can be done in an hour from the gate at the roadside. Good views.

ASCENT FROM WYTHOP MILL
750 feet of ascent : 1½ miles

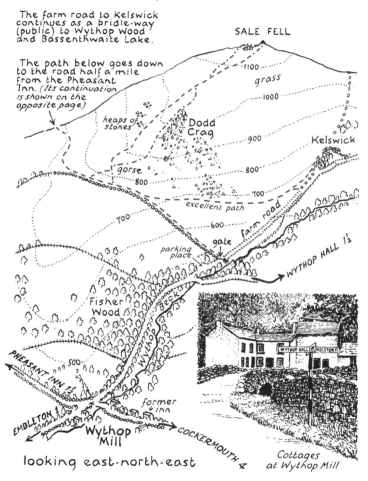

The farm road to Kelswick
continues as a bridle-way
(public) to Wythop Wood
and Bassenthwaite Lake.

The path below goes down
to the road half a mile
from the Pheasant
Inn. (Its continuation
is shown on the
opposite page)

SALE FELL

1100

grass

1000

heaps of
stones

Dodd
Crag

900

Kelswick

gorse

800

800

700

excellent path

farm road

700

600

gate

parking
place

farm road

WYTHOP HALL 1½

Fisher
Wood

WYTHOP BECK

WYTHOP HALL EMBLETON

PHEASANT INN 1½

500

former
inn

EMBLETON 1

Wythop
Mill

COCKERMOUTH

looking east-north-east

Cottages
at Wythop Mill

A sylvan approach gives added pleasure to this
simple climb. As an introduction to the Wythop
Valley (an introduction warmly to be commended)
this route is excellent and instructive.

THE SUMMIT

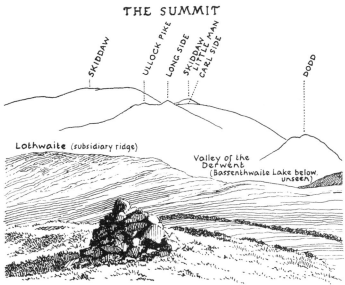

SKIDDAW ULLOCK PIKE LONG SIDE SKIDDAW LITTLE MAN CARL SIDE DODD

Lothwaite (subsidiary ridge)

Valley of the Derwent
(Bassenthwaite Lake below, unseen)

The top is a pleasant grassy pasture populated by sheep
but unfrequented by man — which makes it a desirable
objective on a summers day for anyone who would like
to visit a summit for quiet meditation without, however,
incurring the expenditure of much energy on the ascent.

For ordinary mortals there is nothing of interest in the vicinity of
the cairn, but visitors with geological knowledge might add to it
by doing a little exploring. John Postlethwaite's excellent *Mines
and Mining in the Lake District* contains this impressive paragraph:—
"Near the summit of *Sale Fell*, there is a small mass of very beautiful
rock. It consists of a pink crystalline felspathic base, in which there are
numerous crystals of dark-green mica.   The base is chiefly composed of
orthoclase, but some triclinic, probably oligoclase, is also present. There
is no quartz visible to the naked eye, but small crystals may be detected
under the microscope. There is also a little hornblende present. The rock
is very hard and tough, and in lithological character is unlike any other
rock in the Lake Country."   (with acknowledgments)
 All this is Greek to the poor layman, and he would be no wiser after an
inspection of three possible sites: (1) a rockface in view from the cairn,
(2) a collection of upstanding boulders,
and (3) a scattering of 'white' stones,
although he might notice that some of
the latter appear to have been chipped
by hammers. There is no other rock in
sight, and one of these must be Mr. P's
'small mass', but, in spite of his liberal
detail, which? What is 'orthoclase'? Or,
worse still, 'oligoclase'? Resuming his
meditations at the cairn after this abortive tour, let him now reflect
on the poverty of his education. How much there is to learn about
this fair earth and how little we know! How much beauty is never seen!

stones

boulders   grass

rockface

N

100 YARDS

THE VIEW

The Skiddaw group is the best thing in the view, the top being displayed, not as the usual pyramid but as a long, level skyline. The Helvellyn range is also well seen as a tremendous wall running across the district, but elsewhere the prospect towards Lakeland is disappointing, the higher Lord's Seat nearby concealing the mountains of the interior. The Wythop valley below is very pleasant, a restful hollow of woodlands and green fields. Criffell is conspicuous on a Scottish horizon extending west to the hills of Galloway.

Lakes and Tarns
NE : Bassenthwaite Lake

Principal Fells

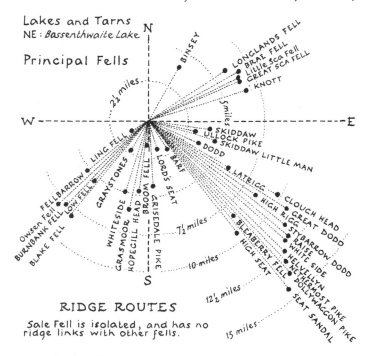

RIDGE ROUTES

Sale Fell is isolated, and has no ridge links with other fells.

A note for sheep fanciers:

The oldest strain of sheep in Lakeland is the Herdwick, a small, ragged but very hardy breed, tough enough to winter on the tops, and producer of the best mutton. Latterly, the Swaledale and the Rough Fell varieties, bigger animals with a heavier crop of wool but needing the shelter of the valleys in winter, have been increasingly introduced. The sheep on Sale Fell used to be a cross between Herdwick and Swaledale, combining the best qualities of each — but only in half-measure.

Scar Crags

the eastern ridge

Scar Crags is the big brother of Causey Pike, topping the latter by 115 feet, but it is the lesser height that captures the fancy, that provides the challenge, that steals the picture and is the better known by far. Scar Crags continues the line of the ridge towards Eel Crag, and does so in rather striking fashion, having a ragged edge of broken heathery crag throughout its length, and, below, an excessively rough slope falls steeply to Rigg Beck. There is a regular and recurring pattern of arete and gully on this southern face, as though the fellside had been scraped by a giant comb: an effect best seen from Ard Crags directly opposite. The north flank has nothing of interest; once however it was the scene of unusual industrial activity, Lakeland's only cobalt mine being situated here in the stony amphitheatre of Long Crag.

West of the summit, the fell drops gently to Sail Pass, a useful crossing between Braithwaite and Buttermere for travellers on foot.

Braithwaite

▲ GRISEDALE PIKE

Stair
●

EEL
CRAG
▲

▲ ▲ CAUSEY
      PIKE
SCAR CRAGS

MILES

0   1   2   3

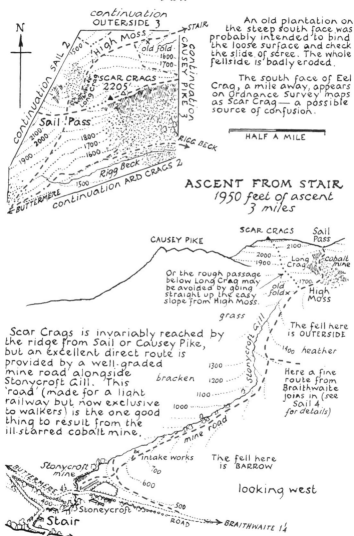

MAP

continuation
OUTSIDE 3

High Moss

SCAR CRAGS
2205'

Sail Pass

Rigg Beck

An old plantation on the steep south face was probably intended to bind the loose surface and check the slide of scree. The whole fellside is badly eroded.

The south face of Eel Crag, a mile away, appears on Ordnance Survey maps as Scar Crag — a possible source of confusion.

HALF A MILE

ASCENT FROM STAIR
1950 feet of ascent
3 miles

CAUSEY PIKE

SCAR CRAGS

Sail Pass

Long Crag

cobalt mine

High Moss

Or the rough passage below Long Crag may be avoided by going straight up the easy slope from High Moss.

The fell here is OUTSIDE

Here a fine route from Braithwaite joins in (see Sail 4 for details)

Scar Crags is invariably reached by the ridge from Sail or Causey Pike, but an excellent direct route is provided by a well-graded mine road alongside Stonycroft Gill. This 'road' (made for a light railway but now exclusive to walkers) is the one good thing to result from the ill-starred cobalt mine.

The fell here is BARROW

Stonycroft mine

Stair

looking west

BRAITHWAITE 1¼

THE SUMMIT

looking down to Causey Pike

Unexpectedly the top is flat, and there is no obvious sign of the double breaking wave formed by the summit-outline as seen from the Keswick area, although this can be identified after a study of the ground. There is a cairn on the highest point and a second cairn fifty yards away to the east. The top is grassy.

DESCENTS: It is usual to descend by the ridge, *via* Causey Pike, but simpler and quicker to go down the north slope (no path) to join the Stonycroft mine road. The south slope is impossible.

RIDGE ROUTES

To SAIL, 2536': ¾ mile : WSW
Depression (Sail Pass) at 2046'
500 feet of ascent
Sail is the next unavoidable obstacle on the ridge to Eel Crag, and calls for a long pull beyond Sail Pass (a walkers' crossroads) on a very distinct path.

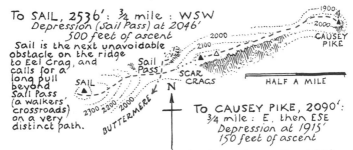

To CAUSEY PIKE, 2090':
¾ mile : E, then ESE
Depression at 1915'
150 feet of ascent

Keeping the steep edge on the right hand, a pleasant track leads down to a depression, beyond which is a short climb and a switchback journey over the several bumps of Causey Pike to the last one.

THE VIEW

The view is good, but its detail is not so well composed as in the panorama from the neighbouring Causey Pike, while the advantage in altitude contributes little extra to the scene; in particular the valley and lake scenery between north and east is less satisfactory. The mountain picture is inspiring, however, especially to the south, and close by in the west the head of Coledale is very well displayed. The more intimate peep downwards to Rigg Beck from the edge of the crags near at hand should not be omitted.

Principal Fells

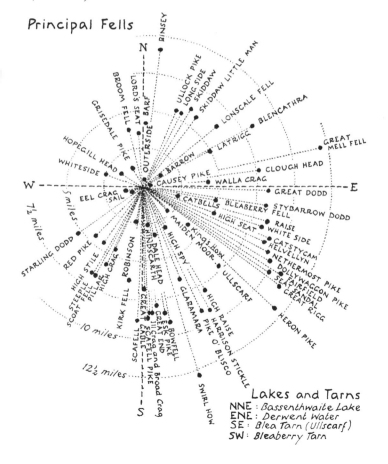

Lakes and Tarns

NNE : *Bassenthwaite Lake*
ENE : *Derwent Water*
SE : *Blea Tarn (Ullscarf)*
SW : *Bleaberry Tarn*

Wandope 2533'

GRASMOOR ▲   ▲ EEL CRAG

WANDOPE ▲
        ▲ WHITELESS PIKE
● Rannerdale

● Buttermere

MILES

0   1   2   3

from Whiteless Crags

NATURAL FEATURES

There is no mountain not worth climbing, and any summit above the magic figure of 2,500 feet might be expected to attract fellwalkers and peakbaggers in large numbers. To some extent Wandope does this, but only because the top almost gets in the way of a popular triangular tour based on Buttermere — Whiteless Pike, Eel Crag, Grasmoor — and the cairn is visited almost as a matter of course (if indeed it is noticed at all) and by the simplest of detours.   The other three, too, feature more prominently in the landscape and are often climbed individually as sole objectives — but rarely Wandope, which is sandwiched between neighbours and too hidden to attract separate attention.   In fact, Wandope is only well seen from the uninhabited valley of Sail Beck, from which it rises in a mile-long wall rimmed a thousand feet above by a line of shattered crags.   The hinterland of the summit is an upland prairie dominated by Grasmoor and Eel Crag, and it is along here that most walkers pass, often without realising that the insignificant swell of grass on the eastern fringe is distinguished both by a name and an altitude above the 2500' contour.

Wandope might be expected to stand out more conspicuously from the greater mass behind, for it is partly severed by two gills which drain from the plateau and immediately form, on either side, deeply carved rifts, one a scree-choked ravine, the other a profound hollow.   These are Third Gill, south, and Addacomb Gill, north, and both go down to Sail Beck. The first is a place to avoid, the second a place to visit or at least look at from the rim of its crater: the profound cwm is Addacomb Hole, a perfect example of a hanging valley, quite the finest in Lakeland, and a remarkable specimen of natural sculpturing. The issuing stream has high waterfalls and the whole scene is a complete geography lesson without words.   Wandope is also a feeder of Rannerdale Beck.

As for the name, old-timers surely approved the Ordnance Survey's decision to abandon Wanlope (for which good authority was claimed) and revert to the name by which so many generations of Lakeland walkers have known the fell.

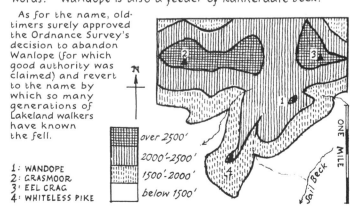

1: WANDOPE
2: GRASMOOR
3: EEL CRAG
4: WHITELESS PIKE

over 2500'
2000'-2500'
1500'-2000'
below 1500'

ONE MILE

Sail Beck

The Addacomb Ridge,
from Sail Beck

The Thirdgill Ridge,
from Whiteless Breast

MAP

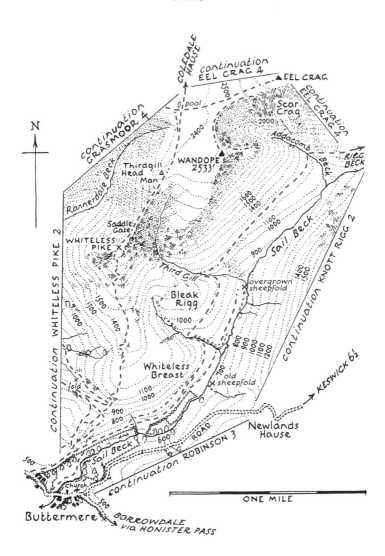

ONE MILE

ASCENT FROM BUTTERMERE
via THIRD GILL

2250 feet of ascent
2¼ miles

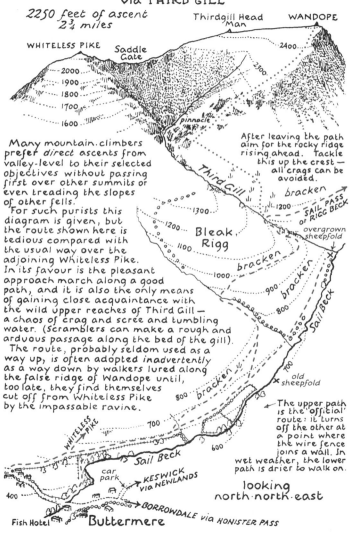

Thirdgill Head Man

WANDOPE

WHITELESS PIKE

Saddle Gate

2400

2000
1900
1800
1700
1600

2200

pinnacle

After leaving the path aim for the rocky ridge rising ahead. Tackle this up the crest — all crags can be avoided.

Third Gill

bracken

1300

1200

SAIL PASS or RIGG BECK

Bleak Rigg

1200

overgrown sheepfold

1100

bracken

1000

bracken

Sail Beck

900

800

Many mountain climbers prefer *direct* ascents from valley-level to their selected objectives without passing first over other summits or even treading the slopes of other fells.

For such purists this diagram is given, but the route shown here is tedious compared with the usual way over the adjoining Whiteless Pike. In its favour is the pleasant approach march along a good path, and it is also the only means of gaining close acquaintance with the wild upper reaches of Third Gill — a chaos of crag and scree and tumbling water. (Scramblers can make a rough and arduous passage along the bed of the gill).

The route, probably seldom used as a way up, is often adopted *inadvertently* as a way down by walkers lured along the false ridge of Wandope until, too late, they find themselves cut off from Whiteless Pike by the impassable ravine.

bracken

800

old sheepfold

700

WHITELESS PIKE

700

bracken

600

Sail Beck

car park

KESWICK via NEWLANDS

BORROWDALE via HONISTER PASS

The upper path is the 'official' route: it turns off the other at a point where the wire fence joins a wall. In wet weather, the lower path is drier to walk on.

looking north-north-east

400

Fish Hotel

Buttermere

ASCENT FROM BUTTERMERE
via THE ADDACOMB RIDGE

2250 feet of ascent
3½ miles

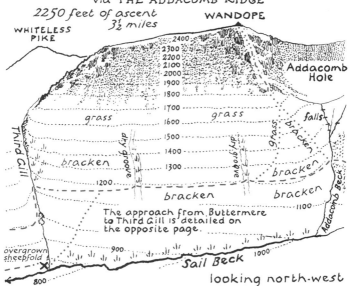

WHITELESS PIKE

WANDOPE

Addacomb Hole

2400
2300
2200
2100
2000
1900
1800
1700
1600
1500
1400
1300
1200

grass

grass

grass

falls

bracken

bracken

old groove

old groove

bracken

bracken

bracken

Third Gill

1100

Addacomb Beck

The approach from Buttermere to Third Gill is detailed on the opposite page.

overgrown sheepfold

900

1000

800

Sail Beck

looking north-west

The path across the breast is part of the through-route from Buttermere to Rigg Beck, Newlands — a grand walkers' way among the hills, avoiding the motor road. A branch goes over Sail Pass to link with Braithwaite.

From the place where the path crosses Addacomb Beck go left straight up the ridge (here ill-defined), or, to avoid overmuch bracken, cut the corner from the second of two rushy grooves. When the first rocks are reached the ridge becomes narrower and a thin track climbs up through heather and bilberry and sundry Alpine flora, with Addacomb Hole sinking ever lower on the right. This section of the ridge is excellent and the route continues first-class to the top, which is reached exactly at the summit-cairn.

If using this route in reverse (or travelling to Buttermere from Newlands by the path) pedestrians hurrying to catch a bus, or desperate for a pint, can save ten minutes by dropping down to the sheepfold at Third Gill and using the lower (straighter) path.

The great feature of this route, apart from the ridge itself (the upper half of which is delightful) is Addacomb Hole — a perfect hanging valley. Only by the gradual gaining of height along the ridge can the proportions of this remarkable half-crater be fully appreciated.

ASCENT FROM BUTTERMERE
2300 feet of ascent : 2½ miles

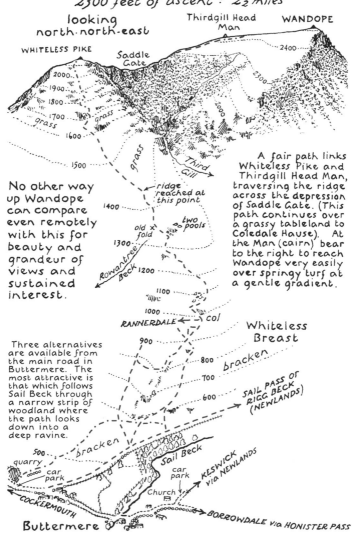

looking
north-north-east

Thirdgill Head Man

WANDOPE

WHITELESS PIKE

Saddle Gate

2400

2000
1900
1800
1700
grass
1600

grass

2100

grass

2000

1500

Third Gill

ridge reached at this point

1400

old fold ✕

two pools

1300

Rowantree Beck 1200

1100

1000

RANNERDALE

col

900

Whiteless Breast

800

bracken

700

SAIL PASS or RIGG BECK (NEWLANDS)

600

No other way up Wandope can compare even remotely with this for beauty and grandeur of views and sustained interest.

A fair path links Whiteless Pike and Thirdgill Head Man, traversing the ridge across the depression of Saddle Gate. (This path continues over a grassy tableland to Coledale Hause). At the Man (cairn) bear to the right to reach Wandope very easily over springy turf at a gentle gradient.

Three alternatives are available from the main road in Buttermere. The most attractive is that which follows Sail Beck through a narrow strip of woodland where the path looks down into a deep ravine.

500

quarry

car park

bracken

bracken

Sail Beck

car park

KESWICK via NEWLANDS

Church

COCKERMOUTH

Buttermere

BORROWDALE via HONISTER PASS

THE SUMMIT

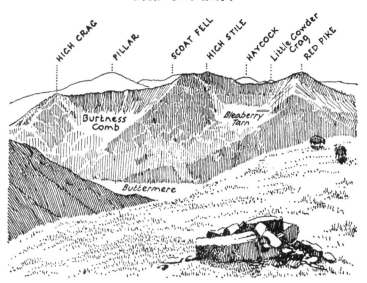

HIGH CRAG — PILLAR — SCOAT FELL — HIGH STILE — HAYCOCK — Little Cowder Crag — RED PIKE

Burtness Comb

Bleaberry Tarn

Buttermere

Apart from the view, the summit is unremarkable, being a smooth grassy parade kept neat and trim by grazing sheep. The stones of the cairn, which stands near the brink of the great downfall to Sail Beck, were obviously not provided by the summit itself, and some anonymous enthusiast must, in days gone by, have laboured mightily in bringing them up from the escarpment.

DESCENTS: The quickest way down (for Buttermere) is by the steepening southern slope, keeping the edge of the craggy east face close on the left until the ground falls more abruptly to Third Gill. There are crags below, which can be avoided, but it is best to break out of them to the left to a grassy slope, which can be followed down to join the Sail Beck path for Buttermere. If time permits, the Addacomb ridge should be preferred — this is useful also for Newlands — or the valley may be reached by a detour over Whiteless Pike, this being the usual course. In mist the Addacomb ridge is least likely to lead to trouble.

For destinations north, there is a very fast descent via Coledale Hause to Braithwaite in 1½ hours.

N

COLEDALE HAUSE (for Braithwaite)

ADDACOMB RIDGE (for Buttermere or Newlands)

WHITELESS PIKE (for Buttermere)

SAIL BECK (for Buttermere)

Third Gill

THE VIEW

Pride of place in the view must be conceded to the Scafells, from here looking magnificent, but scarcely less impressive is the scene eastwards, where range after range of tall fells cross the line of vision to culminate finally in the long Helvellyn skyline. The head of Sail Beck is a striking feature far below. Grasmoor and Eel Crag occupy much of the horizon, appearing dreary and shapeless at such close quarters, and Hopegill Head fits neatly into the gap between.

Ingleborough, Cross Fell, and the Isle of Man are all visible on a clear day.

Principal Fells

10 miles

7½ miles

5 miles

2½ miles

N

HOPEGILL HEAD

BOWSCALE FELL

BLENCATHRA

GREAT MELL FELL

CLOUGH HEAD

GRASMOOR

EEL CRAG

SAIL

CAUSEY PIKE

GREAT DODD

BURNBANK FELL

BLAKE FELL

W

ARD CRAGS

BLEABERRY FELL

E

STYBARROW DODD

GAVEL FELL

MELLBREAK

HEN COMB

HIGH SEAT

RAISE

WHITE SIDE

CATSTYCAM

HELVELLYN

GREAT BORNE

CRAG FELL

MAIDEN MOOR

KNOTT RIGG

HIGH SPY

NETHERMOST PIKE

DOLLYWAGGON PIKE

FAIRFIELD

LANK RIGG

STARLING DODD

RED PIKE

HIGH STILE

HINDSCARTH

ROBINSON

FLEETWITH PIKE

DALE HEAD

ULLSCARF

RED SCREES

GREAT RIGG

CAW FELL

HAYCOCK

SCOAT FELL

PILLAR

HIGH CRAG

HAYSTACKS

KIRK FELL

GREAT GABLE

LINGMELL

SCAFELL PIKE

SCAFELL

GREAT END

ESK PIKE

BOWFELL

ESK HAUSE

ALLEN CRAGS

GLARAMARA

HIGH RAISE

HARRISON STICKLE

LITTLE GOWDER CRAG

12½ miles

S

WETHERLAM

B EP GE GG SP S KF
L
FP H

The Scafell group

Lakes and Tarns
E : Derwent Water
S : Buttermere
SSW : Bleaberry Tarn

RIDGE ROUTES

To GRASMOOR, 2791': 1¼ miles: NW, then W.
Depression at 2375': 430 feet of ascent
An uninteresting journey over wide plateaux

Aim north-west to reach the Coledale-Whiteless Pike path where it skirts the head of Rannerdale. Turn towards Coledale and then left onto the path linking Eel Crag with Grasmere. At one point there is a steep drop on the left looking down into Rannerdale. Along the wide top of Grasmoor, at the head of the slope, the track is more imaginary than real, but the walking, on mossy turf, could not be better; there is a half-mile of it before the top is reached.

To EEL CRAG, 2749': ¾ mile: N, then NE.
Depression at 2420': 340 feet of ascent
A cliff-edge circuit of Addacomb Hole

Follow the semi-circular rim of the crater immediately to the north. The path is faint at first, but soon becomes more distinct. To reach the summit of Eel Crag it is necessary to cut across to the much broader path linking Eel Crag with Grasmoor.

To WHITELESS PIKE, 2165': ⅞ mile: W, then SW.
Depression at 2050': 110 feet of ascent
A good finish along an excellent ridge

Many walkers must have been beguiled by the southern ridge of Wandope into the false assumption that, if they follow it down, it will lead them to Whiteless Pike. Every step along here, however, puts Whiteless Pike further out of reach while bringing it nearer, because of the rough ravine forming between. The southern ridge is, in fact, a snare and a delusion. To gain the true one, aim west from the summit and make for the cairn of Thirdgill Head Man: it is visible from the summit. Here a path will be met; turn left along it and go down a narrowing crest to Saddle Gate for the climb to the Pike, now directly ahead.

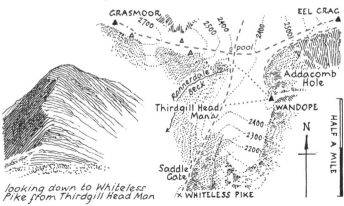

looking down to Whiteless Pike from Thirdgill Head Man

Whinlatter

1696'

from High Lorton

BROOM FELL ▲

CRAYSTONES ▲   LORD'S
                      ▲ SEAT

High ●
Lorton   ▲ WHINLATTER

        Whinlatter ⤢ Pass

                ● Braithwaite

      ▲
GRISEDALE PIKE

MILES

0   1   2   3   4

Whinlatter Pass

NATURAL FEATURES

Whinlatter the Pass, an excellent motor road, is known to many; Whinlatter the Fell, a lonely sheep pasture, is known to few. The abrupt heathery slopes, streaked with long tongues of scree, form an effective northern wall to the pass, and there is little in this rough and forbidding declivity to suggest the pleasant heights above, where an undulating plateau trends downwards to the quiet valley of Aiken Beck. This stream defines the boundaries to west and north; the eastern termination of the fell, among the Thornthwaite plantations, is less distinct. From the top the extent of the afforestation of the surrounding area is appreciated fully: plantations completely encircle the fell, and indeed its own western and northern flanks are under timber. The rough face above the pass, significantly, has not been acquired for forestry.

MAP

N

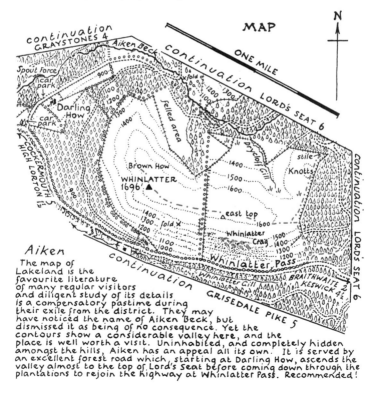

Aiken

The map of Lakeland is the favourite literature of many regular visitors and diligent study of its details is a compensatory pastime during their exile from the district. They may have noticed the name of Aiken Beck, but dismissed it as being of no consequence. Yet the contours show a considerable valley here, and the place is well worth a visit. Uninhabited, and completely hidden amongst the hills, Aiken has an appeal all its own. It is served by an excellent forest road which, starting at Darling How, ascends the valley almost to the top of Lord's Seat before coming down through the plantations to rejoin the highway at Whinlatter Pass. Recommended!

Grisedale Pike, from the east ridge of Whinlatter

ASCENT FROM WHINLATTER PASS
750 feet of ascent : 1¼ miles

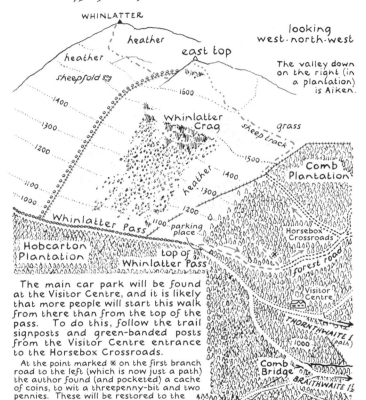

WHINLATTER

heather

east top

heather

heather

sheepfold

*looking
west·north·west*

The valley down
on the right (in
a plantation)
is Aiken.

1400

1300

1200

1100

1000

1600

Whinlatter
Crag

sheep track

grass

1500

1400

1300

1200

Comb
Plantation

heather

Whinlatter Pass

1100 parking
place

Hobcarton
Plantation

top of
Whinlatter Pass

Horsebox
Crossroads

×

forest road

Visitor
Centre

THORNTHWAITE

1000 (path)

Comb
Bridge

BRAITHWAITE 1½

Hospital Plantation

The main car park will be found
at the Visitor Centre, and it is likely
that more people will start this walk
from there than from the top of the
pass.   To do this, follow the trail
signposts and green-banded posts
from the Visitor Centre entrance
to the Horsebox Crossroads.

At the point marked ✳ on the first branch
road to the left (which is now just a path)
the author found (and pocketed) a cache
of coins, to wit a threepenny-bit and two
pennies. These will be restored to the
loser upon receipt of a claim (the
dates of the coins must be stated)
attested by a responsible householder.

Whinlatter tempts few walkers, the steep slopes of
heather and scree above the pass being too rough
to contemplate, but the crest of the fell is entirely
different — a delightfully undulating ridge, a joy to
walk upon.   It can be attained, moreover, by the
simplest of gradients if the direct climb from the
road is disregarded in favour of the forest roads
and paths depicted in the diagram, the whole of
the walk then being no more than an hour's ramble.

THE SUMMIT

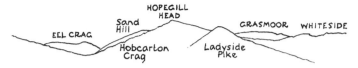

The part of the fell recognised as the summit is the small heathery dome of Brown How at the westerly end of its long undulating top. Here, still in a good state of preservation, is a wall in the form of a crescent, which, if intended as a wind-shelter, seems an extravagance in a place so seldom visited; more probably, considering the ocean of heather all around, it was built to serve as a shooting hide.

The Ordnance Surveyors had no doubts that this was the highest point the fell, at 1696', for only here was a 25' contour shown above 1650', yet the eastern top appears *from here* to be at least equally high. This may be an illusion of the sort familiar to all who frequent mountain-tops, for subsidiary summits often take the trick of appearing higher than the true summit *when viewed from the latter*, the eye having no horizontal level to assist in hilly terrain.   In this case, however, the illusion is strengthened by the distant background to the eastern top, formed by Stybarrow Dodd (2770') with Sticks Pass (2420') to its right — for the line of vision from the main top to the eastern top strikes the background only a few hundred feet lower than the Pass, say at 2000', and is therefore *rising*, from which it follows that any intermediate points on that line (including the eastern top) must be at a greater elevation than the viewpoint. Without instruments allowances must be made for defective vision and mental weakness, while refraction of light and curvature of the earth may be factors necessary to correct the judgement of the eye. The most that one dare bet is that the eastern top should be credited with at least a 1675' contour — an investment worthy of anybody's bottom dollar. (The 2008 Ordnance Survey 2½" map gives the altitude of the eastern top as 525 metres, which is 1722'.)

DESCENTS : Routes down to Aiken Beck should be avoided because of the plantations; routes down to Whinlatter Pass are exceedingly rough except for that described on Whinlatter 4.

THE VIEW

The view generally is inferior to those from neighbouring heights, but in one direction it excels, this being to the south, where the supporting buttresses of the lofty Grisedale Pike-Hopegill Head ridge build up magnificently across the depths of Whinlatter Pass and reveal various lines of ascent that have tended to become overlooked as afforestation of the lower slopes has taken place.

The Vale of Lorton also features well, but here is viewed from the side and is less effective than when seen end-on along its full length.

Principal Fells

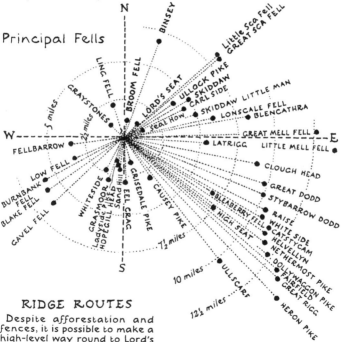

RIDGE ROUTES

Despite afforestation and fences, it is possible to make a high-level way round to Lord's Seat and Broom Fell, keeping above 1500' throughout — a fine circuit of the Aiken Valley. The route is shown on page 2 as far as Knotts and on Lord's Seat 6 from Knotts to Lord's Seat.   To avoid the mud, use route B on Lord's Seat 9.

Lakes and Tarns

The Solway Firth is the only sheet of water in sight, but from the eastern top of the fell Derwent Water makes a charming picture above the intervening plantations.

Whiteless Pike   2165'

from Rannerdale Farm

GRASMOOR ▲   EEL ▲ CRAG

▲ WANDOPE

▲ WHITELESS PIKE

● Rannerdale

● Buttermere

MILES

0   1   2

The popular concept of a true mountain shape is a pyramid, with steep uniform sides on all flanks and a sharp peak. For a short distance along the road near Rannerdale Farm, on the shores of Crummock Water, it seems that Whiteless Pike has the qualifying attributes. But it fails to present an outline of similar shapeliness and beauty to other angles of view, and so cannot rank for stardom. Yet, seen from Rannerdale, surely it is the Weisshorn of Buttermere.

MAP

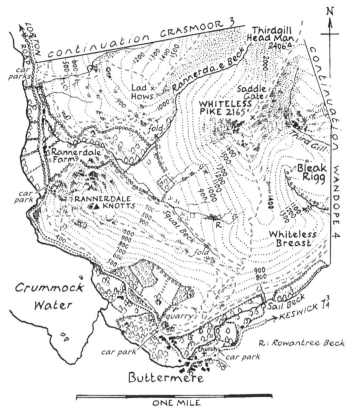

ONE MILE

A peculiarity of the streams flowing down to join Squat Beck is that they become subterranean, sinking in their beds at the 700' contour. The wall from the square enclosure in the centre of the map to Squat Beck is incorrectly shown as a stream on the 2½" Ordnance Survey map.

The face of Whiteless Pike overlooking Rannerdale is too steep to be climbed direct in comfort, but the path of ascent from Buttermere may be joined very pleasantly by following the valley of Squat Beck to its head. It may be remarked here that Squat Beck does not occupy the main valley of Rannerdale as it appears to do: note the course of Rannerdale Beck.

Curiously, the path over Whiteless Breast does not follow the ridge but wanders over to the west and back again.

ASCENT FROM BUTTERMERE
1800 feet of ascent : 1¼ miles

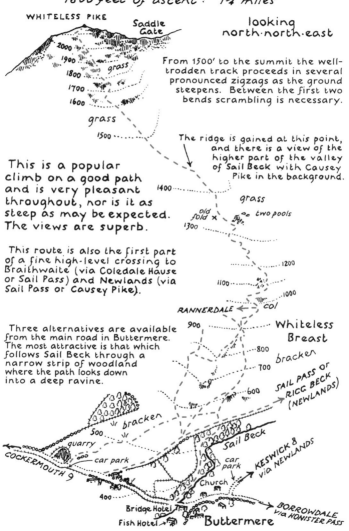

WHITELESS PIKE

Saddle Gate

2000
1900
1800
1700
1600

grass

1500

grass

looking
north·north·east

From 1500' to the summit the well-trodden track proceeds in several pronounced zigzags as the ground steepens. Between the first two bends scrambling is necessary.

The ridge is gained at this point, and there is a view of the higher part of the valley of Sail Beck with Causey Pike in the background.

This is a popular climb on a good path and is very pleasant throughout, nor is it as steep as may be expected. The views are superb.

1400

grass

old fold ×   two pools

1300

This route is also the first part of a fine high-level crossing to Braithwaite (via Coledale Hause or Sail Pass) and Newlands (via Sail Pass or Causey Pike).

1200

1100

1000

RANNERDALE   COL

900

Whiteless Breast

Three alternatives are available from the main road in Buttermere. The most attractive is that which follows Sail Beck through a narrow strip of woodland where the path looks down into a deep ravine.

800

700

bracken

600

SAIL PASS OR RIGG BECK (NEWLANDS)

bracken

500

quarry

car park

COCKERMOUTH 9

Sail Beck

car park

KESWICK 8 via NEWLANDS

400

Church

Bridge Hotel

Fish Hotel

Buttermere

BORROWDALE via HONISTER PASS

THE SUMMIT

WANDOPE

SAIL

SCAR CRAGS

CAUSEY PIKE

The top is small and exposed, with no cairn. Except as a viewing station it has little of interest.

DESCENTS: The only route of descent is by the path to Buttermere, which starts some 20 yards south of the summit. For Rannerdale turn right in half a mile and follow the valley of Squat Beck.

Whiteless Pike, from the Thirdgill ridge of Wandope

THE VIEW

Like Causey Pike, its counterpart at the other extreme of the Eel Crag ridge, Whiteless Pike has a great advantage as a viewpoint, by reason of the small uplifted summit and the abrupt downfall therefrom, which together permit a prospect both wide and deep, a view of valleys as well as of mountains. The Scafell mass is most excellently displayed, and is nowhere better seen than from this northern side of Buttermere, the valley scene below the distant, lofty skyline being very beautiful; indeed the whole rich picture in this direction is crowded with lovely detail. Less rugged but not less charming is the appearance of Crummock Water and Loweswater to the west. In contrast, nearby Grasmoor and Wandope fill up the northern horizon unattractively.

Principal Fells

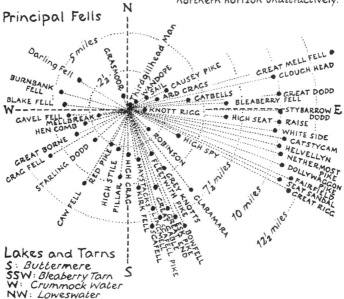

Lakes and Tarns

S: *Buttermere*
SSW: *Bleaberry Tarn*
W: *Crummock Water*
NW: *Loweswater*

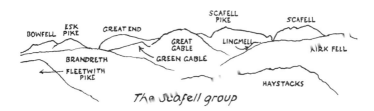

The Scafell group

RIDGE ROUTE

To WANDOPE, 2533': ⅞ mile: NE, then E.
Depression at 2050': 500 feet of ascent

A winding path leads down to, and traverses, the depression of Saddle Gate before climbing up to the cairn of Thirdgill Head Man (which, in mist, should not be mistaken for Wandope). Here desert the path and cross the meadow on the right to its culminating point.

The illustration below shows the ridge rising to Thirdgill Head Man (left skyline). Wandope's summit is on the right.

The illustration below shows the ridge rising to Thirdgill Head Man (left skyline). Wandope's summit is on the right.

Whiteside

2317'

from the road
to Scale Hill

- High Lorton
- Hopebeck

HOPEGILL
▲ HEAD

WHITESIDE ▲
Loweswater
●
● Lanthwaite
▲ GRASMOOR

MILES
0   1   2   3

NATURAL FEATURES

As travellers make their way up the Vale of Lorton, eager for sight of the thrilling Buttermere skyline just around the corner, their enthusiasm is kept in check by the successive buttresses of Whiteside, which descend steeply into the valley on the left and conceal the desired view of lake and mountain ahead. There are three buttresses on this western flank of Whiteside — Dodd, Penn and Whiteside End — and together they form a cornerstone in triplicate to the high fells in the rear, for it is here that Lakeland really leaps into the sky from the coastal plain of West Cumbria. These steep acclivities are rough and stony, and bulky rather than graceful — but many a beautiful picture is seen in an unattractive frame, and so it is here, the gaunt, massive portal enhancing the delicate, exciting scene ahead. The three buttresses rise in convex slopes to a sharply-cut summit ridge, and in a matter of yards the immediate dreariness of the grassy top is succeeded by a dramatic view down the other side of the mountain to Gasgale Gill in its ravine below. This south-eastern side presents an entirely different aspect: here are no sturdy buttresses but a vast scoop hollowed out of the fell, the debris of powerful forces of erosion, a place of shattered aretes, a natural quarry. This is Gasgale Crags, which a rich growth of heather is doing its best to make attractive by softening its naked harshness. From the ridge above, or the stream below, the natural architecture of the face cannot be appreciated, and one needs to visit Grasmoor, directly opposite, to observe the remarkable repeated pattern of aretes and scree-runs. This scene is unique. A splendid ridge from the summit eastwards leads on to Hopegill Head and Grisedale Pike. All waters drain into the River Cocker.

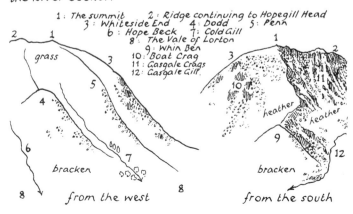

1 : The summit   2 : Ridge continuing to Hopegill Head
3 : Whiteside End   4 : Dodd   5 : Penn
6 : Hope Beck   7 : Cold Gill
8 : The Vale of Lorton
9 : Whin Ben
10 : Boat Crag
11 : Gasgale Crags
12 : Gasgale Gill

grass

from the west

heather

heather

bracken

bracken

from the south

Gasgale Gill

Between Lorton and Buttermere the only route through the mountains is provided by a rough path along the valley of Gasgale Gill, starting from Lanthwaite and leading up to Coledale Hause, at 1900', for Braithwaite. This is an excellent way for walkers in a hurry, Crummock Water and Keswick thereby being linked in a half-day's march. In Gasgale Gill the path runs along the base of Whiteside.

The rockstep

Waterfalls
near the head of the gill

The rockstep illustrated above was encountered just after rounding the corner of Whin Ben while proceeding eastwards. In 2007 it could not be located on either the higher or the lower path. According to the Ordnance Survey Gasgale Gill is the name of the valley, and Liza Beck is the name of the stream.

The lower section

The middle section

MAP

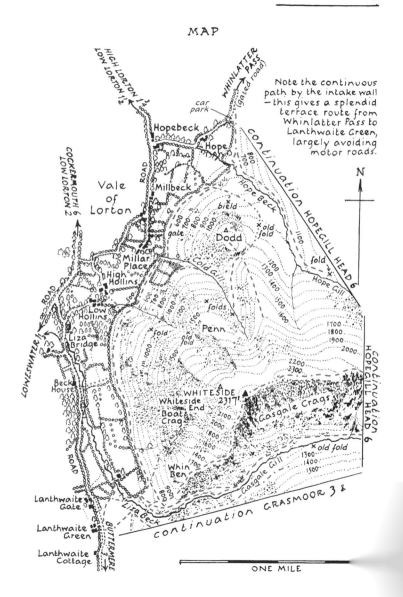

Note the continuous path by the intake wall – this gives a splendid terrace route from Whinlatter Pass to Lanthwaite Green, largely avoiding motor roads.

ONE MILE

Dodd Pass

A pronounced indentation in the ridge of Dodd serves as a pass between Hope Gill and Cold Gill, and is much used by sheep. One side of the pass is a tumble of scree, and it is clear that the rocks still standing here are the remains of what must at one time have been a continuous rampart. A counterpart to this curious gap is to be found at Trusmadoor in the Northern Fells.

Cold Gill

Just above the intake wall, Cold Gill used to be crossed by this tiny stone bridge, possibly the smallest in Lakeland. The bridge has gone now, but the place where the wall is broken can still be seen.

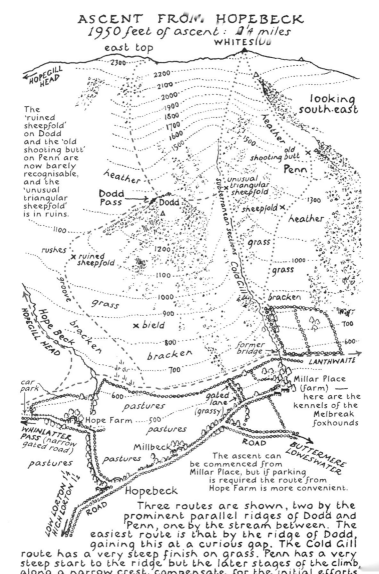

ASCENT FROM HOPEBECK
1950 feet of ascent : 2¼ miles

east top

WHITESIDE

HOPEGILL HEAD

looking south-east

The 'ruined sheepfold' on Dodd and the 'old shooting butt' on Penn are now barely recognisable, and the 'unusual triangular sheepfold' is in ruins.

heather

old shooting butt

Penn

Dodd Pass

Dodd

unusual triangular sheepfold

sheepfold

heather

subterranean sections

Cold Gill

grass

rushes

ruined sheepfold

groove

Hope Beck HOPEGILL HEAD

grass

grass

bracken

bracken

bield

bracken

former bridge

LANTHWAITE

car park

Millar Place (farm) — here are the kennels of the Melbreak foxhounds

gated lane (grassy)

WHINLATTER PASS (narrow gated road)

pastures

Hope Farm

pastures

Millbeck

pastures

pastures

ROAD

BUTTERMERE LOWESWATER

LOW LORTON 1¾ HIGH LORTON 1½

Hopebeck

ROAD

The ascent can be commenced from Millar Place, but if parking is required the route from Hope Farm is more convenient.

Three routes are shown, two by the prominent parallel ridges of Dodd and Penn, one by the stream between. The easiest route is that by the ridge of Dodd, gaining this at a curious gap. The Cold Gill route has a very steep finish on grass. Penn has a very steep start to the ridge but the later stages of the climb, along a narrow crest, compensate for the initial efforts

ASCENT FROM BECK HOUSE
1950 feet of ascent : 1¼ miles

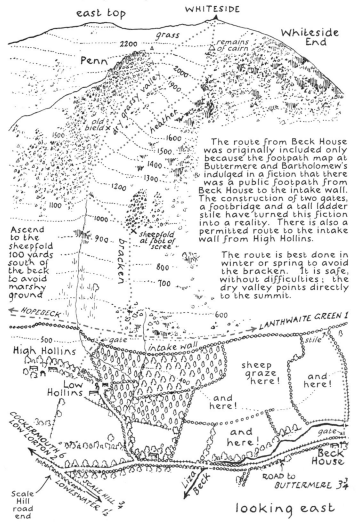

east top — WHITESIDE

Whiteside End

grass

2200

Penn

remains of cairn

2000

1900

dry grassy valley

heather

old bield ×

1500

1600

1500

1400

1300

1200

1100

1000

900

sheepfold at foot of scree

bracken

800

700

Ascend to the sheepfold 100 yards south of the beck to avoid marshy ground

The route from Beck House was originally included only because the footpath map at Buttermere and Bartholomew's indulged in a fiction that there was a public footpath from Beck House to the intake wall. The construction of two gates, a footbridge and a tall ladder stile have turned this fiction into a reality. There is also a permitted route to the intake wall from High Hollins.

The route is best done in winter or spring to avoid the bracken. It is safe, without difficulties; the dry valley points directly to the summit.

← HOPEBECK

600

LANTHWAITE GREEN 1

500

gate

intake wall

stile

High Hollins

sheep graze here!

and here!

Low Hollins

and here!

and here!

COCKERMOUTH 6
LOW LORTON 2

gate

Beck House

SCALE HILL 3¾

LOWESWATER 12

Liza Beck

ROAD TO BUTTERMERE 3¾

Scale Hill road end

looking east

ASCENT FROM LANTHWAITE GREEN
1850 feet of ascent : 1½ miles

When viewed from the road Whiteside looks uninviting and it is difficult to see how a good route can be worked out. The key to the ascent is Whin Ben, reached from Lanthwaite Green. From the post opposite the car park aim for the top of Whiteside and a path will soon materialise. Head straight up the hill from the footbridge, and then follow the ridge. From the Ben onwards the route keeps to the edge of the crags overlooking Gasgale Gill.

Like Grasmoor and many other fells hereabouts Whiteside is richly vegetated and of special interest to botanists.

WHITESIDE

Whiteside End

Boat Crag

striated rocks and prostrate juniper

2200
2100
2000

1600
1500

heather

Whin Ben

heather

COLEDALE HAUSE
BRAITHWAITE

Gasgale Gill

800
700
bracken

600

heather
1000
900

700

fall

weir

Liza Beck

grass

cattle grid

ROAD
GORTON

Lanthwaite Green

car park

500

BUTTERMERE 3

GRASMOOR rises very steeply on this side

From Whin Ben onwards the views of Gasgale Gill are tremendously impressive.

looking north-east

The central portion of the weir has been washed away.

The first problem is to locate the footbridges, as neither of them is visible from the car park.

This ascent, which promises nothing but a hard grind, turns out instead to be a delightful and interesting climb. It is incomparably the best route up the fell.

THE SUMMIT

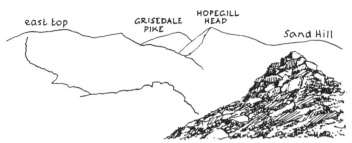

east top   GRISEDALE PIKE   HOPEGILL HEAD   Sand Hill

The cairn is well sited at the end of the ridge, just above the steepening drop to Crummock Water, and on the edge of an abrupt downfall of crags. But there is little doubt that this is not the highest point of the fell: the first pronounced rise on the ridge eastwards certainly seems to have an advantage in altitude — looking back from here the official summit fits into the same horizontal plane as Blake Fell, 1878', four miles in the background, and therefore the view of it is downward.

The top is grassy, away from the rim of crags. The only other cairn is prominently seen 300 yards in a westerly direction.

DESCENTS : The best way down is to Lanthwaite Green via Whin Ben, keeping the steep edge on the left throughout; a fair track soon materialises. In mist, a complete stranger to the mountain would be better advised to aim northwest and descend the grassy valley there found: it has no difficulties, and leads down to the intake wall. This route is also to be preferred to the Dodd and Penn ridges in bad weather.

The summit rocks
from the south   from the east

THE VIEW

Whiteside is the finest viewpoint for the coastal plain of West Cumbria, the Solway Firth, and the hills of Scotland beyond: a magnificent uninterrupted panorama crammed with detail; it is surprising to find the intervening Fellbarrow range sunk into complete insignificance from this elevation.

In other directions the view is patchy. The Skiddaw and Helvellyn ranges are well seen but the best skyline in Lakeland (south to the Scafells) is completely hidden by Grasmoor.

More intimately, the glimpses down the aretes of Gasgale Crags to the gill far below are very striking.

Principal Fells

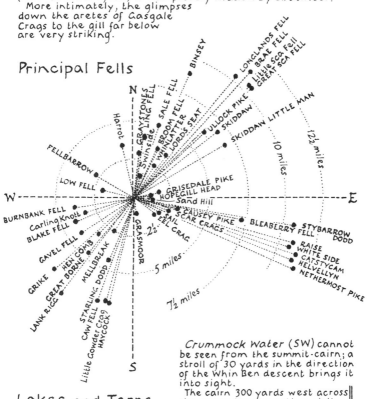

Lakes and Tarns
NNE: *Over Water*
    (a faint trace only)
W: *Loweswater*

Crummock Water (SW) cannot be seen from the summit-cairn; a stroll of 30 yards in the direction of the Whin Ben descent brings it into sight.

The cairn 300 yards west across the grassy top is worth a visit — from this point Loweswater and Crummock Water are both seen in a comprehensive valley view.

RIDGE ROUTE

To HOPEGILL HEAD, 2525′ : 1⅛ mile : ENE, then E.
Main depression at 2200′ : 360 feet of ascent

An exhilarating high-level traverse with a grand finish.
The path is sketchy, but the sharp rim of the great downfall
to Gasgale Gill is an infallible guide. The best part of the walk
is the final depression, where a narrow heathery crest with
a distinct track leads across to the pyramid of Hopegill Head.
Approach this depression down the grass to the left of the rocks
of the ridge.

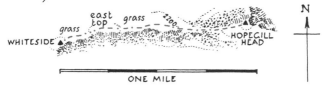

ONE MILE

*Whiteside, with Whin Ben (right)
from Lanthwaite Green*

Gasgale Crags, Whiteside   from Dove Crags, Grasmoor

looking east along the ridge to Hopegill Head and Sand Hill

THE NORTH WESTERN FELLS

Some Personal notes
in conclusion

When concluding Book Five I expressed the opinion that the north Western Fells were the most delectable of all, and, after two years in their charming company, I hold to that view. In other areas I have sometimes tired a little of repeatedly tramping the same tracks, but not here. Times without number I came off the hills faced with a long trudge down Whinlatter, or along the Coledale mine road or newlands, until every stone and every tree became familiar, but never, rain or shine, did I do so wearily, but only regretting that another day was done, that another week must pass before I could return. always I was lingering, always looking back.

All this territory is wonderful walking country. much of it, south of the grisedale Pike ridge, is well known and needs no introduction (although I have just completed nearly 300 pages doing that!). Even so, there are many corners rarely visited, many excellent routes rarely trodden, many interesting features rarely seen. several of the lines of ascent described in this book are as good as anything else in Lakeland, which is saying a lot, yet the majority of walkers are unaware of them. Searchers after traces of ancient history or old industrial activity will find much of interest. Geologists and botanists are well catered for here. Photographers cannot fail to produce beautiful pictures.

On the whole, the walking is quite excellent. The hills are easier to climb than their abrupt appearance suggests: the secret is to get on the ridges early, because it is the ridges, not the fellsides, that provide the best travelling underfoot and the finest views, and give the area its special appeal.

Newlands is a privileged valley, not only extraordinarily pleasant in itself but ringed by grand fells; for a quiet fellwalking holiday there is no better centre. Borrowdale we all know and love, but this valley is not so well placed for the area, and is nowadays so busy with cars that its joys are best experienced in winter. Buttermere is beautiful, but a better base for the western

Fells than the North Western. I ought to put in a good word for Thornthwaite Forest, to the north of Whinlatter, which, in spite of much afforestation, is a fascinating place to explore. I never saw a soul here in eight months' weekend wandering, except once when I found myself mixed up in a foxhunt. Nothing in this region pleased me more than the shy Wythop Valley, so easy to walk, so charming and unspoiled, a little tranquil world apart.

Several times I came down to Buttermere, and it was hard to deny myself an occasional excursion to the magnificent mountains on the far side, but now the time has come when I am free to do this, and Book Seven will tell of High Stile and of Great Gable and Pillar and others that yet remain unrecorded. If I say that I start upon the last book in the series with mixed feelings, many of you will know what I mean.

AW

Autumn, 1963.